ON BOARD
WITH
THE LORD

ON BOARD
WITH
THE LORD

SMOOTH SAILING IN ROUGH WATERS

HANS UITTENBOSCH

TATE PUBLISHING
AND ENTERPRISES, LLC

Published by Tate Publishing & Enterprises, LLC
127 E. Trade Center Terrace | Mustang, Oklahoma 73064 USA
1.888.361.9473 | www.tatepublishing.com

Tate Publishing is committed to excellence in the publishing industry. The company reflects the philosophy established by the founders, based on Psalm 68:11,
"The Lord gave the word and great was the company of those who published it."

Book design copyright © 2011 by Tate Publishing, LLC. All rights reserved.
Cover design by Shawn Collins
Interior design by April Marciszewski

Published in the United States of America

ISBN: 978-1-61346-754-1
1. Biography & Autobiography / Religious
2. Biography & Autobiography / Personal Memoirs
11.12.06

DEDICATION

To my beloved wife, Trudy, who has given me loyal support and encouragement during our many years of Ministry to Seafarers, and who became my capable teammate in our Ministry to Seafarers.

    To our precious children Marcel, Selwyn, and Desiree, who from their earliest years have given of their time and talents to Seafarers from around the world.

ACKNOWLEDGMENTS

Our Lord and Savior Jesus Christ for the call to the Ministry to Seafarers and for his extraordinary guidance.

The officers, staff, and crewmembers of the ships for their exceptional graciousness and friendship.

The numerous churches and loyal individuals for their prayerful financial support, enabling us to establish the Seafarers Centre in Montreal, and for their continuing support of our Ministry to Seafarers.

Ms. Gien Janssens, our capable administrator, for having given her all in the service to Seafarers.

Mr. Hilbrand and Mrs. Willy Ten Wolde, who relocated long term to Montreal to become outstanding house parents in our Seafarers Centre, and were much loved by the Seafarers.

Mr. Peter and Mrs. Jenny Vermeulen, who as dedicated volunteers sacrificed much for the Seafarers.

The many dedicated Christian staff workers and volunteers for their diligent work and for their loving outreach to Seafarers.

My wife Trudy and our dear friend Stefani Kauffman, for their patience and their tireless efforts in the editorial and administrative design of this book.

TABLE OF CONTENTS

PREFACE

"Wherever the Word of God has been spread into the world there have always been predictable consequences:

- It is normal to see a high level of cultural organization.
- There is usually a reasonably consistent legal system.
- There is some understanding of the value of human beings.

Work is taken up with some long term goal in mind and is often valued for more than its immediate financial returns."

"Most educational and medical institutions were established, or are still being supported and run by Christians."

—**Allen Stares** as published in the March 24, 2010, issue of the Christian Renewal.

CBC News correspondent Brian Stewart, having traveled to many of the world's troubled spots during his forty-plus years as a journalist, noted that he had been struck by the rather blithe notion, spread in many circles, including the media, that organized mainstream Christianity has been reduced to a musty, dimly lit backwater of contemporary life, a fading force.

From what he calls his "ring-side-seat" over decades, he clearly articulated that there is nothing further from the truth.

> Christian volunteers have been a faithful witness to truth, the primary light in the darkness, and so often the *only* light. I have found there is no movement or force closer to the vast human predicament than organized Christians in action.
>
> —**Brian Stewart,** as published
> in the Nov. 26, 2008, issue of the Christian Renewal.

This book is characterized by a distinct Christian perspective. The Christian dimension in the national, political, economic, and personal lives of the citizens in our multicultural society may indeed *seem* muffled. But what you will find throughout this book, illustrated in the lives of people, some of them at work on board of ships, is that the biblical principles have a profoundly redemptive and restorative effect.

Deep down in the hearts of all people there is the question:

"Is there a word of the LORD for me?"

In the variety of encounters in the lives of both passengers and staff on the ships this book reflects that the answer to this question is: "There is!"

INTRODUCTION

The seafarers are well-trained people with exceptional graciousness and courtesy, expressed in their relationship with passengers and visitors. They represent more than one hundred different nations. They are ordinarily only for a brief period of time in our country. In more than 700 ports throughout the world, they are hosted by Seafarers Centers, which provide them with excellent services.

Their place of work on board ships is far away from home, family, and their social circle for long periods of time. Like all of us, they experience spiritual and emotional needs, frustrations, injustices, difficulties, and disappointments that demand to be addressed.

As a pastor to seafarers, it has been my concern to provide distinct Christian care, encouragement, and support to those I meet on board. That care is expressed admirably in the Sacred Scriptures. With its extensive variety of conclusive answers the light of Christ illumines every situation.

For a number of people the world of *cruise ships* has some familiarity, as the personal care for each passenger on board leaves an indelible mark of the excellent service of the staff.

The world of the *crew of cargo ships* remains an unknown entity to most people, aside from the highly publicized confrontations with pirates.

A forty-five-year Ministry to Seafarers cannot be portrayed in one book. So I have limited myself to an autobiographical and a cursorily anecdotal account highlighted in some notable contacts. The approach to those might well be of inspiration in your life.

It has been my conviction, and the facts have borne this out, that what God has to say in his Word has thoroughly changed, inspired, enriched, and encouraged the lives of many seafarers we have contacted.

For their absolute protection, I have spoken about my contacts totally anonymously. I believe that the displays of their commitment to the call of God might well inspire *you* to discover the meaning of the lessons that are reflected in every chapter.

- I also hope and pray that committed Christian pastors will come forward to be stationed in some of the busiest ports, to minister to the seafarers and particularly to the vast numbers of staff working on board of cruise ships.

- It would be a blessing to see chaplains, who have a distinct biblical insight, appointed on board of cruise ships with the specific assignment to minister to the staff.

- Dedicated Christians, residing in port cities, might wish to search out existing Seafarers Centers in order to extend their voluntary support to function as ship-visitors and as hosts and hostesses in these centers.

- I ask the churches and individual Christians to remember in prayer the officers, staff, and crew of the ships coming to the ports. Remember those who know the Lord, and those who do *not* know Him, that all people may come to know His name and acknowledge Him as their Lord and Savior.

In the dedicatory prayer for the temple, King Solomon referred not only to the people of Israel, but he mentioned specifically the foreigners. This section could well be applied to the seafarers:

As for *the foreigner* who does not belong to your people Israel but has come from a distant land because of your name—for men will *hear* of your great name and your mighty hand and your outstretched arm—when he comes and prays toward this temple, then *hear* from heaven, your dwelling place, and do *whatever the foreigner* asks of you, so that all the peoples of the earth may know your name and fear you …

I Kings 8:41–43

THE CALL
TO MINISTRY

In my parental home in the Netherlands, it was the custom to read a chapter of the Holy Bible every day at the conclusion of the meals. I grew up in a generation where all members of the family assembled around the table in the dining room for dinner. No one rushed out to a meeting, to a soccer game, or to a concert. Television had not yet been introduced. We all experienced the sense of "family" and "communication." This contributed to the dimension of belonging; it inspired confidence.

At the conclusion of the meal, the word of God, embodied in a large Bible, was placed on the table and a chapter was read from either the Old Testament or the New Testament. The entire Bible was read in sequence. Ordinarily it was my father who read. My mother would read in his absence. That had something to do with the theological orientation and training in reformed circles. The parent, biblically speaking, was reflecting the "priestly function" in leading the devotions for the family. That was an excellent idea. It was part of your function as a parent.

Later in my life, that pattern changed: When my wife and I were married, we decided to each take a copy of the Bible and to take turns reading through the chapter. The advantage of that is it helped us to concentrate on the reading. We heard it, spoke it, and constantly saw it before our eyes. Our thoughts would not drift to something else.

My parents read one chapter at the time. That prevented us from getting an aversion to the reading. One day it might be a bit longer than the next. In fact, there were times that I wished to have the next chapter read as well, because of the intrigue of the story: How would it end?

We did not always understand every aspect of the reading, but we felt at ease with it. I preferred the Old Testament. It has such fascinating stories. One of them is found in Judges 6. It tells the story of Gideon, who asked the LORD God for a visible sign to get confirmation about his task of saving Israel from their attackers.

Gideon placed a fleece outside on the threshing floor. He then challenged the LORD God: "Please make it soaking wet with dew during the night, but let the ground around it remain totally dry. Then I will know that you will indeed be with me in this battle." God did it. Gideon still had doubts, so he asked God to repeat the same show the next night, but in reverse: The fleece was to be totally dry and the ground around it soaking wet. God did it again. I was amazed that God just played along with this doubting character.

It also intrigued me that throughout the Bible—and especially here in his approach to God–the familiarity and openness of people to directly address the living God, displayed a real closeness between God and the individual. Both inside and outside of the community of churches, the search for this close interaction with God should be encouraged.

In my case, I needed certainty about the direction of my own future. I figured if Gideon dared to do this even twice, I should be able to do it once. I was ten years old at the time. I needed confirmation in my mind if I should become a naval officer or a preacher. My bedroom was on the third floor. A steep roof was right outside my window. The gutter could support the nice, little Persian prayer rug, which was lying in front of my bed. The rug had to stay dry of course. My mother would have a fit if it should get wet.

So one night, I challenged the LORD: "A dry rug means I'll become a naval officer." When I woke up the following morning, I ran to my window, threw it open and looked out. There was a soaking wet roof, but no rug. The wind had blown it into the garden and I found it there among the bushes, as soaked as its environment and covered with old leaves and mud. I sneaked the thing back into my room, tried to clean it as well as I could, and let it dry under my bed. My mother never found out.

I concluded, "No naval officer, but a preacher," although I didn't like it that I did not get a clear indication. Unlike Gideon, I did not dare to ask God for a second show. After all, the first one had fallen flat and wet.

Some twenty years later, I realized why. The LORD had a combination of the two professions in mind for me: I was scheduled to become a naval-preacher. I never thought of that when I picked up the little rug in the garden. At that time, I did not reflect theologically. My main concern then was how to get this thing back into my room. In fact, I was frustrated with the manner in which God had gone about it. If it had to be wet, He could have simply left it on the roof and drenched it there.

Had it remained on the roof, I could have dragged it inside without running the risk of getting caught by my mother. Of course, in many instances we feel that our interpretation of what God *should* have done would have been better, but in my ministry I became aware of an interesting principle: In displaying his presence and his purposes for my life, at times accompanied by signs or symbols, I learned that God had his own program for my life, with his kind of signs and signals. I had to learn to interpret them. A drenched, muddy rug was to remind me that the road to and in the ministry would not be smoothly paved. I would run into a lot of dirt.

I did!

TRAINING IN EVANGELISM

Shortly after the last World War, my father—a banker by profession—organized monthly meetings for the well-situated residents living in our neighborhood. The purpose was to introduce people to God who has appeared to us in Christ Jesus. The theme of the meetings was "Significant Questions in Life." The meetings were held in one of the ballrooms of a well-known hotel in the immediate vicinity of the residences of the invited people.

People would not have to travel far, and they could sit comfortably at nicely decorated tables, enjoying coffee and a variety of desserts. My father worked in a secular environment, so he was very sensitive to people who were irreligious. He wanted to challenge them with the call of our LORD.

When you wish to become evangelistically involved, both the kind of people you seek to approach and the setting to which you invite them are vitally important factors demanding harmony. People unfamiliar with the gospel are not inspired by an invitation to a church hall as they would suspect that you would want them to join your church.

The sessions organized by my father always featured a very well-known Christian speaker: a professor of one of the universities, a philosopher, a medical doctor, or a scientist. They would discuss a topic of current interest such as "The Problem of Depression," "Euthanasia," "The World of Islam," or "Death."

In his speech, the speaker would articulate the biblical and Christian view on these matters in a sensitive way. Questions were always solicited. It was hoped that through these meetings, the Spirit of God would touch the hearts of at least some of the attendants to the point that they would come to an awareness of Christ as "The LORD of Life."

Miraculously, some hearts were touched and some people became quite interested and reacted by writing on the response card that they would like to get further information about the subject that was discussed. Further clarity about the relationship with Christ came about in social get-togethers at our house and through correspondence or telephone contact with the speaker.

As a thirteen-year-old, I was not only involved in the preparation of these meetings, but I witnessed at close range the entire process of "curiosity" in the lives of a variety of attendants. I was delicately coached in the process of evangelism. Sixty years ago the idea of "sharing" was not popular. In fact, the word was not used at all. One hardly spoke openly about one's faith.

I always played a large part in the preparations for these meetings. The programs had to be stuffed into envelopes and delivered to the homes in the neighborhood. Many of these homes had high fences, large gates, long driveways, and purebred dogs.

At the hotel, I functioned as a receptionist and usher. More than one hundred people showed up most evenings. What fascinated me was the joy of my parents about some of the reactions of the people who had responded. They also facilitated an immediate contact with the speaker or even set up a "social contact" in our own home to encourage the inquirers.

Thus, I was introduced to evangelism, not by attending any organizational meetings or by following a syllabus or by attending any study courses. I did not go to any weekend meetings with dynamic preachers or speakers either. Instead, I was inadvertently brought into contact with an intriguing *personal* model of sensitive witnessing in the relaxing atmosphere of a classy ballroom, organized unobtrusively by my own parents.

In many instances, when people become aware of a notable activity or a model of operation, the urge develops to explore one's own territory with the question: "How can what I have seen and experienced be used in my own circle on the level on which I move?"

I was a student in a secondary school, and I had three friends in our neighborhood who were committed Christians. They were all somewhat familiar with the monthly meetings in the hotel. When we talked about what went on in that hotel, we decided we should start something like it among the young people attending our school. We proposed to do it in one of our homes. By turn each of us would give a thoroughly prepared speech about some lively subject of current interest among young people, such as "Intimate Relations." (The word sex was not used in those days in our circles. "Intimate Relations" was a courteous and civilized word for the same thing.)

Since I lived in a house in which the living room, dining room, and den were all adjacent to each other, we held the first meeting there. My mother exhausted herself throughout the week with baking, which undoubtedly explained the added number of young people who attended meetings held during subsequent weeks. Thirty-seven students showed up on the first night. The number increased to one hundred and four nearly every time after that first meeting.

There were students who became inspired by the Spirit of God, and several of them came to know Christ as their LORD and Savior. We met on Sunday nights, but we got so excited about it all that we came up with a variation for Saturday nights.

We noticed that a lot of young people would hang around the four movie theaters downtown. We looked around and found an abandoned restaurant for rent. It was close to two theaters. My father suggested that I should approach a particular, well off church member for help to rent this place one night per week. I did just that and informed this particular man of our vision.

He picked up the entire tab. We got into the restaurant. We cleaned up the place, we dressed it up with some paintings and artifacts from our basements and we organized our mothers to provide refreshments. We were all set.

We put Bibles and New Testaments on every table, as well as a variety of Christian literature, all free for the taking. The most popular "tract" proved to be a pamphlet we had put together under the title "Simple Suggestions to Remain Unhappy."

We went to the long lineups at the four-movie theaters in the city and began to invite the young people to join us for a lively discussion with refreshments in our "café" (the term "coffee-house" had not yet been coined) at no cost to them. These last five words were without a doubt instrumental in getting the place filled on the first night. Many of them were intrigued by the fact that we would simply sit around tables, eat, drink, talk, and then let them leave with whatever literature was available. The decorations and the props—the Bibles and Christian literature—were instrumental in getting the conversations going along the lines we intended. We talked about the real values of life in Christ. We did it courteously, but with conviction, at all times respecting the comments and objections of our guests. It was an inspiring experience each and every time.

Many of the young people actually thanked us for the unexpected, but intriguing evening, and said that they would like to come back the next week. Some of our guests found the LORD. That is of course an inappropriate statement. The LORD had already found them, but perhaps in and through our meetings, they woke up to the fact that he was looking for them.

It reminded me of a famous evangelist who, following one worship service in a church, was approached by someone who asked how many people had been converted as a result of his preaching. The preacher responded, "Two and a half." The questioner wondered about this odd answer and suggested that he might mean two adults and one child. The preacher said, "No, I mean two young people and one old man. The young people have their whole life still to give to Jesus, but the old man has only half a life left."

One summer, a well-known German evangelist and preacher invited a number of us to assist him in his crusade in Cologne, Germany. Having just survived the five-year-war in Holland, we had seen destruction, but what we saw in Cologne defied description: total devastation. There was not a single building left intact except, miraculously, the Cologne Cathedral. Though damaged, it remained standing. "Was it not in this Cathedral where they had found a statue of the Christ, all broken in pieces?"

When they repaired the statue, they were unable to find the hands, so they left it unfinished, without hands, and placed a small plaque at the bottom.

It read, "You are the hands of Christ."

In this chaotic city we set-up a huge army tent. Hundreds of people came to the tent every night while we functioned as ushers. It was a moving sight, people coming out of their destroyed homes, some of them walking long distances since there was no public transportation, all seeking healing for their hearts. They were on the right track!

The prophet Isaiah had already prophesied years ago, that Christ had come "to bind up the broken hearted," ... and ..."to comfort all who mourn ... ," (Is.61:1,2). That, in essence, was the message of the evangelist.

This experience, repeated every single night for three straight weeks, deepened my own faith as I saw the power of the Gospel's dynamic message affect and change the lives of many attendants. It inspired me anew to dedicate my life to the proclamation of the gospel and specifically to evangelism. In what form that would come to expression was not crystallized at that time, but the power of the Gospel in the lives of people who had been devastated during the world war, as well as a compassion for them inspired me enormously.

LESSONS DURING
THE CROSSING

In a magazine, I happened to read that it would be possible to study and work at the same time in the United States of America. I decided to pursue this. Gordon College and Seminary in Boston, MA, accepted my application and became my sponsor. Arrangements were made with the owner of a shipping company, who was a member of our church, to get passage for me on a cargo vessel headed for the USA from Rotterdam.

On the night before my departure, my father came up to my bedroom on the third floor. Characteristic of his brevity with words he made two remarks. First he said, "You have decided to go to the USA to study Theology. If for some reason you should change your mind on the subject, you have my blessing, but do not come back home without a degree of some sort." Secondly, "You are going with God. Stay with Him." He then knelt down on my prayer rug and simply said, "I shall now pray for you." He did!

The following morning, in a wild rainstorm, I boarded a freighter in the port of Rotterdam, along with three other passengers. It was an excellent ship of the "Liberty class," very seaworthy and in good shape. However, we wrestled across the North Atlantic for the next fourteen days in unbelievably rough seas.

The crossing on a cargo vessel was actually a prelude to my career on board of ships as a chaplain to seafarers. I learned a number of valuable lessons even though, at that time, the "Ministry to Seafarers" was not an item on my agenda.

First, almost every day a lot of time was spent discussing and debating the dynamics of the gospel of Christ. I was used to this since I had, by then, quite a bit of experience as a result of the projects we had had with the students and the young people in my home town. Here I was on a ship and the crew raised the issues. Was it because I had told them that I was on the way to the USA to study theology? Perhaps. The hurdle that turned up again and again in the discussion was the demand of God to harmonize ourselves with his commandments.

This was such an enormous hurdle that some of the seafarers suggested that because of it, they would stay away from the Christian religion. It put you in a harness and forced you to live by a set of laws. All my talking about "freedom in Christ" ran smack into this. Who would understand this freedom to be a deliverance from the bondage of sin? Who would be willing to commit himself to the demands of the LORD to live by his laws? It would seem to stifle one's life.

It often appears to be this "hurdle" that prevents so many people from "committing" themselves to acknowledge Christ as LORD. In an emotional setting, people might be prepared to do this. The fact that we hear about recommitment or rededication at a later stage indicates, that many people have begun to realize the short fall of their original commitment, the need to *obey* Christ. Yet, Jesus tells us, "If you love me, you will obey what I command" (John 14:15). It is an odd combination of course, love and obedience, especially today when we have taught ourselves to do our own thing; feeling free to do what we want and like.

The whole philosophy of moral education has a tendency to go into this direction. However, the Bible tells us that obedience is in reality far more liberating. The focus is to be on seeking the honor of Christ.

A second lesson this voyage taught me was the awareness of an overwhelming sense of "loneliness." Being at sea for days on end and not seeing a single ship anywhere gives you the feeling that you are totally forsaken. In the language of a lot of people that word is "amplified," but the most fascinating aspect is that, if you actually should bring God into the concept of being forsaken, the reality of it evaporates. "God so loved the world, that he gave his only begotten Son, that whosoever believes in him should not perish, but have everlasting life" (John 3:16). This is the best known verse in the Bible. It is printed, in most of the world's languages, in the very front of the Gideon Bibles, which can, (or could) be found in hotel rooms and in the cabins on board of cruise ships. The sensation of being forsaken is real, but go by the facts: *God* does not forsake anyone in the world he so loves.

The people at sea are living for months on end without their family. Wife, children, parents, all their relatives are just not there. That is terrible. To be away from home for half a year, or as is the case for many of them, for nearly a year, is totally devastating. The father goes home and his own child runs away from him because, after such a long absence, the child does not recognize his father.

His wife has been in charge of the family, the household, the total operation of what he calls his home. Then, the husband returns with his agenda. Despite the bond of love it takes time to "adjust" after having been gone for so long. He was lonely at sea and to his stunning amazement, he discovers that he feels at times excluded and "lonely" on land as well, even within his own family.

Years later I heard a seaman say to me in jest that he was a DP—a displaced person. When a person jests, there is frequently a hidden truth in it. I began to experience a sense of that myself. It was in the early fifties. From that point on my family was accessible only through correspondence and an occasional—and expensive—telephone call. Prior to that, I had just looked at the adventure of the voyage and at what lay ahead.

Sailing rips you away from your social life, your life ashore, your friends, and the people with whom you were associated in many different ways. None of them were here. No one would meet me on the other side of the ocean. In North America there would not be a single individual who would say: "You have been waved out in Rotterdam. I am here to wave you in." My whole social world had collapsed.

For the Christian seafarer, there is also the absence of the church, the religious community. It just is not there. Trying to form a "church community" on board is a tricky business. There is a great variety of religious backgrounds: "He is a Catholic, I am a Protestant, that man there is a Hindu, and the tall one over there is not a believer." To form a fellowship of Christians demands that there are at least some others who believe in a somewhat similar vein as you do. They must also be willing to "stick their necks out." They are on board of a ship twenty-four hours a day. If a person drops a sledge hammer on his toes and swears, he then feels he would not be accepted by a "Christian fellowship" whose members watch what they say and are worshipping God.

As one of my friends once remarked: "The best display of your Christianity is when you are skating and take an awful fall on the ice, almost breaking your leg, and you are screaming with pain, to then get up and utter, 'Praise the LORD!'" We are not always on that level. Moreover, who would want to show off being religious? We are too inhibited, too ashamed, or too hesitant to say anything about our link up with the church.

Being away from home and its context is also instrumental in the cave in of the relationship with the church. The relationship just peters out. Many people prefer to be "incognito" where it concerns their religious orientation.

It is very difficult for the professional seaman. Here he is on a ship; he did not choose its "social setting." He might not be able to get along with the people with whom he is sailing. Yet he must work, even eat, and associate with them in his off hours. He is stuck with them.

Friendships and associations, which the seaman had carefully built up over the years ashore, have disappeared. He is all alone here. When he is frustrated about his life or worries about his family, to whom can he talk? The people on board are all "in the same boat." They do not need the problems of someone else. Each person is in a particular slot on a ship. The person, you perhaps may wish to talk to, has a higher or lower rank than you. Professionally, you can—and at times must—talk to him, but you cannot talk with him about your personal life and anxieties. That just won't work.

I remember the Philippine radio officer who was hired because he was familiar with English. On a cargo ship with more than twelve people on board, the law required the presence of a radio officer. Everyone else on board was Polish. They spoke Polish at the breakfast, lunch, and dinner table. They spoke Polish on their time off. They had Polish newspapers and Polish books. They also had Polish food, because they had a Polish cook.

The Philippine radio officer, aware of his responsibilities, stayed on board, but felt totally isolated. In fact, he was at the point of crying. I encouraged him in the LORD and reminded him that the prophets in the Scriptures were lonely and isolated people too. He was not only a prophet, but his very function on board was of such value, that the lives of the Polish community depended on him and on his actions.

A Belgian master, with whom we had sailed, joined us one night for dinner at our home. He suffered a similar kind of pain of isolation and frustration. He had nicely scheduled his holidays for the time that his youngest daughter was going to be confirmed in the church. He had missed the last Christmas, even though he was scheduled to be home in time. The ship ran into a furious hurricane and his arrival at home was fully six days late. His wife and family were very unhappy. He had not been home at Christmas during the last nine years, so they certainly had expected him to be home this time.

Now he sat at our dinner table. He had just received notice that he had to extend his contract for two more months. His relief captain was unable to relieve him, so he had just phoned his wife to inform her that, even though his heart went out to her and to his daughter, who was going to be confirmed, the Company had ordered him to stay on board.

His wife was crushed. "You are the captain, aren't you?" she shouted. "You are the boss of the ship. You can say to the office, 'My daughter is counting on my coming home. My sailing schedule has been made up already a year ago to allow for this.' You cannot stay away. Tell the company."

"I cannot tell the company even though I am the captain," he said. "If I would tell them, 'get someone else, because I am not doing it,' the company will say, 'Dear Sir, Come home on the first flight to pick up your last pay check.'" My wife is ready to divorce me. I am stuck on the ship. To whom can I talk? Imagine being on board on the very day that my daughter is confirmed. Horrible, absolutely horrible..."

I often see seafarers standing at the ship's railing, staring out over miles and miles of water and no one out there to talk to.

The third lesson I learned at sea was the frightening power of the Atlantic Ocean. This kept my attention during the entire voyage but, it came to a climax when we experienced a furious hurricane which lasted for days on end. My cabin was mid-ships. To get to the dining room I had to walk across the open deck. I noticed the incredible height of the waves next to the ship in a half-moon shape, and the depth of them along side. In my naiveté, it inspired me to walk towards the railing, which was fortunately made up of steel posts, with three steel cables all along the ship.

I bent over to observe the half-moon shape of the wave along-side. Its enormous height towering above the ship was impressive. It was an incredible sight, but only for a few seconds. Then this towering wall collapsed, partly on the ship's deck, and it slammed me against the cables with such enormous force that I figured I would not survive. I grabbed the cables, while an enormous suction was pulling me off the ship. A steel post prevented my body from slipping between the cables.

Hanging on for dear life with all my might, I realized that the living God was displaying his mercy to me in preventing me from being swept overboard. Arriving totally drenched in the dining room, I learned that at that very same time the cruise ship, the Andrea Doria, was in deep trouble about one hundred miles away from where we were. SOS signals had been picked up by our ship. It was feared that the ship would sink. Even though our ship attempted to sail in her direction, the fury of the storm prevented us from reaching her in time. The Andrea Doria did sink in the North Atlantic.

During the years that Trudy and I sailed on both cargo ships and cruise ships and in our ministry to the seafarers in the Port of Montreal, a thousand miles away from the most furious part of the North Atlantic, we learned to deeply respect the power of the oceans.

A group of Croatian seafarers, headed by their master, came walking into our Seafarers Centre with only one request: "Do you have a chapel in this place?" We had a beautiful chapel! As I ushered them in, I asked if I could be of service. They replied, "We have come here to thank God. We went through hell on the North Atlantic. The ship was in ballast and we figured we would not make it, but we did. So we want to thank God. Please, pray with us."

I visited the ship later that day. The captain, temporarily residing in a small guest cabin, ushered me into his own cabin, which was totally destroyed, as if someone with a sledge hammer had smashed his desk, chairs, and wall furniture.

I asked him what happened. He said, "The storm ripped my 1000-pound safe out of the wall and it rolled for thirty-six hours back and forth in my cabin while the ship constantly heeled over some forty-five degrees, destroying everything in sight. Imagine, Reverend, I had to get out of my cabin, because I was being chased by my own money."

Years later, I recalled a chief officer on board of an English ship. I had a serious conversation with him and the subject of overwhelming storms came up in that conversation. I pressed the matter of the need to acknowledge God. I had a hard time getting him "on board" with my sermon, but then he suddenly said: "Padre, I am well aware that I am trying to almost 'argue' with you, that I do not need God and that I am quite self-sufficient. But I do admit to you," and he stood up, came close to me and whispered in my ear, "when you are out there at sea, in your little steel box, even though it may be over 100,000 tons like this ship and you are out in a ravaging wind force, and seas with a height of twenty-five to thirty feet waves, it is so frightening, you will *want* to believe in God."

THE CHALLENGES
OF MY NEW COUNTRY

When you sail on a cargo ship, there is not always absolute certainty that you will arrive at the port you were aiming for. I arrived in the coal yards of Newport News, VA. The year was 1952. Most immigrants to the USA sail into the main port of the USA: New York, NY. The first thing that strikes them is the Statue of Liberty, which bestirs the hearts of anyone sailing by. It conveys a message: It makes you deeply aware that you have entered the country where liberty is the very foundation of society. I had not seen it as yet, but I had heard about the unique symbolism of the Statue of Liberty.

In Holland, I had become acquainted with Indonesians, who had come shortly after the war to live in the Netherlands. Our home was located across from a huge residence, which had just been vacated by the Germans. Six Indonesian families moved in. It was not surprising. About nine houses further down the street was an enormous estate with thirty-six rooms, which had also been taken over by the Germans, but was now vacated as well. It had belonged to a very wealthy person. I believe well over a dozen Indonesian families took residence in it.

We befriended them, particularly the young people with whom we got along very well. In school, moreover, we had some Chinese friends. So ever since I was young, I was accustomed to a somewhat cross-cultural climate.

I never really reflected on the fact that some of my friends were dark skinned. In fact, I was somewhat jealous of them, because as a redhead I had very white skin. The sun did not darken me like my Indonesian friends. The sun fried me instead. Yet race and color made no difference to me at all.

I discovered that some of my friends had exceptional talents, so I was intrigued with the gifts God had given them. Religiously, we talked to each other with respect, but with great conviction.

Upon arrival in Newport News, I managed to get a taxi to the train station, since I was headed for Boston. Two heavy suitcases and fifty American dollars made up all of my earthly possessions. When I found the right train, I boarded the first car I came to, due to the weight of my suitcases. The car was only one-third full. I noticed that the people, who were all black, smiled at me as I dragged my heavy suitcases through the car to a comfortable seat. I figured they could see a mile away that I was a new arrival in the USA, because of my heavy bags.

I noticed their smiles and their rather curious looks when I passed by. They reminded me a bit of my Indonesian friends, although I did think that these people were considerably darker and had bright, white teeth. My teeth had become discolored, due to lack of proper nutrition during the war. I found a seat where I could sit alone; I did not dare to communicate with any of the people, because I did not speak English well enough.

A few weeks later, in college, I was asked to give a speech about my personal belief and about the community I came from. So I began by saying, "I lived in Holland close to the tulips." The entire student body burst out in spontaneous laughter. I did not understand why they laughed, so I quietly carried on with my speech. When it was finished, someone came up and congratulated me on my presentation, even though it had left much to be desired. He explained that the laughter had been occasioned by my pronunciation of the word "tulips." It had come across as "two lips." What really impressed me was the gracious manner in which he explained to me my lack of proper pronunciation. I have experienced this gracious reaction from so many in North America, and I have always deeply appreciated it.

In the train I sat by the window and I was fascinated by the beautiful scenery of my new country. Then a conductor showed up. I had been on trains throughout Europe and had met all kinds of conductors—happy ones, sour ones, arrogant ones, young, and old ones—but the behavior of the conductor, who now appeared before me, defied description. He started to shout at me as if I had committed a very serious crime.

He shouted so loudly and his speech was so fast that I could not figure out what he was saying. I finally gathered that I was in the wrong car. I thought, "What have I done? Did I get on a train that is headed for Dallas instead of Boston?" He grabbed me by my coat, dragged me to my feet, and started to pull my suitcases down. I thought, "My good man, are you planning to kick me off this train while it is moving at sixty miles an hour?" Watching him, I collected whatever was lying on my seat.

I heard him repeat himself and then he pointed to all the people in the car, who quietly and somewhat anxiously, listened to the conductor's explosion. He tried to make clear to me that I was sitting in the wrong car. I still had not figured things out. Why get excited when there was lots of space and I was sitting alone in a compartment with six seats? While he, with one suitcase, and I with the other proceeded towards the exit, he pointed to a sign by the exit. It read: "For colored only."

I could not believe my eyes. If I would have come to America with some of my Indonesian friends, could we not have sat together on this train? Would I have to sit in a car with white people and they would have to sit with colored people? All of us were going to Boston.

The next car had white people in it. They did not smile when I came in. They did not seem to care who I was, why I was on the train or what the reason was that I started to look for a seat half an hour after the train had departed. The conductor threw my suitcase down and took off with the angriest look he could produce.

I reflected on what had just happened. What was the reason for the extraordinary fury of the conductor? Why did he have to scream? He could have quietly sat down next to me and said, "Young man, you look like a foreign student with your heavy suitcases. Am I right? You may not be aware of it, but here in Virginia, and on this train, black people have to sit in one car and white people have to sit in another car. That's the law of this part of the land, so you will have to move to another car. Shall I help you with your suitcases? I'll show you the way." But, that had not been his reaction at all.

Perhaps the LORD let this happen to teach me a lesson. If you deal with a situation that is not as it should be, you ought to approach the person quietly, reasonably, respectfully, and explain the situation as clearly as you can. Then keep your mouth shut. The second lesson he taught me was a bit more difficult. There are not only conductors, but all kinds of people who, when they run into a complexity, try to set it straight by yelling, screaming, and gesticulating, frightening everybody in sight. React to them with the utmost of calmness and quietude. Nowadays we would say, "Keep your cool!"

So, the train sped to Boston, white cars and colored cars, holding hands as it were, all running on the same rails in the same direction and all pulled by one engine. I wondered if it was a white or a colored engine.

LESSONS LEARNED
FROM THE POOR

We called it the "Poor House." It was a hospital for the poor and homeless supported by the state. I managed to get a job there. I was attending the theological school and needed money to keep myself in reasonable shape.

The first night I was trained, along with another seminarian, by a lovely, somewhat older nurse, who had been graced by God with a heart of compassion and an attitude of understanding. Such people make an indelible impression on you. She instructed us in giving injections to people who were suffering from diabetes. The seminary student and I practiced on each other, under her watchful eye, and she decided within a few minutes that we could be on our own. In a subtle way, she conveyed genuine love for people. She displayed it beautifully with the one patient, who was still awake. He was blind, deaf, and dumb. She instructed me to get "in touch" with him through touch. It was impressive: God must have planned this!

That night, and years later in my ministry, in my congregations as well as among the seafarers, I have benefited from the training by that nurse. The job, I recall, paid one dollar per hour, but because we were on night duty, we received a special rate of $1.03 per hour.

After half an hour of training, coaxing, and orientation, I assumed she would either stay with us during that first night or at least put us together in one ward. She did not. She said that she was in charge of the entire hospital during the night and there were five wards. My companion left for another ward and I was now in charge of the entire ward in which we got our training.

There were thirty-eight men, nine of whom needed injections. Six of them needed to be washed and cleaned up every morning. Diapers for adults had not reached the market yet. Three of them needed to be fed, and the place had to be as clean as I could make it.

It was a challenge. The stench certainly let me know that cleaning and washing had priority. I attacked the problem with vigor, starting at four in the morning. To keep myself sane and positive, I had a touch of ether put on a napkin and tied it around my nose and mouth. I liked the odor.

I decided that I should do the job in the joy of the LORD. These poor creatures couldn't help it that they were in the condition they were in. I was the only diversion they had. That meant that I had to be in top shape to help make their lives bearable. They were stuck in their beds and in this ward. My manner of conduct had to bring to them rays of the glory of Christ. That was not only my job, but the job of everyone who calls himself a follower of the LORD.

That's a huge effort. Today in the postmodern climate, there is a strong tendency to concentrate on our own happiness first and foremost. We are to be catered to. We are to be encouraged, get our rest, our share, our satisfaction before we are prepared to concentrate on another person.

I shall never forget this one white haired, white bearded man, who was my last person in the cleaning routine. When I had hoisted him back into his bed after I had washed him and provided clean sheets for his bed, I sat him up and adjusted the pillows behind him. I believe he was paralyzed from the waist down. To encourage him, I concluded my session with him by saying: "Well, sir, you are nicely washed up, you have clean sheets, one even has flowers on it. Imagine you're lying between flowers. So are you happy now?"

His straightforward answer, without the slightest smile on his face was: "How in hell can anybody be happy in the poor house?"

I agreed with him that "in hell" you could not be happy. But I reminded him that this poor house was not "in hell." I also suggested that we should focus on heaven. You could not be happier anywhere else!

The gentleman in charge of the meals would come in at four in the morning. It was a simple breakfast he prepared, a few slices of bread with a thin slice of meat between them and some diluted orange juice. We were, after all, in the poor house.

He made it a point to prophesy who would pass away during the next night. It meant that I could extend some extra care, physical as well as spiritual, before it happened. He was usually right in his judgment. Here I was a young seminarian, and almost every night I walked with others on that narrow edge between life and death with people who had no one on earth who cared for them, other than the staff of the poor house.

I still see the blind, deaf, and dumb man. He dressed himself every morning as properly as anyone can be dressed in a poor house. Then he exerted himself in making his bed and in cleaning up his little table next to the bed, refreshing the water glass and watering the plant that had been there for ages. Think of it, he couldn't even see the color of the flowers, but he took care of the table, the bed, the plant, his night slippers under the bed, and his pajamas so that his world would be in proper order. He could not see, hear, or talk. We just communicated by touch.

There is a lot of language that can be put in that touch. His language conveyed the thought: "I do not question God, why I am the way I am. God must have his own reasons. It's not my business to pry into his purposes. But, I am thankful that I am in a place that provides me with a roof over my head, a decent bed, a little table next to it, and my slippers under it. I have three meals a day as well as a late-evening snack of a dehydrated donut. God be praised for his mercies. And those people who are here every day, the nurse and the others, they communicate with me. I can even figure out who is who."

It was a sight that touched my heart. Sometimes I thought I could see Jesus in him. I didn't have to ask him if he was happy in the poor house. To him this was not a poor house. His thoughts and actions displayed that he was in touch with heaven. Fifty years later his testimony still rings in my ears.

LESSONS LEARNED
FROM PRISONERS

In Romans 15:20, Paul says, "It has always been my ambition to preach the gospel where Christ was not known…" That has been my compassion too.

I always searched for settings where I would be able to come into contact with the people who are not—as yet—in Christ and whom I might be able to challenge to obey his voice. Before I entered the International Ministry to Seafarers, I found myself in a congregation in Kingston, Ontario. It presented quite a number of exceptional opportunities. We had members who worked in the psychiatric hospital, students who attended Queens University, as well as some who studied at the Royal Military College. All six of them always attended church in their splendid bright red uniforms. Besides the engineers, merchants, construction workers, and farmers, there were guards working in one of the four prisons.

In the church we had one hundred and sixty-two young people who lived in the context of their predominantly conservative, immigrant homes and in the climate of the various schools which they attended. God must have assigned this wide variety of people to Trudy and me in order to prepare us for the ministry to people from around the world.

It was in the maximum security prison, called KP, Kingston Penitentiary, that Trudy and I became involved with people whom we thought belonged to the category referred to by St. Paul.

Trudy became a member of the Elizabeth Fry Organization. It gave her access to the Maximum Security Prison for Women in Kingston. Many of the prisoners were young women. Just before their release, they were allowed to visit someone on the outside in order to bring them into contact with the outside world again; a rather frightening concept after their long imprisonment. So Trudy invited some of these girls, one at a time, to our parsonage. To visit in a relaxed setting would be a meaningful experience for them, and to get a taste of the Christian lifestyle might well prove to be an added benefit.

I became involved with KP as a result of a visit to a member of our denomination from another city. He was incarcerated there and scheduled to spend several more years in this prison. I had found it extremely frustrating to talk to this nineteen-year-old lad in a setting where I was on one side of a glass wall and he was on the other side. Next to us, on our left and right, were other people as well as two guards. The same was true for the prisoners on the other side of the glass partition. It had become a shouting match among us to reach the person on the other side.

Since I had come into contact with the chief chaplain at the local ministerial association, I asked him if it would be possible for me to use his office for a more personal pastoral contact with this prisoner who had gone off track. He consented. This gave me access to the inside of KP, where I visited this young man regularly.

Sometime later the chaplain invited me to attend one of his early morning Sunday services in the men's prison, as well as in the women's prison, in order to become acquainted with the different aspects of the chapel ministry, as he called it. He had organized art classes, reading classes, discussion sessions, and Bible studies. I was fascinated.

One day he called me into his office and asked if I would be willing to preach the sermon sometime within the next two weeks. I agreed and came out to preach. We stood again in his office in anticipation of the clock moving to zero hour. He led us in prayer and ushered me to the door leading to the absolutely packed chapel with some two hundred and fifty people in attendance. With his hand on the doorknob, he looked me in the eye and said, "Do not pussy-foot. Sock it to them straight. They need the word of God." So there I had my terms of reference.

I was impressed by his love for his people, his devotion to his job, and his biblical focus. I liked the man. Perhaps it was mutual, because a few weeks later he called me in while I was visiting the prisoner of our denomination. He told me that he was scheduled to be away for half a year on the West Coast of Canada to meet with chaplains, to train them, and to visit a number of prisons. Would I be willing to fill in for him during his absence?

So I became the deputy prison chaplain because, as he explained to me, I had to have a proper title in order to have access to this federal institution. I did not understand that, but it became clear when I was called to visit a prisoner in the high isolation security area. I was asked to inform him that his father had died. I entered the secluded area and finally the highly secure, solo cell of this man. It was a dismal setting. After I had introduced myself, I approached the subject for which I was assigned to come and informed him that the LORD had called his father out of this life.

Without a trace of emotion in his stone hard face he responded: "Who is my father?" A man ripped away from his family and any relationship of love with his father and mother, he had dug his own grave of isolation, since I believed he had committed crimes which may have caused others no longer to have a father. In this utterly bizarre climate, I attempted to say something about a Father we may not recognize, but who for sure knows us even in isolation in KP.

"Who is my father?" It was the first time I heard that question. In the course of my ministry for the next forty-five years, I have heard it over and over. When I referred to "Our Father," I discovered that there are countless people who do not know him at all. It convinced me that I should stick to my calling in order to remind the world around me that our Father is still in search of a lot of his sons, and is longing to celebrate with them.

When his sons come back to him in confession, this Father has only one observation: "…this 'son of mine' was dead and is alive again; he was lost and is found." One of them was in isolation in KP.

Part of my responsibility was to have interviews with many prisoners. There were over eight hundred in this prison. As I interviewed many of them, there were three things that came to the fore:

1 Many of those who were incarcerated were between the ages of eighteen and twenty-five.

2 In almost all instances, the crime committed by the individual was committed with someone else.

3 In very many instances, the crime was committed while the perpetrator was under the influence of alcohol or drugs.

So in summary, the vital message is: watch your conduct, especially when you are young; watch the company you are keeping; and watch what you are drinking or taking.

What inspired me particularly in this ministry was that I saw the Spirit of God miraculously at work in the hearts of people. I remember especially a twenty-four-year-old young man who had killed someone and was now scheduled to be imprisoned for as many years as his current age. Imagine!

I knew him quite well since he worked in the chaplain's office. He attended the Bible study and there it suddenly happened: He was touched by the mysterious working of the Spirit of God. That confirms again that in the last analysis it is God himself who calls us out of our darkness and sets us in the brilliance of his light. He submitted himself to Jesus Christ and proudly proclaimed that he had become a Christian.

One day I came into the chaplain's office terribly frustrated because I had prepared an exciting newsletter for my congregation in prison as well as for the women in the women's prison. The duplicating machine, an antiquated Xerox machine, had crumbled up the original and had totally destroyed it.

As I marched into the chaplain's office, I threw my bag on the desk, and walking over to the corner to hang up my coat, I vented my frustration saying: "That rotten machine destroyed my newsletter, and here I had prepared such a good letter. Boy, am I ever depressed about that." My converted Christian friend, who was polishing the desk, put his cloth down, walked around the desk and stopped directly in front of me.

Then he said, "Padre, it does not become a Christian to be *ever* depressed." His remark floored me. When a prisoner, committed to Christ and in a real spiritual sense set free by him, is scheduled to be locked up for many years and makes a remark like that, you keep silent. To be a Christian *should* make a difference. My words of depression were indeed totally out of order. They were part of my old sinful nature that had obviously not yet been crucified. He sounded accusatory, but he was right. It was another lesson in my training. It made me think that he was one of the flowers in the wilderness of KP. I developed a real love for the ministry to prisoners and served my deputy time with excitement.

About two years later, when we had started the Ministry to Seafarers in the port of Montreal, the chaplain asked us to come down to Kingston and join him for dinner. Trudy and I had dinner with him and his wife. I figured it was to express appreciation for the time I had served in KP on his behalf. But there was more to it. He offered me a position in the maximum security prison in Montreal or, if I did not want that, a position in a brand new prison in Alberta. But our LORD had committed us to the Ministry to Seafarers and that had taken deep roots. So we declined. He suggested that, when we were in Kingston, I should at least come in one Sunday morning to preach the sermon once more. I looked forward to that and I did preach. The place was still packed. No one had left.

After the worship service about eleven prisoners, with whom I had had a bit more meaningful contact, crowded around me. One of them said, "What are you doing now Padre, are you back in your church?"

I said, "No, I have accepted a position as chaplain to Seafarers in Montreal."

This was met with deathly silence. Then, the one who had asked the question exclaimed, "A chaplain to what?"

I figured that they were not familiar with the word "Seafarers," so I explained: "I work with people who work on ships."

He asked, "You mean sailors?"

I said, "Yes, you could call them that."

Again deathly silence. Then one of them remarked, "Whatever got into you Padre, to start working among *that* kind of people?"

Here my friends, all committed to a maximum security prison because of the nature of their crimes, looked down on the profession of sailors. In their view, sailors are people who do not measure up. They are seen as rowdy, drunken, piracy oriented individuals and not as the professionals they are, bringing ships, cargo, and passengers from one part of the world to another. So I had a half hour discussion with them explaining who sailors really are and what it means to bring the gospel of Jesus Christ to people from around the world, so that they come to acknowledge him as their LORD and Savior.

It was another lesson in how people, despite their own shortcomings, view others with preconceived notions. *These* kinds of people and *that* kind of people are all called by *this* LORD and Savior to commit *themselves* to him and to his glory! "I say to every one of you: Do not think of yourself more highly than you ought, but rather think of yourself with sober judgment, in accordance with the measure of faith God has given you" (Romans 12:3). Not an easy word in our somewhat stuck-up society.

THE STRANGERS
IN OUR GATE

Seafarers come to our ports on cargo and on cruise ships. They are not homeless. The mere fact that they sail for months on end testifies to the fact that they seek to support their families. They are not destitute. They get paid for their duties, but they are *isolated* from their homes, their friends, their churches, (if they belong to one) from their culture, and their country.

Their endless voyages make them go from port to port in countries many of us have never visited. It may look so romantic, traveling the world and visiting all those foreign countries. You can drink in the atmosphere as you stroll through the cities. You can pick up characteristic souvenirs. You can benefit from their technical sophistication.

The Seafarers are caught up in this stream as well—not for a brief vacation, like the tourists—but for months, for years on end. There is nothing romantic in it for them anymore. They seek *human* contact.

The services of Seafarers Centers in many ports are of inestimable value in their care for and contact with the Seafarers. They provide them with an excellent response to their needs in communication and in personal provisions, but *human* contact is also characterized by spiritual exchange. As representatives of God we, as chaplains, have an invaluable task to address this need. This is what we are called to. Then we make contact on a level, which is beyond the business model and approach them as people, who are, like we ourselves, created in the image of God. We are to call them to live to the glory of *his* name.

According to the Scriptures, there are three major categories of people who demand the special attention of the church:

- The Poor

  Christ reminds us, "…The poor you will always have with you…" (Matt. 26:11).

- The Widows and the Orphans.

  "Religion that God our Father accepts as pure and faultless is this: to look after orphans and widows in their distress…" (James 1:27).

- The Strangers.

  The seafarer belongs to this category. Throughout the Bible we see God's profound concern for the stranger. His rest, recreation and refreshment are mentioned in the fourth commandment (Ex. 20:10). His protection is highlighted on the basis that God's people themselves have been strangers in Egypt (Ex. 22:21). His access to the Almighty is clearly incorporated by King Solomon in his dedicatory prayer for the temple (1 Kings 8:43).

So the "stranger in our gate" needs to be personally welcomed, especially by us, the chaplains, to meet Christ. Does not God summon us to listen carefully to something like the telephone voice of almost any company?

"The menu has *not* changed. (It is still the message of the Bible) Your voice not only, but especially your *actions* will be monitored for quality control."

MINISTRY ON SHORE VERSUS MINISTRY ON SHIPS

Before I became a pastor to seafarers I served two congregations. Ministry in a congregation is *structured* unlike ministry to seafarers. In my first congregation, God showed me what I thought was a large part of the whole range of human conduct in its glory and in its misery. . The congregation was made up of recent immigrants, all from different parts of the Netherlands. Many of them believed they were the authority on how the church ought to be run, and how the pastor ought to preach. For me, it was a unique place to learn humility.

Fresh out of the seminary, before I was even ordained, my congregation went through a crisis: There was an explosion in the magnesium mine, in which one young man from the congregation died and one father of many children got burned on almost two thirds of his body.

In that climate, I experienced how God triumphed in the lives of young and old with his grace and with his love. It began to dawn on me that Christ is the Good Shepherd and that he was leading the flock. I was there to feed the flock and to show them the good pasture of the LORD.

The very last act in my ministry there was again a funeral because suddenly, my most gracious elder, who had ushered me through the "maiden voyage" of my ministry, was called to his eternal home.

In my second congregation, a congregation twice the size of the one I had just left, I was in charge of three worship services every Sunday. Two neighboring congregations were without a pastor. When the chaplain at the maximum security prison asked me to deputize for him for half a year, it increased my load to five worship services every Sunday.

The city where I served had three hospitals. Six students from the Royal Military College belonged to our congregation as well. In the sixties, the pattern of a clergyman's life was clearly defined. Besides five or six Sunday worship services, hospital visits were expected. I was also expected to teach the Bible and the Heidelberg Catechism to the young people. The catechism is a document that reflects the doctrinal position of the Christian church.

All the families of the congregation expected to be visited at least twice a year. The telephone rang on a daily basis. Council meetings and a variety of other meetings demanded my presence. Church secretaries were unknown in the churches I served, so the administration fell to me as well. The task was overwhelming and exhausting, but clearly spelled out.

What I did see was that God was teaching me another lesson, "I can do everything through him who gives me strength" (Phil.4:13). This lesson had been illustrated in what I thought was a bit childish, yet also highly effective way by my Old Testament professor in the seminary: "Remember, gentlemen, here you are learning Hebrew and the Old Testament, but in the congregation there will be times, when you will be excessively stressed." At that moment he stretched a piece of elastic between his hands almost to the breaking point. Then he continued, "Remember that God allows that stress, to remind you that he is in charge and that he goes with you to the breaking point."

There he left it, but it reminded us to think theologically and to conclude: Not *through* but *to* the breaking point. *Christ* went through it: His body was broken for us. So, we have to keep in mind that he is in charge. We are told to bear up to the breaking point.

It was the Professor's poetic way of saying—and displaying—that we were headed for what we call today "stress." In the late fifties that word was not yet in popular use

In ministry to seafarers structure totally disappears. The telephone does not ring anymore. Instead, we must seek to create some kind of pattern in this highly mobile and changing world. Today there may be four seamen in the hospital. Last week there were thirty-nine.

When a Seafarers Center is operated some guidelines are of course necessary and Sunday worship services should be scheduled, but because we minister to different ships every day of the week, we have no identifiable congregation. We never know who will come to the church services. We do not know what languages they speak or if they are even familiar with the Bible or with the protocol of a church service.

I have come to the conclusion that the unstructured character of the ministry to seafarers has a very serious influence on the performance of the pastor. In many instances, he might concentrate exclusively on the operation of and the support for the Seafarers Center. This is a monumental task in itself.

As the senior staff member, he becomes chaplain *and* Director. If he has no support staff, he is responsible for every aspect of the operation of the center. As a result, the distinct pastoral and evangelistic character of the pastor to seafarers is replaced by the need to manage the Seafarers Center. It is of course easier to address clearly identifiable needs than to go on board of ships and to seek occasion to proclaim the gospel to people who might not necessarily be interested in what you have to offer.

On board you come into contact with another world. Here are people from different nations, who are perhaps unable to understand or to speak English comfortably. They are by and large, extremely gracious and actually very fascinating people I have come to love. But they are not always waiting for you, a pastor. They are not looking for your message. They do not immediately express their specific need, which you could address. So, you are left in mid-air.

You may hang up a notice on the bulletin board stating that there is a Seafarers Center and that a bus will be arriving at a specific time. You may put down some reading material, both secular and sacred, and notice that it is greeted with a mixture of reactions. . This is not very encouraging to you. So as pastors to seafarers we must focus on our calling, for that is the crux of the matter.

The Rev. I Frivold, former pastor of the Norwegian Seamen's Church in New Orleans, LA, in a speech to seafarers' pastors, concluded her remarks with the observation: "As missionaries, we can easily stray and be tempted to get involved in matters, which are not ours to perform. Our main task must remain the spreading of the Word of God."

WHO ARE THE SEAFARERS?

On my former business card it said "harbour chaplain." A harbor is a distinct, industrial complex like an airport, or a steel mill, or a car factory. It involves thousands of people, all doing different jobs. It is a secular complex. The days are measured in terms of time, over-time, double time, even triple time, not in terms of weekdays and LORD's days. Although to the outsider it appears as a unit, there are sharp demarcations, which are carefully observed.

The most obvious one is the one between seafarers and long-shoremen, also called dock-workers or stevedores, the people who work "along the shore." The former run the ships, the latter, under the former's supervision, load and unload the ships. Seafarers, apart from pure business relationships, do not ordinarily associate socially or otherwise with longshoremen. We shall not examine the reasons for this. It is simply a fact.

My position as chaplain brings me into superficial contact with longshoremen. I pass them by on my way to and even on the ships. I also come into contact with the port authority officials in order to obtain information about the ships. I often meet the port police, especially in emergencies. I meet the port agents on board as well as ashore. My ministry is ordinarily not directed to any of them. It is directed specifically to seafarers. They are the professional people who work and sail on cargo ships, tankers and on cruise ships. They are my congregation. My heart goes out to them.

There are of course seafarers on all kinds of other ships as well:

- On fishing vessels and floating fishing factories
- On rescue and escort ships, like the Coast Guard and the Water Police
- On off-shore oil platforms
- On scientific and research ships
- On ferries and on private yachts

Then there is the naval world, which represents a country's defense force at sea.

Seafarers are ordinarily referred to as "sailors." Though they all *sail*, as the expression has it, the word "sailor" actually only refers to the category of seafarers, who work on deck, under the supervision of the boatswain. The people on board of freighters and tankers are classified in three departments:

- The Deck Department, comprised of deck officers and sailors
- The Engine Department with the engineers and their assistants
- The Catering Department, providing and maintaining food and lodging

Until recently, with its highly developed technical breakthrough, all ships with more than twelve crewmembers had a radio officer on board. Classified among the deck officers, he was in fact separate from them. He was there primarily for safety reasons and wireless shore communication. The radio officer used to have his private communication office. His wall was decorated by a clock marked with red and green sections of three minutes.

During these periods of time, no vessel anywhere in the world is permitted to broadcast any message, either by voice or by Morse code, except in case of emergency. That means that the entire world at sea is silent for twelve minutes every single hour of the day and night. In the event that there should be a ship in serious trouble, which would be able to send out only a faint SOS message, it could be heard by other ships easier and more clearly during this "Silent Time." Any ship in its vicinity could then hear the emergency call uninterruptedly, note the ship's location, and attempt to come to its rescue.

It is a testimony to the concept of community in the most desolate place on earth: The High Seas. I have often thought: *Imagine if we should apply this concept to every individual on board and ashore and suggest that for a period of twelve minutes every hour—well, let's make it every day—we should remain silent and listen.* What would we hear? Who knows, we might hear the cry of one of our neighbors and detect that he has sailed into trouble and is in crisis, perhaps in total despair. He might be "sinking." We could then rise to the occasion and come to the rescue. We could conceivably lead him to the Light in the Word of God. Who knows but that God is calling out to us in that silent time, and above all the world's cacophony calls us to note what is happening in the lives of others.

He could even alert us to change our own "sailing course" and review the chart he gave us, in order to get the correct harbor in focus ourselves, especially when we have drifted off course.

I think there is more to that clock of the radio officer than meets the eye.

On cruise ships, there are people who in all quietude and in their own way, seek to acknowledge God while they are on board. Every now and then they page through an old crumpled devotional, given to them by their mother or wife, and kept in their pocket ever since. That's why many of them so appreciate the weekly devotional, "Our daily bread," which I often distribute liberally. They need encouragement. They need to know that they are part of the Christian church and are upheld by our prayers. Isolation and spiritual loneliness, on board ships, are fierce enemies. That's why part of our ministry is, of course, pure pastoral care.

Then there are those who are deeply moved by our interest in the well-being of their souls. They appreciate the time we take to offer prayers, blessings, and the LORD's counsel when they are on a break from their station. They work on the bridge, in the officers' lounge, in the bar, in the galley, in the dining rooms, in the crew's mess room, in the individual cabins, in the hospital, on the stairway, in the garbage collection area, in the laundry rooms, in the repair shops, in the offices, in the stores, in the casino, in the performance shows, in the engine room, on deck, at the security stations, in short, they may work anywhere. It means that we must move around constantly, be visible and go to where they are, so as to alert them to our availability to be in touch at their convenience.

There are others who are just curious about our presence on board. The church's care intrigues them. Carefully, gently, and graciously, we attempt to get them to become sensitive to the presence of the LORD and his approach to them through his Word.

There are those, who at all costs, wish to steer clear of any involvement in matters of a religious nature. They deliberately avoid any contact with the gospel, or with the chaplains, since chaplains are the evident representatives of the church and of the gospel. These seafarers are very few in number, but they are also on board. They behoove our prayers, that the Spirit of God will touch their hearts and that our display of love and concern may reflect the love of God for them.

There are those who are in crisis because they are away from home for up to nine months. Or they may be in crisis on board in their job which in almost all instances is extremely pressured. They may be in crisis because of their fleeting relationships on the ship. Their hearts or their consciences may plague them. For them our presence becomes a sounding board for advice, for direction, for a word of wisdom, or consolation.

There are the passengers. They "see" the presence of the church in us. They notice in the daily programs that worship services, meditations, and pastoral council sessions are part and parcel of the menu at sea for them. There are not merely the entertainment shows, the lecturers, the musical performances, but also the opportunities to worship God, to reflect in studies of the Bible, and to interact with other Christians. The presence of the pastor on board may well be a testimony that the church is, and indeed needs to be, identifiably present in these floating hotels, which are home to hundreds of seafarers for months on end, and to thousands of passengers for only a few days.

PROTOCOL ON BOARD

The world of ships, freighters, and cruise ships alike is marked by protocol, cooperative behavior, and dedication. The ship must sail, "the show must go on." Everyone must rise to the occasion, or to use a naval expression, "turn to." I discovered that, in order to function effectively on board, I must make myself acceptable in appearance as well as in the manner of communication.

Although it is not the tradition in my denomination to wear a clerical collar, or to preach in a gown, I do wear a clerical collar and I do preach in a gown. To the people on board, it is an identifiable link with the historic Christian church. The Roman Catholic Church has set the tone in this. Today, however, there is a tendency to shed the clerical garb and to dress casually, like everyone else.

On board with freighters, the uniform has been replaced by ordinary clothing. On cruise ships, one is dressed according to one's function or position. The clerical garb not only fits in well and is appropriate on cruise ships, but it helps with identification. It inspires confidence.

The guard at the gangway, everyone at work on deck, and all people I meet inside the ship immediately recognize me as a minister. That places me in the correct position. I am not the agent, neither am I a vendor, nor a casual visitor.

I am a man of God. I represent Christ and His Church. That's how I am to be identified. Only once did someone mistake me. It wasn't a seaman. It was a passenger. When I was in discussion with the chief cook in one of the more sophisticated restaurants on a cruise ship, during the time that it was officially closed, a passenger marched in and asked me if I happened to be the Maitre d.'

It was a reasonable question. I decided to shift the term to the spiritual level, so I responded: "Yes I am, but not of this restaurant." I felt justified. Although I did not say it to the passenger, I thought: *After all, I do provide the place, the occasion, the setting to be fed by our* LORD, *who said*: "I am the bread of life. He who comes to me will never be hungry, and he who believes in me will never be thirsty" (John 6:35). I know of no restaurant where the menu is that satisfying!

On board of cruise ships, it is expected that one wears clerical garb. The master wears his uniform. Every officer is characterized by his rank, indicated on his uniform. The cook dresses like a cook, the steward like a steward, so it is fitting that I, as the chaplain to Seafarers, dress like a chaplain.

It also means that in my contact with officers, staff, and crew from a wide variety of nations I maintain the correct relationship. I am not a supervisor, I do not work for the company, I am the pastor for the people. Most people are aware of what this means. It gives them a unique opportunity to speak in total and complete honesty about whatever it is that burdens them.

The physical contact likewise is to be restrained. In some nations one shakes hands. In others, one prefers to simply bow. That is their culture and tradition. We ought to be sensitive to this.

Keen observance of specified rules of conduct facilitates the communication. On Greek and Slavic ships, for example, it is significant to remember to shake hands with the owner of a cabin, either inside or outside of it, never across the threshold. That superstition is presumably based on a rather fascinating story found in the Bible:

The ark of God had been captured by the Philistines, who placed it in the house of Dagon, one of their gods. Dagon collapsed in the middle of the night. His head and hands broke off and ended up on the threshold. "That is why to this day neither the priests of Dagon nor any others who enter Dagon's temple at Ashdod step on the threshold" (1 Samuel 5:5).

When I approach people with the liberating news of the gospel of salvation, I would not begin by dislodging such superstitious belief as not shaking hands across a threshold. The belief in the all embracing power of the presence of God will do that in its own time. Its proclamation has priority.

On board it is ordinarily the custom to refer to each other either by title, or by the last name. It is interesting that some people, who work in the same ship for months on end, know others on board only by their title, rather than by their name.

On cargo ships I also developed the habit to address anyone, who does not wear a uniform, with the title, "chief." In the merchant naval world the word "chief'" goes as high as the rank of second in command. So in addressing a person with the word "chief" I have aimed for just about the highest position: chief officer, chief engineer, chief cook, chief steward, chief purser, and so on. If he happens to be indeed the Chief in his department, I have hit the nail on the head. Only once did I fail because the person, upon my inquiry if he were the chief officer, responded, "No Sir, I am the captain." I duly apologized.

The familiarity of the use of first names is only slowly entering the world of ships, although among the higher ranks it is still almost non-existent. When I boarded a Korean freighter, I noticed that seamen did not give me their first name, nor their rank, but their last name. It was prefaced by the word Mr., "I am Mr. Kim."

For years, we invited senior high school students and college students to come and spend a weekend ministering to seafarers at our Seafarers Centre, a magnificent place, characterized by class and distinction.

The students joined us as we went on board of ships to invite the seafarers to an evening of worship and fellowship at the Seafarers

Centre. Many seafarers are young people, so there was easy contact right from the start. For the students it was a profound cross-cultural and missionary experience. They met people from Latvia, Iran, Bulgaria, the Philippines, Egypt, Korea, Russia, Turkey, and half a dozen other countries.

In a relaxed setting following the worship service, to which everyone had been invited, they were able to give account of their faith. For seafarers it is significant to see that the worship service, conducted by what they would consider the professional, the pastor, is confirmed and supported by the people in the audience, especially the young people.

For the students, it was a valuable experience to be able to speak to a total stranger, a foreigner from another country, in this social setting of a club about the Christian faith and the reasons why one believes. It was a unique challenge. Reference is made in the Bible to precisely this: "Always be prepared to give an answer to everyone who asks you, to give the reason for the hope that you have" (1 Peter 3:15). Then a very significant and very wise remark is added: "But do this with gentleness and respect…"

It is extremely valuable to take note of *this addition*. In the minds of many people, Christian witness is associated with an inconsiderate insistence to have the individual make a spiritual *decision* as speedily as possible. This is not marked by gentleness or respect. We live in an age of *instant* response and *instant* satisfaction. That is contrary to the biblical approach of the LORD Jesus himself. He placed before the person his proposals in direct form, or via the record of a story, and he did it graciously and respectfully. The hearer could make up his mind and react with a commitment at whatever time he felt ready.

In our contact with seafarers we have at all times been striving to maintain this type of respectful approach. We are aware that, in the hearts of many seafarers, there is an awareness of the reality of God. It is our responsibility to get in touch with that and so to address the undeveloped area of his relationship to Jesus Christ. Only then will he find genuine peace. That is honorable to God. In the last analysis it is not only the individual salvation of the person, however significant that is. The message of the Bible is that all are to bring glory and honor to God the Father. He, as the very center of the universe, calls for acknowledgment of his power and dominion by all people. That brings praise to his name.

For the young people it was always a moving experience, particularly since many of the seafarers did question them about their belief. A number of them, through their encounters with seafarers from other countries, became inspired to get involved in full-time missionary employment.

But one simple lesson has to be learned, a certain propriety in dress needs to be observed. The seafarers, particularly those working on cargo ships, dress up when they are invited to a social evening at the Seafarers Centre. When they are aware that some form of religious service will be conducted, they especially wish to be correctly dressed.

The current "come as you are" philosophy is not embraced by all people from foreign countries. That should inspire us to follow suit. At times, some young people felt constrained to tell me that religion is not expressed in what one wears. I know that very well, but cross-cultural awareness is significant here. One's witness to the gospel should not be negated by a lack of sensitivity. Respect for the visitor's culture is a vital link in the effective communication of the gospel.

I have also learned the value of being able to greet people in their own language. Seafarers are, in that respect, different from foreigners who have immigrated to our country. The latter, in many instances, prefer to be identified with the community in which they now live. They hesitate to use their native language, despite their accent in English. Assimilation is the key in the process of immigration. Total amalgamation with their adopted country is therefore vital for them.

Not so with seafarers. They come from around the world. They are proud of their country. They may be able to speak English very well, but their heart and soul are in their native land. Their heritage is deeply valued. Many of them are only temporarily at sea. So, it is significant to get as close to them as is possible in the limited time we have. That's why I greet them in their own language. Their reaction invariably is highly positive.

I also learned the incredible value of being able to readily identify the nationality of the seafarers. It took me years to get to this point. Particularly among the Asiatic people, it took me extra time. With the continued shifts in nationalities on board this can become a perplexity. But it is helpful to acquire the art.

People are extremely sensitive to this. If I am Irish, I really do not like to be classified as English. The Japanese, whenever they go to Korea to deliver a speech on any subject, are in the habit of apologizing, in their opening remarks, for the misdeeds, which have been committed during the last world war some sixty years ago. Those misdeeds make a Korean feel very uncomfortable, if he were classified as Japanese.

One ship I remember especially. It was an Israeli container ship with crewmembers from fourteen different nations on board. It was noon. In the crew mess room, the seafarers were in the process of getting their lunch from a table in the center in the room.

As I entered, there were three people standing behind the table. They were filling their plates from the buffet and were moving slowly along. The first one was from Poland. I greeted him in Polish, supporting my very limited Polish vocabulary with a firm handshake and a Polish wish for "bon appetite." His face lit up with a big smile. "Your accent is very good," he said. He then moved shyly along. The second one I greeted with a little bow instead of with a handshake, because he was Korean. I exercised my Korean greeting as best I could, indicating in Korean that I was the pastor, because looking at my clerical collar, I sensed he suspected I was a priest.

He was stunned and with amazement he responded with three words, interestingly in English, "You speak Korean?" I recognized the third man standing at the table as Croatian. "Dobroh Daahn" was my limited message in Croatian. Again I noticed surprise and a broad smile.

Out of the corner of my eye I noticed an Israeli seafarer seated at the table. He was the boatswain, the man in charge of the sailors who work on deck. He was in the process of bringing his soup spoon to his mouth. In fact, his mouth was already half open. But he kept following me with his eyes as I moved from one person to another. He seemed surprised that I had identified the nationalities correctly and had even greeted every one in his own language.

I then turned to him and extending my hand, greeted him in Hebrew with "Shalom, Shalom, Uvraga." It elicited not a response to my greeting, but rather an exclamation of surprise. He rose to his feet, grabbed my outstretched hand and bellowed, "You must be a Prophet!"

That is exactly what I am … a prophet. The Oxford Dictionary tells me that a prophet is "an interpreter of God's will" and "an expounder of the Scriptures."

Many seafarers have spun out of the church's orbit. A considerable number didn't belong to the church. They did not grow up in it, or with it. There are also many who, by birth, heritage and tradition are linked up to non-Christian religions.

Against this background stands the Ministry of Seafarers. It's a unique position in the missionary world. People from around the world come into contact with the delivering message of the gospel and many of them accept the LORD Jesus Christ as their Savior. And then to think: *They are returning to their homes, their native land, their cities, their villages, their communities, with a unique "treasure,"* along with the treasures they obtained in the electronic markets or shops in our countries.

THE SEAFARERS CENTRE

Dr. Roald Kverndal has written a voluminous book entitled, *Seaman's Missions: Their Origin and Early Growth*. It is a contribution to the history of the Church Maritime (William Carey Library, Pasadena, CA).

It is not my purpose to examine in detail the history of this ministry, its clergy, its chapels, and its centers, as this has been done exhaustively by this author. I merely refer to the very essence of the Ministry to Seafarers, as a ministry of the Christian church, with anecdotal references.

Historically, it has been the laity of the Christian church that has given impetus to a ministry among seafarers. The seafarers' world, representing thousands of people of over one hundred nationalities, is characterized by two specific factors that make it distinct from other industrial worlds: The seafarer lives where he works, on the ship at sea. He travels from one place, or country, to another one…

The Christian church was convinced that the proclamation of the Word of God and the administration of the Sacraments should therefore be brought to their members at sea. Seafarers chapels, ashore and even afloat, known at times as "Bethels," were built by various societies in many seaports.

Clergy were called and assigned to preach in the ports at home and abroad. Churches established seasons of prayer for the sailing members of their congregations. In an article of the *Boston Seamen's*

Friend Society in 1828, we read: "The object of the society shall be to furnish regular evangelical ministrations for seamen. This is an unalterable article which embraces a fundamental principle."

In the annual report of the *American Seamen's Friend Society*, dated 1829, it is noted that The Rev. David Abeel, of the Dutch Reformed Church, became the first chaplain ever sent out to preach the gospel to seamen in a foreign port: Canton, China.

The Rev. John Diell became chaplain in what was, at that time, the Kingdom of Hawaii. "Through the providence of God" he was favorably received by the king and the principal chiefs. His job description read, "…next to the keeping of your own heart, the committee wishes to have you make the salvation of seamen the great object of your prayers and labors. To accomplish this objective they wish you to treat them with frankness, affection, and fidelity. Preach to them Jesus Christ with plainness, warmth, and tenderness and an avenue will be found to the seaman's heart."

That same year, the New York Port Society, organized in 1818, and chartered by the Legislature in 1819 for the purpose of "proclaiming the gospel among seamen in the Port of New York," built the Mariners Church in Roosevelt. This was the first edifice ever reared on land for the purpose of preaching to the men of the sea.

In the annual report in 1834 of the *American Seamen's Friend Society* we read:

> "It is an affecting truth that sailors have hitherto been overlooked in the prayers of God's people to a painful extent. While prayers have been offered up for almost every nation and kindred and people and tongue, those who traverse the mighty deep have been forgotten. But we trust a brighter day has dawned, and we hail with gratitude the establishment of a "meeting for prayer in concert" on the evening of the third Monday in each month, when the cause of the sailors shall be spread out before God and laid down in the light of His countenance."

The book in your hands seeks to highlight this original spiritual dimension.

The Seafarers Centers in former days were characterized almost exclusively as a place of worship. Almost every Seafarers Center, which has been set up by the church, has a chapel. Way back in history the word "Bethel," which means "house of God," was used.

The merchant ships used flags to identify the ship's registry or to convey a message. The "Bethels," therefore made use of flags as well to invite the seafarers. The Bethel flag designed by a ship's captain became very popular: The dark blue background represented the high seas. The star in the upper left corner referred to Christ and the dove represented the Holy Spirit. The word "BETHEL," in large letters, was displayed in its center.

The story is told of two seamen walking in the port of Boston nearly two hundred years ago. They were looking for the place where the famous Methodist "sailor-preacher," the Rev. Edward T. Taylor, was preaching. One of them suddenly spotted the Bethel flag and slowly spelled the letters out loud ... B-E-T-H-E-L. Not theologically nor grammatically trained, he exclaimed, "Ah, that must be the place of Father Taylor, who else could beat hell?" Hell surely is beaten when we are in touch with God.

Later on the seafarers centers used to be called the "Seamen's Mission," based on the original name used by the Anglicans. The Roman Catholics refer to their centers as the "Stella Maris," the star of the Sea. Their ministry is called "Apostolatus Maris," the Apostleship of the Sea. The ecumenical movement tends to obliterate the particular denominational connotations. As a result, names like "Anchor House" or "Mariners House," denoting a Seafarers Center, have become current. The name "Seamen's Mission" is still very prevalent both ashore and on board. It's an appropriate name in terms of the ministry.

There is, nowadays, a tendency, however, to look at the Ministry to Seafarers, not primarily as a "mission field," but rather as an organization providing services for seafarers who are briefly in port. When they sail on cruise ships, especially, they are pressed for time. A Seafarers Center located close to the port or even in the port and providing bus service from the ship to the center, is a unique place for the immediate needs of seafarers. There they find telephones in private booths and e-mail stations in a quiet area. The centers have after hours banking facilities and store services. They provide transportation back to the ship. The mobility of seafarers is extremely restricted. That is why Seafarers Centers near the berths, where cruise ships dock, are vital and greatly appreciated.

In one of the Seafarers Centers I conducted, from time to time, brief worship services for seafarers from cruise ships. I informed them that the entire worship service would last no longer than precisely five minutes.

Trudy and I had been making television speeches lasting three minutes and thirty six seconds under the title, "Thought for Today," for the Quebec Television Network of CBC. A five minute worship service was therefore quite possible since we had discovered how much can be said in three and a half minutes. It was always appreciated by the seafarers that a *spiritual dimension* was brought into the business place where they had made a telephone call and mailed their letters. I still recall one gentleman, who telephoned his wife in the Philippines after my short worship service and reported, "I have just attended church."

To maintain the *"spiritual dimension"* of the Ministry to Seafarers is highlighted in this book. It has been our message during the past forty-five years.

The Logo of the Anglican Mission to Seamen was a flying angel with what resembled a copy of the Bible in his hands. This, I believe, was based on Revelation 14:6 "Then I saw another angel flying in midair, and he had the eternal gospel to proclaim to those who live on the earth, to every nation, tribe, language and people."

I liked the symbol and the message: Biblically, there were angels present at the three key events of Christ's life on earth: at the announcements of the birth of Christ, (Luke2:9–13), at the declaration of his resurrection. (Matthew 28:5–7) and at the proclamation of Christ's return (Acts 1:11).

Some time ago a change has come about in its name and in its logo. Appropriately the name was changed to, "The Mission to Seafarers." With an increasing number of women joining the ships, cargo ships as well as cruise ships, this is understandable and well chosen. The word "Mission" was retained. Was that because of the historical affinity and the real public familiarity with the word, or because the church felt it should maintain its mission to proclaim the message of Revelation 14:7?

The Logo has also been changed. There is still a flying angel but without the book in its hands. I often wondered why this change.

The chapel, as the House of God, continues to be central in the Scandinavian Seafarers Centers. Their centers are called "Sjomanskirken" which means "seamen's church." The design of almost all their centers clearly displays the centrality of the church as a place of worship. Libraries, newspaper racks, telephones, e-mail stations, postage and banking facilities, souvenir areas, and pool tables are all surrounding this central worship area. Upon entering, one senses immediately that this is a place dominated by the presence of the church.

In the construction and in the design of their places, the Scandinavians have at all times highlighted the atmosphere of their native country, their church, and home. Every one of their centers reflects class, style, tasteful decorations, flowers, and subdued light. One is aware of a certain elegance and good taste.

These have also been determining factors when Trudy and I set up our own specific Christian Seafarers Centre in Montreal, a one million dollar building, which I dedicated to God in a festive service in October, 1985. In this center the proclamation of the gospel of our

Lord was central. This was reflected in every aspect of its services. Here, seafarers have come to acknowledge the Lord Jesus Christ as their Savior and were baptized. Bibles in every possible language were offered. The testimonies of dedicated staff members and volunteers have enriched the lives of many seafarers who visited it.

It was a building with an extraordinary history. Originally the most notorious tavern in the city, called Joe Beef's, it was eventually beautifully restored. Joe Beef's tavern used to be a wild place, but in the end the Spirit of God did triumph over the mockery of Joe Beef, who ridiculed the clergy and cared nothing for God nor for the Devil.

A minister from a nearby Presbyterian church insisted on bringing the message of the gospel into this loud, secular place. Initially the Reverend was discouraged by Joe Beef. He tried to scare the pastor, saying that his clientele would chase him out of the tavern. The Reverend, John Currie, stood his ground and preached the gospel. Though mocking at first, one day Joe Beef himself was touched by the Spirit of God. He was suddenly changed and in the middle of the sermon announced, "Anyone who wants to go with Rev. Currie to the service in his church will receive free bed and breakfast here."

Some sixty-five men followed the Reverend to his church. For some seven months this minister continued to preach the gospel in Joe Beef's Tavern in the beginning of 1900.

In this totally renovated, but historic building, we had the privilege to set up our Christian Seafarers Centre. We set up the place with class, so as to be able to welcome masters and senior officers from the most sophisticated cruise ships and cargo ships as well. In this setting, officers, staff, and crew members of every ship were heartily welcomed.

In our ministry, representing Christ, we felt that the physical appearance of the Seafarers Centre should reflect beauty, dignity, and excellence in every way. Aware that seafarers longed for a "home-away-from-home," we gave the place the appearance of a private residence, avoiding most nautical signs and symbols such as flags and anchors. We wanted the seafarers, who are at sea for long periods of time, to breathe another "spirit" while ashore in our country for a few hours. So we furnished our Seafarers Centre, instead, with carpets on the floor, comfortable new couches, chairs, and round tables. We brought in real plants and real cups and saucers. Trudy sewed countless lace curtains for the many windows of the two stories of our spacious Seafarers Centre. Beautiful paintings were hung and when all was completed, we invited some two hundred and fifty guests, who were as excited as we were about our seafarers, to a moving Dedication Service in which the newly opened Seafarers Centre was dedicated to God and to His service. The "spirits" of Joe Beef's Tavern were exorcised and "The Holy Spirit" was brought in. With His dominance, we have seen miracles happening in the lives of many seafarers from around the world.

How was all this financed? We had asked God to allow us to raise the necessary funds in two years time. The LORD decided to make that five years. Every other weekend, I would pick up Trudy at the Christian High School where she taught. Trudy and I would fly to some city in Canada or in the USA to inform the congregation about the lives of the people on board, the loneliness, the problems, and perplexities our seafarers faced on a daily basis. We never mentioned money. Instead we shared the countless, often heartrending experiences of our seafarers, as well as their gratitude for any service rendered, no matter how small.

We were amazed at how God provided. He touched people's hearts from coast to coast and the money started to come in, two dollars perhaps or five or ten or more. For every gift we thanked the LORD and the giver.

It was a huge effort on our part, but in five years time the LORD performed the miracle of allowing us to raise, with His help, one and a half million dollars. Our beautiful one million dollar Seafarers Centre was then completely paid off! The half million dollars were used for the staff of the Seafarers Centre. Three luxury apartments on the third and fourth floors of the building paid for its upkeep.

For the operation of the Seafarers Centre, we recruited committed Christian staff most of whom did indeed see their task in the light of a "ministry as unto Christ." In this specifically Christian Seafarers Centre, the Seafarers from around the world found not only a "home away from home" but also had the opportunity to get in touch with the LORD Jesus Christ, who will give them an eternal home.

Once when we visited the Seafarers Center in St. Petersburg, which at that time was still called Leningrad, we ran into some seafarers who, upon learning where we had come from, expressed their appreciation for the home-like atmosphere of our "Church Centre," as they called it, in Montreal and for the warm reception there.

Dr. J. Harold Ellens Ph.D., who served as a ship's lecturer on one of the cruise ships visited our Seafarers Centre and was moved to leave the following testimony on behalf of the staff of the cruise ship he was sailing on:

> "Your Seafarers Centre has been and continues to be a most congenial and welcome place for the seamen and women, who are largely young people under the age of thirty five, with spouses and children at home, hailing from Portugal, Italy, the United Kingdom, Mexico, various other countries in Latin America, Indonesia, Malaysia, China, the United States and Canada.
>
> They have found there the psychologically refreshing experience of a home-like feeling and atmosphere which is an essential change for them from their rather austere accommodations aboard. They have found the kind tenderness of your congenial hostesses and assistants to be emotionally rejuvenating after their long days of fourteen hours duty at sea for these long months.
>
> This is a humanizing and healing experience for them. They have found the superb elegance of your Centre and its highly developed aesthetic appeal to be

a dramatic and inspiring change from the usual port images and impressions that impose themselves upon our personnel in the usually dreary facilities of most ocean piers and ports, as you know. The social setting in which our officers and crews are able to enjoy quiet conversation, personal reading, times of devotional meditation, distracting games and rest is essential to their mental, emotional, psychological and spiritual health.

Most importantly and most dramatically is the impact of your very attractive worship center. The opportunity for our people to take the time for worship, contemplation and Scripture exposition with you has enhanced the quality of their lives. It has confirmed their faith and strengthened their sense of the presence of God. You cannot imagine how important that is for them during the long days and nights at sea. It gives them a spiritual lode star to which to keep their inner compass directed, and guide them through the confusion, distraction, temptation and loss of meaning that long periods at sea attended by extraordinary hours of hard duty brings.

Your Centre is a spiritual and psychological oasis for us. We are grateful. I heartily commend you and wish you to know that you are highly esteemed here for your unique ministry to us."

Some sixty thousand seafarers have come through the doors of our Seafarers Centre during a period of seven years. People have come to the knowledge of Jesus Christ as LORD and Savior. People have professed their faith and they have been baptized there. Thousands of people from as many as eighty-four different countries have left this place with the Word of God in their own language and in many cases it was the first copy they ever saw and ever owned.

They left with prayers, encouragement, blessings, and directives into the way of salvation, that " … all the earth shall be filled with the knowledge of God, even as the waters cover the sea" (Is. 11:9). Here we have the "raison d'etre" for our Christian testimony.

It is very interesting that precisely this dimension had been perceived so clearly by many seafarers. In fact, this Christian atmosphere and care even inspired Turkish seafarers from one ship to invite us to come to Istanbul to encourage the government of that city to start a center "like this one."

SAILING AMONG
THE CLIFFS

Seafarers Centers provide a vast number of excellent services. These are greatly appreciated. It reflects a sound understanding of the message of the Bible: "Love your neighbor as yourself."

St. Matthew 25:34–40 gives the specifications: "Provide care, food and drink, clothing and shelter, as well as pastoral visits." In the modern application this biblical instruction may of course take on a somewhat different and more complex form. In almost all centers, telephone lines and internet facilities are providing opportunities to reach home. The rapid changes in the communication facilities have been of enormous benefit to the seafarers. For people who are away from their families for six to nine months telephone and e-mail contact is an absolute priority. Many Seafarers centers provide transportation to the centers and to shopping malls.

For twenty-seven years I ministered to seafarers in the port of Montreal, Quebec out of two Seafarers Centers. During that time I became the president of the International Council of Seamen's Agencies, which gave me the opportunity to visit almost every Seafarers Center in North America and in the Caribbean.

When we specialized our ministry to cruise ship ministry, some twenty years ago, we had the opportunity to make three world cruises which enabled us to come into contact with Seafarers Centers from around the world.

The vital element in a Christian Seafarers Center is not the number of services it provides. The kind of port, the support base of the ministry, and the physical structure of the building are determinative factors in this.

In three areas, however, the character of a distinct *Christian* Seafarers Center is expressed:

A In the maintenance of the original focus, that the agenda remains founded on the Word of God.

B In the commitment of the Chaplain/Director, his staff and volunteers to faithfully uphold that agenda.

C In the presence of a Board, that reflects its commitment to that agenda.

The Rev. Michael S. C. Chin, the general secretary of ICMA in 1994, expressed it very well in his welcoming address to the one hundred and sixty-eight Seafarers Centers' delegates at the seventh Plenary Conference in Helsinki, Finland. He said, especially to the chaplains present:

> "Although our work is intimately linked up to the Seafarers Centers, none of us would want to be seen simply as providers, directors, and advocates of welfare services and social justice. Our "ministry" is something more than these. Central to our understanding is our sense of calling to share in Jesus' work of reconciliation, of pastoring, and of finding the ninety and nine, who are lost. We see the confession of faith and the baptism as fundamental to this task.
>
> Yet there are few signs of concern about the fact that many seafarers have not made this confession, and that they have not been baptized. Whenever we talk about "ministry" there is great reluctance, if not total

amnesia, to that responsibility. Is it not important to ask how Seafarers may become Christians? Don't we want them to become Christians? God does!"

The original focus has shifted. Some illustrations may highlight this:

We came to a Seafarers Center for a brief visit, as our ship had docked in the vicinity. A very gracious and courteous chaplain welcomed us, but almost immediately retreated into his office.

It is our custom to sit down with seafarers. Six of them were seated around one table. They were the only visitors present, all from India. Their welcoming smile clearly invited us to join them. So we did and they were delighted.

After the customary introductory exchanges, the conversation turned to spiritual matters. They asked us some thoughtful questions about the resurrection of the dead and about reincarnation. Since we were visitors there we did not come "equipped" with copies of the scriptures, but, because we needed to refer to some specific sections of the New Testament, Trudy got up and asked the chaplain for some Bibles which we could use for clarification and possibly leave with the visitors from India.

The chaplain immediately rose from behind his desk and began to look for a Bible in a nearby bookcase. After a few minutes he appeared with one used Bible. He handed it to her, with the remark that we could use it, as long as we would be kind enough to return it when we were finished with it. We thanked him for his help. It turned out that there were no Bibles available for presentation to visitors. Here we were in a *Christian* Seafarers Center, which offered over-the-counter toiletries, sweets, greeting cards, and souvenirs, but no Bibles or any daily devotionals. *Perhaps it might be good to have a supply of Bibles on hand, preferably in a variety of languages.*

We continued our discussion, which became very animated with everyone participating. We concluded our talk about the resurrection with the support of 1 Corinthians 15, and 2 Thessalonians 4. They all seemed to be intrigued and thanked us for the explanation.

One of the seafarers then pointed to a door with a small stained glass window and asked if we knew what was behind that door. They had noticed that staff members would pass through that door on Sunday mornings. They assumed that they were having a staff meeting on the very day their ship was in port. We said that it was most likely a chapel and we explained its use. Then they told us that their ship returned to this port every other Sunday, but they had never attended a church service there.

Upon our inquiry from the chaplain, we learned that on Sunday mornings they did indeed have a Sunday service in the chapel and it was open to everyone. We assured the seafarers that they would be most welcome. They were pleased to hear this. They had assumed that it was a private meeting, which they as visitors, would not be allowed to attend. *It might be helpful to specifically invite all those present to any church service.*

Another Seafarers Center also had a small chapel, which could seat about twenty people, but I never noticed a religious service being conducted there. So, with permission from the chaplain, I conducted five-minute religious worship services. I considered this a unique challenge.

I found some Bibles there and displayed them on a table. At the end of my service I proposed that anyone, who would like to have a Bible, could pick one up.

One seafarer had picked up a copy of the Bible and walked out of the chapel with it under his arm. Consequently, I was informed that in this Center it was *not appreciated* that anyone walked around with a Bible under his arm. When I returned a day later, I discovered that the remaining Bibles had been stowed away. So I explained that earlier in the day I had had a discussion with that seaman on board of his ship. I had told him that the answers to his questions could be found in the Bible. When he came to the Seafarers Center, he decided to slip into the chapel. At the close of my brief service, I directed him to the sections in the Bible where he could find the answers. He subsequently walked out of the chapel with the Bible under his arm.

In Europe, I visited another Christian Seafarers Center. I was the chaplain on one of five cruise ships that had docked in this particular port. Since I had run out of Bibles, I went to this Center in the hope of finding some Bibles in Russian, in English, as well as in Hungarian. The place was a seven-minute walk from the ship.

Interestingly, a group of Russian seafarers standing around the gangway of their ship, located next to the ship I was sailing on, called me and asked why I was passing them by. Could I not stop and speak to them? I stopped and spoke. Then they asked if I could offer prayers for them. I could and I did. Out of the blue they asked for prayers.

When I arrived at the Seafarers Center, half an hour later I was welcomed by two courteous volunteers. We chatted nicely for a few minutes. The chaplain had been engaged that morning on board of a freighter, where they had some difficulties, and now in the afternoon he had left for his residence. So I telephoned him to say hello. He allowed me to step into his office to search for some Bibles. I found one in German and a few in Ukrainian. I decided to take four copies. The kind ladies handed me a little plastic bag. They did not want me to pay for them and were ready to wave me out.

Just then a girl walked in. She asked if they had any batteries for her watch. When the ladies told her that they had none, the girl thanked them and turned to the door. I noticed that she was from the Ukraine, so I called her back, saying, "Please wait a moment, I have something for you." I ran back to the chaplain's office and picked up two Ukrainian Bibles, which I presented to her with the remark, "Here is one for you and one for your friend," assuming she had a friend on board.

She exclaimed, "Thank you! This is exactly what I need. I received a Ukrainian Bible in Marseille, but I gave it to my mother, who had none. Now I have one for myself again. Thank you very much!"

I thought this had been a unique opportunity presented by the LORD. When I turned around to pick up my own bag, the scenery had changed.

"That was not right, Reverend, what you did there," said one of the ladies. As I looked at her in utter amazement, she continued, "It is against the policy of the Center to hand out Bibles to Seafarers."

The other lady tried to come to my rescue by saying, "Didn't you hear that the girl said, 'This is just what I need?'"

"But," said the first one, "it is the policy of this Center to not ever give a Bible to seafarers, unless they *expressly ask* for one."

Imagine: That was the *policy* of this *Christian* Seafarers Center! I mentioned that I was totally unaware of that policy. As I came into contact with other centers it turned out that a number of them had the same policy.

In 1969, I participated in the formation of a worldwide organization extending services to Seafarers Ministries of every denomination and became a founding member. The name of this organization is "International Christian Maritime Association."

I will never forget how shocked I was that various voices at *that* meeting proposed, that in view of the multi-faith orientation of the Seafarers Ministries throughout the world, the word "Christian" should perhaps be eliminated. Think of it: that was voiced already in 1969, almost half a century ago. Fortunately, the word "Christian" remained as part of its name.

In one state where the Seafarers Center was located far from civilization between towers of containers, in a totally "dead'" area, a group of seafarers who had been picked up from their ships were making telephone calls and relaxing in the facilities of this well supplied Seafarers Center.

A Chinese officer approached me and told me that he had just become the father of a son. He was all excited about the birth of his son. Rejoicing with him, I immediately searched for and fortunately found a Chinese New Testament. As I was inscribing it for his son, he said, "Write a Christian name for him, because I would like him to become a Christian." So I did, after which I presented the New Testament to him and offered prayers.

Since there were about a dozen seafarers in the center, I thought it might be appropriate to lead a brief worship service in connection with this festive news. I approached the manager on duty with my request. He responded with, "I regret to inform you that since the Seafarers Center is on federal property, you will not be permitted to hold a religious service here. It is against the law of separation between church and state."

It was nine o'clock in the evening. In this Seafarers Center, hidden among containers in a deserted section of the harbor, we were not allowed to praise and thank the LORD for His gifts without offending the law of the State. Is this happening in North America where the foundations were laid on the basis of the Sacred Scriptures, the Christian tradition? "In God we trust," it says on all American dollar bills.

"Blessed is the nation whose God is the LORD (Psalm 33:12)," was the motto of the Kingdom of Hawaii. We do well to remember it!

One summer, we exchanged our residence for two months with a couple living in a large port in Europe. We looked forward to visit seafarers during our time there.

In this port, there are national and international Seafarers Centers, well equipped, graciously staffed, and accessible to all seafarers. With an enormous number of ships, docked in a large variety of bays and inlets, we figured we would be heartily welcomed, especially since it was summer and vacation time. I had notified one of the chaplains that we would be delighted to be of service and assistance during this busy summer season.

Upon our arrival we were invited to meet the clergy of all the Seafarers Centers. There were about eight people present. They represented different denominations. We had already met a number of them, when I presided at the World Conference of the North American and the World Organizations of Seafarers Ministries in New York City.

After a brief introduction we expressed our readiness to be of service to them. We noticed though, that there was a rather tense atmosphere. We could not explain the reason for it. Ordinarily at these meetings there was a pleasant atmosphere, characterized by a readiness to exchange ideas. These meetings were usually enriched with refreshments, but not this time. Not even a cup of coffee or a glass of water was available for the gathering.

Everyone around the huge table remained silent. One of the chaplains, aware that we had set up a magnificent Christian Seafarers Centre in Montreal, asked us if we intended to do something similar in this port. We responded that it was not at all our intention to do so. After all, the port already had several Seafarers Centers, so there was absolutely no need to add another one. We would be there for only a few months, and we thought we could be of help wherever they needed assistance in any one of their Seafarers Centers, or in any of their programs. Besides that, we planned to visit ships in that vast port.

Without asking us any further questions and for no identifiable reason, the chaplain said: "If you have come to our port with the intention to evangelize, you are not welcome." We were absolutely dumbfounded. Here, a colleague, without any reason or explanation, expressed an overt opposition to evangelism in the port. I thought, "Perhaps I did not hear him correctly," but Trudy assured me that he meant exactly what he said. The meeting was then adjourned.

Still in a state of shock, we lingered a bit. Some of the clergy were asked, if they could visit the seafarers in the hospital during the period that the chaplain on duty for the next month would be away on vacation, but all of them seemed to have engagements of one kind or another. So, in our rather naïve enthusiasm, we suggested that we would be willing to visit the seafarers in that hospital, but the immediate response was, "It is better, that *you* do not go there." Amazed I asked, "Why not?" The reply was, "The social worker of the hospital has said specifically, 'Do not have anyone with a distinct Christian orientation and message visit seafarers, because that might upset them.'"

Not ready to give up, I asked if we could be of help in any other way. One chaplain responded that a Sunday worship service was scheduled in the chapel of one of the Seafarers Centers the following morning at ten o'clock. We were glad to hear that. If we wanted to do them a favor, we could bring notices to four ships, located in a particular bay. But we had to make sure to obtain the exact number of people, who wished to come to the church service. We were told to notify the person in charge of the vans of the exact number of seafarers to be picked up.

In my years on the waterfront in Montreal, I had learned that notification of the evening worship services could be responded to by a few or by many seafarers and you never knew exactly how many people would actually show up until you finally arrived with the van at the ship. But I was willing, despite my misgivings about such an unusual demand, to go by their rules.

So we left for that particular area, where we found the four ships. One was from Japan, one from Germany, one from Greece, and right behind it was one from Egypt. Though we had a courteous reception on the Japanese ship, no one indicated a desire to come to a church service in the Seafarers Center. I did not find that surprising. Ordinarily Japanese seafarers need to be invited about four times before you could expect a positive response. On the German ship there were some people from the Kiribati islands. They were all Methodists. Three of them promised to come. On the Greek ship no one committed himself, because they thought they were scheduled to sail, but they appreciated the invitation.

When we came to the Egyptian ship, we were welcomed with a "wailing" scene. Ahmed, at the very top of the gangway, functioning as the guard, bellowed at us before we were even on the third step of the gangway, "Have you visited Mohammed in the hospital?" He had been brought to the Seafarers Hospital with pain in his chest, so those on board were afraid Mohammed might die. Everyone we met on the ship asked us the same question, "Have you visited Mohammed? He is in room 357."

We explained to them, that we had just arrived in the city, but we promised to visit him. We then told them the purpose of our visit. Two gentlemen, both belonging to the Coptic Church, the oldest Christian church, assured us that they would definitely come to the church service. We spent time with many of the seafarers at their mid-afternoon tea break. We talked, testified, and left. When we returned home, we reported that about five people could be expected to come to the worship service for sure.

On the way home Trudy reminded me that every hospital has visiting hours, during which we were free to visit Mohammed. So, promptly at six o'clock we arrived at the hospital and headed for room 357. It was a ward. There, in the corner, along with some twelve other patients was Mohammed. I exhausted my limited Arabic vocabulary and greeted him in his own language.

He was delighted to see us and to hear his own language. He had been unable to communicate with anyone, and as a result was very anxious. We assured him that he would be properly taken care of. I made contact with the nurse, who informed me he was improving, so he would most likely be released in a few days. He calmed down and began to relax. I offered prayer for him, which appeared to give him quietude and peace. I then provided him with an Arabic Bible.

As we prepared to leave the ward, the gentleman in the next bed said, "It is good that you came to visit him, for he has been unable to communicate with anyone. Are you a pastor for seafarers?" When I said, "Yes, I am," he pointed to the room across the hall and said,

"There are also seafarers in that room. Perhaps you would like to visit them as well?" We did visit them. One was from Brazil, one from Ghana, and one from Peru. They too were delighted to have us come. Trudy had quite a talk with some seafarers in the little lounge, where we finally ended up with about half a dozen people for evening prayers, uninterrupted by summoning nurses or social workers.

On Sunday, not two, but thirteen Egyptian seafarers stood ready to be picked up for the church service, along with the three people from Kiribati; and surprisingly, eight Greeks, since their ship had not left as yet. So they had decided to stand by the gangway hoping to be picked up. The driver was forced to make three runs to the same area instead of one.

The Chapel was packed to overflowing. Many of the attendants had to find a seat in the lounge. They were joined by all others for refreshments after the service. The Greeks sat together, the Egyptians needed two tables, and the Kiribati, true to their nature, had found a table in the back. One of them had a guitar and they softly sang one of their Methodist hymns. They have the gift to sing in high soprano and deep bass, reflecting a full-fledged choir. They emanated a sense of peacefulness.

Since we had met many of those present on board their ships, we sat down with the Egyptians and then with the Greeks. Near the counter where the refreshments were served stood two of the chaplains we had met at the meeting. We approached them and inquired if we could be of further service. Their response took us by surprise. "You have not correctly informed us about the number of seafarers who would attend today." We explained that only five seafarers had definitely wanted to come. All the others had decided at the last minute to join them, as they were leaving for the Seafarers Center.

Personally I was thrilled that so many seafarers stepped into the chapel to hear the Word of God. Here they heard the gospel of our LORD and Savior Jesus Christ!

The chaplains then expressed their concern about our going from table to table to socialize with the seafarers, whom we had invited the previous day. We were amazed. When one has invited guests, is one not expected to function as host?

Reflecting on this behavior and comparing it to a similar reaction we had noticed in different parts of the world, we concluded that their reluctance to sit down with seafarers could possibly be caused by a language barrier, cultural differences, or timidity. Many people do feel awkward about spontaneously approaching strangers. So, our amicable conversation and interaction with seafarers from different parts of the world may have appeared to them almost like a criticism of their conduct. Yet, communication is *so* essential for seafarers, who are isolated on their ships for weeks on end. Even a smile or a handshake is effective in establishing contact, as are gestures. *So let's give them a warm welcome!*

And it is precisely through communication, that one becomes a witness for Christ. In Romans 10:14 we read, "How can they believe in the one of whom they have not heard? And how can they hear without someone preaching to them?"

As the Rev. Michael Chin said,

> "…We cannot endorse certain approaches to witnessing and to the presentation of the gospel. However, it is one thing to avoid pitfalls. It is quite a different matter to regard it as an option, or to abandon it completely. Without an adequate response few, who are shaped by non-European and American experience, will ever take us seriously. We tread the path of death and rejection, when we cease to be concerned about communicating and giving a reason for our faith."

A Chinese chief officer from mainland China had sailed around the world. In the process, he had visited many Seafarer Centers, yet no

World War. My home town was only ten miles away from where Ann Frank and her family were hidden. I have never forgotten the very last sentence Mr. Frank spoke to all the members of his household when the German soldiers finally caught up with them in their secret hideaway. As he handed each member of his family a small paper bag with some essential items, such as a tooth brush and some toothpaste, he said: "For three years we have lived in fear. Now we shall live in hope."

In response to opposition one might well obtain inspiration from what is written on the new baptismal font, installed in Salisbury Cathedral, England. It was created by William Pye and dedicated in 2008, seven hundred and fifty years after the Cathedral was consecrated in 1258.

The font is three meters wide and designed in cruciform shape, combining both movement and stillness, with water flowing from its four corners while maintaining a perfectly still surface of water which reflects the complete peace we have in Christ Jesus the LORD.

The words engraved on the four curves of the font are particularly moving. The first sentence reads: *"Do not fear for I have redeemed you"* (Is. 43:1). That's what baptism is all about. It is the firm basis on which we stand and in our ministry we call everyone else to stand on it as well.

In the second sentence we see clearly, that God is personal: *"I have summoned you by name, you are mine"* (Is.43:1). I tell my seafaring friends, "There is no isolation at sea. You may think or feel you are isolated, but stay with the facts: God knows you by name and you belong to him."

The third sentence is even more encouraging: *"When you pass through the waters, I will be with you"* (Is.43:2).

The fourth statement expresses that irrespective of the troubles you may run into. You are not going to be overwhelmed by them, either in life or in death: *"And through the rivers, they shall not overwhelm you"* (Is.43:2).

That leaves us with one final matter in any and every kind of "opposition" you may face. In the LORD's Prayer there is one sentence which the LORD Jesus highlights especially when he repeats: *"For if you forgive other people when they sin against you, your heavenly Father will also forgive you"* (Matthew 6:14). Especially when he clarifies that one sentence: "And forgive us our debts, as we also have forgiven our debtors" (Matthew 6:12). If he forgives us, we also should forgive our debtors. If you don't, he won't!

That is the most difficult prescription imaginable. You cannot handle *that* alone. You won't have to, if you get on board with the LORD!

REACTION OF SEAFARERS
TO THE BIBLE

In the minds of many Christian people, Ministry to Seafarers is accomplished predominantly in worship services, in which the Bible is preached. This may still be a small part of the Ministry to Seafarers in some centers, but in many Seafarers Centers it is no longer prominent. Worship services may be scheduled at stated times, or conducted at the request of a seafarer, but they are declining, both in frequency and in attendance.

In the traditional, formal worship services, the Bible was treated with profound respect. It was carried into church ostensibly and with dignity. It was read, either from the lectern or in the middle of the congregation. In some churches and chapels the Bible was kissed at the end of the reading. I deeply appreciate this last mentioned display of respect, but I have not adopted it. The only time I kissed the Bible was when I was ordered to do so by the judge at the time I was sworn in as a Canadian citizen. All of us had a copy of the Bible in front of us and were asked to take it in our hands and to kiss it. Because I was under orders of the judge, I did as I was told. It was not a very passionate kiss. It was a Gideon Bible, a courtroom copy, which undoubtedly had been kissed already by many people, but it did not bring the Word of God closer to our hearts—to our lips, yes.

Whenever I conduct worship services for seafarers however, I seek to maintain the respectful treatment of the Bible. I grew up in a setting where it was considered improper to mark the Bible by underlining certain verses, or by inserting one's private commentary in the margin. But the times have changed. Bibles, even when brand new, come to us with special markings.

So I succumbed to marking my Bible with lines and comments and references, but once in a while something happened. I had preached in our chapel of the Montreal Seafarers Centre. Our Seafarers Centre was known by the seafaring community as the "Church Centre." To convey to the audience that the Bible is a book that needs to become part of our lives, we had copies on display in the bookcases along the wall. We advised all visitors that these Bibles were there in a wide variety of languages and were free for the taking. The free distribution was intentional. An English Bible could be purchased for about a dollar and a half. An Indonesian or a Thai Bible might cost between twenty and thirty dollars. So we established the policy that absolutely everyone, irrespective of either the cost of the Bible, or the seafarers' own financial situation, should have ready access to the Bible and be allowed to take it back on board and consider it her or his personal property. No one should have to be embarrassed by being unable to pay for a Bible.

We told the people in the churches, "You are not able to board the ships. But you can meaningfully participate in the Ministry to Seafarers by paying for the Bibles we distribute. We have to obtain copies in some fifty different languages. We purchase these Bibles from a variety of Bible Societies. If you pick up the tab, you have become co-missionaries with us." The "church" rose to this occasion magnificently.

In our chapel, we had installed comfortable chairs with an appropriate little rack on the back. Copies of the Bible, and a Book of Praise were inserted there, ready for use in the chapel service.

The forty-five-pound pulpit Bible, a magnificently embossed copy, donated by a devoted supporter, was neatly mounted on the center table or "altar" as it was called. Two candles, one on either side, were lit at the opening of the worship service, this to illustrate that the proclamation of the Word of God brings light, since it is centered in the One Who *is* the Light of the world.

Only at one time was this Bible formally brought into the auditorium. It was at the Dedication Service of the Seafarers Centre. A young gentleman from Afghanistan carried it. He had come to know the LORD through the reading of the Bible. He had been baptized in the name of the Triune God. We gave him the honor of carrying the Word of God to the very center of the altar, in the very chapel, where he had come to know Jesus Christ as his Savior.

That Bible, opened at Isaiah 55 with its ringing testimony, reminded us all that here is the very source of the need for Ministry to Seafarers. When I conducted those chapel services I used my own private Bible. I felt comfortable with it. The sections I wanted to read were clearly marked. Certain parts were highlighted with lines to enable me to refer to them easily.

In preaching the Word of the LORD, I used plain, non-colloquial British-English, and illustrated my sermon with understandable examples. In surveying the audience every time, again I realized that most of them spoke only little English. The nature of the material I talked about was in many instances quite foreign to them, demanding their total concentration. I reminded myself of Oswald Chambers' age-old devotional, "My utmost for His highest," to get *their* utmost for His Highest."

On many occasions the chapel was filled. When I read the Scriptures and held my Bible in my hand while I preached I sensed the tension and prayed that the message would get across. After the worship service, I ordinarily moved about to find out from a variety of attendees if they had understood what I had talked about. In many instances, presumably because English is also my second language, the response was very positive. In terms of what the message was all about, a further word of explanation was often necessary.

On two occasions there were unusual reactions: The first one took place at the Feast of Pentecost, admittedly not as dynamic a feast as Christmas or Easter, but in reality the most dynamic day on the Christian calendar. I had preached about the Holy Spirit and his coming. I waxed eloquent, because of the dynamics of this extraordinary event. Two Polish stewardesses looked very disturbed, while I preached. So I asked them, after the service, if they had understood the message, because I suspected that they had difficulty with the English language. They did, but not in the manner I thought. "You speak Spirit all the time. Why do you speak Spirit?" I explained again, that I had spoken about the third person of the Holy Trinity. Then they began to understand. But they told me that the word "Spirit" in Polish refers to whiskey. That's why they had become confused and upset. Why had I not been consistent in my use of "British-English" and had used the words: "Holy Ghost" instead?

The second occasion took place when two junior officers, who had sat in the first row, approached me after the service. They were from Pakistan. They looked severely upset, almost angry. Pointing to my Bible, which I still had in my hand, they asked: "Did you say that this is the Word of the God?"

I answered, "Yes, I did." They continued: "Did you say that the whole book is the Word of the God from cover to cover?" I admitted I had said that too. "Then why," asked one officer, "do you put lines in the Book?" I explained that I found it easier to locate verses quickly when I had marked them.

He then said something I have never forgotten: "If this book has the Words of the God, what right do *you* have to judge the God by considering some of His Words more significant than others?" They had another question: "Why do you disgrace the Word of the God by putting it *behind* your back on the chairs?"

It was interesting that they used the article "the" in their reference to God. Biblically speaking there is no article. God is Spirit, but the distinct characteristic of God is that he is personal. That's why Christians speak about God and not "the" God. He stands in a personal relationship to us as Our Father.

In our modern Western society, we could readily answer both questions about the treatment of the Scriptures, but we would answer as Western people. It is incumbent on us to remove every vestige of offense. Since this incident, whenever I proclaimed the Word of God in the chapel, I picked up the forty- five pound Bible from the altar and read from it. We were reminded once again that people observe our conduct and the manner in which we show respect for "sacred things." But the decline in a liturgical perception of life has influenced many to the point that they simply do what they *feel* is right.

In the world on board ships and in the Seafarers Centers, we are dealing with people from around the world with different languages, different religious orientations, and different forms of behavior.

When I was on board an Egyptian ship, very early in my career, I talked with a group of people in the narrow confines of a small cabin. The discussion was about the Christian religion. I took a small New Testament out of my pocket and I quoted some pertinent sentences from it. Not wanting to give the impression that I was finished with the conversation, I placed the New Testament in an upright position on the floor against the leg of my chair. By this action I thought I was indicating to them that I would continue to refer to the Bible. Instead the conversation started to fade. One after another the Egyptians in the circle excused themselves and left. Only one person remained behind. I asked him if he could explain why everyone had left. Was it because they had to return to their work? He said, "No, but you quoted from that Bible," and he pointed to my chair leg, "That Bible is on the level of Almighty God. You said so yourself, but then you took it and placed it not only *below your waist, but on the floor!* That was disgraceful."

So the authority of my message had evaporated. That's why everyone felt that it was not worth listening to me any longer.

Therefore they left. It pained my soul. The very presence of God did not only become obscured to my friends. In their eyes I had also brought shame on the LORD.

This was a lesson of great significance. When I come with the key to the way of salvation, with the door to the Truth, with the springboard for renewal, I should conduct myself beyond reproach, especially in the manner in which I handle that "Key."

There are other aspects to this: According to people who carefully analyze the market, the Bible is the most frequently sold book. That may well be the case, but is it the most frequently *read* book?

Among the people I meet I have discovered that many are totally unaware of what the Bible says. That's not surprising. The respect for the Bible as the Word of God has seriously declined. In our North American society, rooted in the Christian tradition, it is not even allowed to be read in public schools. It is not used as a guide in governmental declarations. It may not be given as a graduation present to students. It may be used in the courtroom, to be held, when one swears an oath, but it is never opened nor read.

That is restricted to the confines of the church.

Some publishers highlight the Bible with elaborate covers, which are extensively decorated with symbols, scenic pictures, or the cross.

Shortly after the collapse of the communist system in the Soviet Union I was asked by a Bible publisher if they should publish a Bible in Russian. Up to the time of the collapse we used copies of the Russian New Testament in micro print. I proposed that they publish a simple, plain New Testament in an updated version with the Psalms and Proverbs, especially for distribution among Russian seafarers. They were after all the very people, who could and would carry the Word of the LORD back to their native country in voluminous amounts.

So a modernized Russian New Testament with a black cover was published, but on its cover was placed a golden orthodox cross. That is a cross with two bars across, one horizontal, the other one at a thirty-five degree angle. The publisher thought that this was a fitting reminder of the history of the people. In that he was right. The Soviet people have their roots in the Orthodox Christian Church. For seventy years they had been forbidden to link up with the church. So the cross might well bring back fond memories.

I was concerned however. We had dealt with Soviet people in the port of Montreal for almost a quarter of a century before communism fell. We had smuggled Bibles and New Testaments to them in various ways for years. But a New Testament with an orthodox cross on it was not the wisest choice at this time. The Russian seafarers picked them up, as many as they could carry. But when I boarded some of the ships, I noticed that in several cabins the New Testament, with its beautiful cross, was placed, closed, as an icon on the lamp above the bed, or in the center of their little desks, or even in the port hole, if there was one in their cabin. The person coming in would bow, or nod towards the cross and would feel protected, especially in the storms at sea, because of this religious symbol above the bed.

Of course this sort of superstition is found in many places. Crosses or other icons are hanging around people's necks or from the mirror in their car. But the New Testament, the Word of God sitting decoratively on the light above the bed or pasted against the port hole? That does not serve its purpose.

Some people tell me that they do have a Bible. Their mother gave it to them when they went to sea years ago. They faithfully bring it along to every ship they board anywhere in the world. Do they read it? No, but they assure me it is under their pillow on the bed. In the minds of many people it is associated with protection during the most vulnerable time—when you are asleep. Then you are consciously not in control. Moreover, it is pitch dark in your cabin and you are on a ship. You are not on solid ground. You need all the help you can get.

But there are also many people on board who do have a Bible and who read it. They have discovered that in sailing on the turbulent waters of life, as well as on the oceans they need the "chart" of the Word of God.

In their case Psalm 139 becomes alive, " ... If I dwell in the uttermost part of the sea, even there will your hand guide me, and your right hand will hold me fast ..." They realize that they need that "guiding hand," especially on the ship, where they are in association with hundreds of people of every possible background, and experience all kinds of influences. That's where the directives of the Bible zero in on the reality of life.

When I introduce the Bible into the conversation and carefully note their initial verbal or bodily reaction and then delicately focus on the call extended to them by God, I am almost always encouraged. In many instances there is genuine interest. It is similar to what the Bible states, "Is there a Word of the LORD for me?" They would never put it in those words, but their whole demeanor displays this type of reaction. So, here is that unique combination of the proclamation of the Word and the mysterious working of the Holy Spirit.

The Second Engineer came with six other South African officers and crew members to our house for dinner. Our dinner is normally concluded with a time of Bible reading. Every family member has a copy of the Bible and all participate in reading a few verses. This has been a tradition in our family. Our children were incorporated in it at a young age. Our guests receive a copy as well. They too become active participants.

The Second Engineer, upon receiving a copy of the Bible, fell apart. He said, "This is the first time in my life that I have a Bible in my hands!" He was deeply moved and he did read when it was his turn.

The astonishment of the Second Engineer dominated the rest of the evening as we got involved in a discussion about the presence of Jesus Christ in our lives. The discussion had special significance for this engineer. He had sustained severe traumas in his life because of deep personal tragedies. In fact it became painful when he almost cried. Imagine, here he was with his fellow officers and us at the table. But it enabled us to highlight that God responds to our tragedies, with his words of consolation…"You, whom I have upheld since you were conceived, and have carried since your birth…, I am he who will sustain you…" (Is. 46:34). With God in your life, you are able to pull through. We gave the Second Engineer a Bible. The book he had never touched is now the guide in his life.

Aside from the personal expressions of delight from seafarers, for whom the Bible has become a dynamic inspiration, it is remarkably encouraging to note the e-mails which give testimony to that same inspiration. Here I record just a few:

- Yesterday I received the beautiful Bible you sent me. I thought you had forgotten me, but to my great surprise, I found it on my desk. I was reading it. It is an amazing book…

- Every day I read the New Testament. With this you have given me a sense of the future. In fact it gives me power in my difficult life.…

- I would like to thank you for this Bible which you gave me. From the first moment I received this wonderful book I started to read it.

- It helps me immediately and already the same day I started to feel much better.

- I met the men you suggested I might wish to talk to. All nine took a Bible as well as a "Jesus" video. I have also been able to share with all of them. They will be here for some time, so I am hoping to continue with teaching. (pastor R)

- Thank you for your assistance. I hope to contact the two addresses you gave me. The lack of scriptural materials in a variety of languages is definitely hampering our ministry to seafarers. We are expecting 47 cruise ships calling at our Port. (A call from a Seafarers Center)

They had just arrived from the airport. All seven of them came from South America. Three were engineers, one was a special cook, and the other three were deck officers. We sat down in the garden of the Seafarers Center as I welcomed them. Mysteriously we started to talk about certain aspects of the Bible, when one of them got up and walked to his suitcase standing nearby, opened it, and returned with his Bible. He wanted to know in detail where mention was made of the "writing on the wall" in the palace of King Belshazzar, and the consequences. We studied Daniel and in chapter 5 we found the record.

Two others went to their luggage as well and managed to get their Bibles. That left four people without a Bible. Sheepishly they looked around feeling out of touch with their shipmates. I tried to cover up their embarrassment and suggested that in the event they had no Bible with them I would be glad to get one for each person. It was greeted with enthusiasm. So we ended up with a Bible study in the garden. I told them that the history of the human race actually started in a "Garden" as well.

Renzo Dorati is an Italian second officer on board of one of the huge cruise ships which came into the port of Montreal on a regular basis. A young, vivacious, positive, somewhat humoristic character, he swung into the Seafarers Centre for the purpose of making a telephone call to his family in Italy. Struck by the beauty of the place, he walked around, inspected the store area, paged through some of the magazines on the huge magazine rack and finally came to rest with an interesting article in one of the magazines about racecars.

We have always made it a part of our responsibility to gently suggest to all our visitors that a copy of the Bible in their native language can be found on any of the bookshelves. We would then point out that they are indeed free for the taking and in many cases, we urged them to take a copy along. Why would we urge them?

Fundamentally for two reasons:

First, it would be an opportunity for them to take note of what the LORD is saying to them in his Word, and since his Word will not return void, according to Isaiah 55:11, it might well become instrumental in reaching their hearts to the point that their lives would conform to our LORD and Savior, Jesus Christ. After all, that's what the Christian life is all about. People must come to the point that they glorify the LORD with their lives, committed in obedience to his word.

The second reason is altogether very simple. Most people would feel that it is tantamount to stealing to just remove a book from the library shelves, and to take it to their ship. But if we come with a copy of the Bible, in their language, in our hands, and present it to them, it will be a lot easier for them to accept it.

So, I picked up a copy of the Italian New Testament and decided to offer it to Renzo, suggesting he take it along, together with the magazine about racing cars. Our young, vivacious officer thanked me for the magazine, but firmly refused the New Testament. He made it clear, in no uncertain terms, that he was not a Christian. In fact, he did not even believe in God. He despised the church for what he called its 'money-making business." And utterly satisfied with himself, he declared that he only believed in himself, and in no one else.

So, thank you, but no thank you! He kindly suggested that I give it to someone else, who might really want it, but *he* wouldn't give it a second thought. *He*, Renzo, reading a Bible? The thought was laughable. When I put it on the desk in front of him, he bent down and gave it a little shove, with the racing car magazine, pushing it toward the center of the desk, thereby indicating, that this was not for him.

Then he dove into one of our telephone booths with a glass door, smiling cheerfully, and in a true Italian manner, telephoned his family, talking excitedly and lively for about twenty minutes. When he had finished his call, he came out almost singing with joy and evident happiness. Obviously, it was a good telephone call. He paid for the call, left a generous tip for the Seafarers Centre, and armed with his car- racing magazine, raced out of the door, an almost unforgettable character...

The Spirit of the LORD thought so too. I have seen the Spirit of the LORD working ahead of us. That is of course biblical. After all, what would we do without him leading us? We pray for that regularly. *How* the leading of the Spirit unfolds is always surprising, but that keeps it exciting. In some cases, the Spirit is in "full swing," even when we have retired, given up, turned our backs, abandoned the thought of further pursuit, and are quietly grumbling that we wasted our time and effort.

Renzo's blunt refusal was a case in point. Surely I had a good time with him. We laughed, joked, and danced around each other with words, but he left, making me feel very strongly, that my offering of a copy of the Bible was really a ridiculous exercise. Without a deep conviction, that we stand in the service of the master and are guided step by step by the Spirit of the LORD, the exercise was indeed ridiculous.

"Not by power (i.e. our effort) but by my Spirit, says the LORD" (Zach.4:6).

The Seafarers Centre filled with people from the cruise ship, all eager to phone home, kept us busy. They were bustling about, nervously pacing the floor, purchasing souvenirs, cards, and toiletries, sipped their coffee, and waited for their turn. We talked to them, encouraged them, and assured them, that they will get a turn as soon as possible, and so the time flew by.

But, suddenly, the door burst open and in raced Renzo. He rushed to the desk, where the little Italian New Testament was still lying, undisturbed, grabbed it with a sweeping motion and as he turned around without stopping, bellowed: "I forgot to take this along." Then, as I escorted him to the door, and as he stood by the front door, he whispered in my ear, almost apologetically, "I am taking it, because you never know."

Renzo Dorati is now "racing through" the Scriptures. When that great and final day comes we'll find out if he is part of that great assembly that "won the race."

THE FEAR OF THE LORD
IS THE BEGINNING
OF WISDOM

Particularly among seafarers from Afghanistan, Iran and the Soviet Union I discovered a strong desire to get hold of some good Christian teaching material. They wanted to become better acquainted with the Christian religion and to discover how to apply the Bible to the practicality of their lives. Many of the seafarers were not impressed with the materials I had given them. These were often oriented to the North American cultural climate.

I came out of the Reformed tradition. I was educated with a document called the "Heidelberg Catechism." When I visited Heidelberg in Germany several years ago and attempted to find out if anyone in that city was familiar with this document, I did not find a single individual who knew anything about it. In fact no one there had ever heard of this Catechism. However, during my seminary days I became intensely acquainted with this almost four hundred year–old document and discovered its enormous value.

It has fundamentally three sections. The first one deals with the misery of us all, caused by the disease called sin. The second section deals with deliverance out of this sordid climate. The third section deals with gratitude. But all this comes after a most ringing and exciting opening paragraph, which answers the question: "What is your only comfort in life and in death?"

The inspiring reply puts it in one stunning sentence: "That I am not my own, but belong—body and soul in life and in death—to my faithful Savior Jesus Christ!" Then there is a more detailed explanation of what it means to belong to Jesus Christ. It is put in simple crystal clear language, supported by some twenty passages from the Holy Bible.

So I gave a copy of the Heidelberg Catechism to one of the seafarers from Afghanistan and to one from the Soviet Union. That was in the days that it was still strictly forbidden for Soviet people to come into contact with anything related to the Sacred Scriptures. I said: "I believe I have found something that you might appreciate." On the following day both of them told me with great excitement, "With this little booklet you have given us a clear, direct explanation of what the Christian Faith is all about."

I discovered a pleasant looking booklet, called the *Compendium*, issued by the Back to God Ministries International. It has become extremely popular among small groups of committed Christians, who wish to maintain a regular Bible-study on board of ships.

At the request of an organization exclusively concerned with the proclamation of the gospel in Russia after the collapse of the Communist reign there, I recommended that they translate and distribute the "Heidelberg Catechism." They did and it became an overwhelming success in different parts of the former Soviet bloc.

Now there is one "Question and Answer" in this document that continuously pops up in the lives of many people I come into contact with. It is Question and Answer #21, "What is true Faith?" The answer is, "True Faith is not only the knowledge and conviction that everything God reveals in His Word is true. It is also a deep-rooted assurance, created in me by the Holy Spirit, through the gospel, that out of sheer grace earned for us by Christ, not only others, but I too, have had my sins forgiven."

In terms of the *knowledge* I as preacher, ship-visitor, and teacher have the responsibility to promote it. That's why I am on board, moving about, contacting as many people as I can. For that purpose I got my training. If he doesn't get the knowledge part straight I have to repeat my message in clearer terms. I am well aware of the difficulties involved: I must speak in simple English. Secondly, I must speak in such a manner that what I say is clearly understood. In most cases I am not talking to someone who has a background in the church. So he or she is unfamiliar with church language. Words like salvation, sin, grace, forgiveness, and mercy are loaded words understood in the Church, but not necessarily understood on the ship.

I shall never forget one night in our beautiful Seafarers Centre. There were some sixty five seafarers bustling about, talking on the phone to their families, buying souvenirs, talking to the volunteers. Some were playing snooker. A Chinese captain, who had come alone several nights in a row, furiously tried to finish a huge and very complicated puzzle. One man, from South America played the classical guitar and had half a dozen people attending his private little concert. Some sat around a low table with four of five copies of the Bible. They were in earnest discussion with some volunteers trying to figure out who God is, and what He really expects from us.

At the end of the evening, quite late at night, we were ready to bring our seafarers back to their ships in our vans. I informed everyone that the time to return to the ships had come, but that we did not wish to bring them back without first asking for the blessing of God upon them all. I also told them that one of our guests from Cuba had just received notification of the death of his father. Another one from Macedonia had just learned that his wife was scheduled to go to the hospital, and one man from Italy, full of joy and happiness, had just found out that he had become the father of a little boy.

With whom can they share their emotions? In my prayer I encouraged the ones in sorrow to entrust themselves to the LORD's consolation and care and I thanked the LORD for the baby boy.

For the new father, we prepared a package with a toy and with an inscribed copy of the New Testament. We assured him that his child would do well throughout his life if he would follow the ways of the LORD, clearly marked in that magnificent book. I asked everyone to briefly sit down. I then read a few lines from the Holy Bible: "If we claim to be without sin we deceive ourselves and the truth is not in us. If we confess our sins, he is faithful and just and will forgive us our sins..." (1 John 1:8–9). Three times the word sin popped up. After a short word of explanation I asked all of them to stand and said, "Let us pray." This always created a reaction characterized by an approving mumble. I concluded my prayer with the LORD's Prayer, supported by some soft voices of those who were familiar with it. It was a moving moment—I stood by the door with our staff and volunteers to shake hands, and to bow politely to the Koreans and the Japanese, wishing them all a blessed night.

There was one deck officer from Nepal. He spoke reasonably good English. He had listened to the verses that had been read from the Bible. Three times he had heard the word "sin." When he shook hands, his question in dead seriousness was, "What is sin?" That question had popped up more than once. It behooved an answer. His knowledge had to be broadened with an understanding of both the word and its influence in his life. So he did not get into one of the vans in order to return to the ship. He had another coffee and we had a serious discussion about sin for at least an hour. It related to the commandments of God, rough stuff, but we supplemented it with the assurance, that we are forgiven through the sacrifice of Christ's death on the Cross.

"Good Evening Mr. Officer from Nepal! Christ Jesus the risen Son of God, Who died upon the cross, forgives sins, yours and mine! It's an almost unbelievable story, but a true one. And it applies to everyone. So, *out* with sin and *in* with obedience to God … You will discover that the world around you begins to change, because the Spirit of God is changing *you*."

He eventually crawled into the van with a copy of the New Testament in Nepalese and with a copy of the Compendium of the Heidelberg Catechism. Imagine, close to fifteen thousand miles away from his native country this man runs into the Savior, in our "Church-place." Two hours ago he did not even know what sin was. Now he knows about *sin* and *salvation*. His agenda from now on will be one of *service*.

AN EXCEPTIONAL
SHIPPING COMPANY

Most major ports have a type of Ships Traffic Control Center. It's like an Air Traffic Control Center. It enables one to determine which ships are in port, which ones are in the process of coming in, and which ones are leaving. To me this Control Center has always been a help in determining my day of ship visiting.

Early one Monday morning I checked in to get their latest information. The officer in charge at the time was very excited. He alerted me to what he considered to be the most exceptional situation he had ever run into in his entire career.

"Late Saturday night," he said, "a call came in from a ship, which had just entered the St. Lawrence River. She was on her way to Montreal with a cargo of magnesium oxide. Instead of continuing her journey up the St. Lawrence River to Montreal, she asked permission to stop and go on anchor in the St. Lawrence River."

When the Control Center officer got this call, he asked if there was a problem with the ship. Did they have difficulty with the engine or with the steering mechanism? Was there some other emergency to force them to anchor the ship rather than to sail straight through to Montreal? The reply from the ship was that a telex would be sent explaining the situation.

The control center officer exclaimed, "Now Reverend, in all my twenty five years at this Control Center I have never received a telex like this one. Look at it. I think it is utterly exceptional. I am happy you are here, because I would like to ask you to board that ship the moment she has arrived. She should be here sometime today at berth 59. Find out what kind of people are on it. You would certainly know what kind of a captain and what kind of an odd crew this is. Here is the telex. Take it along, and then be absolutely sure to come back and report to me."

The telex was in French. Canada is a bilingual country and in the Port of Montreal the main language spoken is French. I read it. It said: "*Navire avise qu'il ne navigue pas le dimanche, parce que l'equipage est chretien.*" Translated it says: "The ship advises that it does not sail on Sundays, because the crew members are Christian."

I was stunned as well. I toyed around with the idea of calling CBC-TV before going on board. TV ordinarily does not film anything that is normal and acceptable, but something out of the ordinary is readily publicized. I decided against it and thought that it might be better to first find out what was going on there.

It was a small coastal vessel with a crew of only twelve people. I boarded and walked into the general mess room where officers and crew usually ate together. In a little alcove behind the officer's table was a Bible. I picked it up and briefly paged through it. It looked well used. At one side of the mess room there was an opening above a counter, enabling the cook in the galley to place the meal inside the mess room. The cook working there saw me pick up that Bible and examine it. He came into the mess room to set the tables and said, "The captain reads that Bible to all of us before the noon meal every day." I thanked him for the information, and made my way upstairs to the captain's cabin.

After I had introduced myself I related the surprise of the officer in the Control Center, who had received the telex. I indicated my own surprise as well. I asked him how all this had to be interpreted. He explained that he was part of a company which owned nine ships. This company was positively Christian and employed, if at all possible, Christian officers and crew members. He then continued, "We believe that the commands of the LORD are very clear with respect to the Christian's conduct and specifically with respect to the maintenance of the Sabbath. Face it, that's what it says in the Bible, just look at Isaiah 58."

I knew Isaiah chapter 58 very well. Thousands of years after this was written, Isaiah 58 still rings a bell "If you keep your feet from breaking the Sabbath, and from doing as you please on My holy day... and if you honor it by not going your own way and not doing as you please... then you will find your joy in the LORD..." (Is.58:13–14). So, it's not the product of someone's imagination. It is God Himself who is talking!

Imagine the application of all this in today's world. What do I observe near the cruise ships in the port on the day of the LORD, the Sabbath, His holy day? Thousands of passengers are disembarking from half a dozen huge cruise ships. Bus loads of new passengers are coming in. Trucks are unloading tons of supplies. Suitcases are brought off and on the ships by hundreds of porters. Airplanes are on standby and are flying in and out to absorb the enormous volume of people and to bring them to their destination all over North America.

The seafarers, who have a few hours off, are scurrying around to get some much needed supplies for their personal use. And what about the millions of seafarers who are at work on cruise ships and freighters and tankers, and fishing vessels and oil-docks throughout the world? To them the Sunday is not known as a Sabbath unto the LORD. The traffic directors, the police force, the security are all working on overtime. The Sabbath is broken here and everywhere.

I need not limit myself to the world of ports. On the Holy Day of God, don't many people do more or less as they please? They pump gas and race to the store, to the stadium, to the theater and expect everyone to attend to their needs.

My captain continued, "On this ship, on Sundays we ordinarily knock off and do only what is absolutely necessary. After breakfast I invite the crew to come up into my cabin for a brief time of worship. They all come, including the chief engineer. I believe he is not a Christian, but he respects what we do and in order to maintain the spirit of unity on the ship, he always joins us and quietly sits in.

I read a few passages from the Bible, as I do every day at high noon, just before we have our dinner in the dining room. We then listen to a cassette with a sermon of some preacher. Afterwards we go around with an offering plate to collect money for an orphanage. We figure, we are here at sea without our wives and children, but it is for a limited time. Those kids are always without their father and mother! Finally we sing a hymn and I conclude the service with a prayer. It all lasts about twenty minutes.

Then I say, 'The day is yours.' Just about everyone is able to relax, sit on deck, get some sunshine, write a letter home or read a book. No loud music, no pressure, no stress, Biblical Sabbath rest' if you will. Human beings need the change. Did not God himself show us that pattern? Did he not rest on the seventh day? There is more to life than to work day after day. We need some sort of spiritual renewal, as well as physical rest, because we are not robots. On a ship especially, we are involved in a constant operation and must work 24 hours a day, so this pattern makes sense, don't you agree?"

I thanked the master for his lucid explanation, offered prayer for him and for his crew, as well as for their families thousands of miles away. I told him, "I should like to see the chief engineer," to which he replied, "By all means, in fact I am extremely pleased that you place as number one on your agenda the person who has not as yet committed himself to Christ."

He continued, "Be sure, however to also meet the other crew members. You might even wish to read the Bible at high noon and briefly speak to the men. It is so significant that we see a preacher on board. We need to be encouraged. You would call that pastoring, wouldn't you? So go to it!"

It developed into a fascinating day. The chief engineer indicated his surprise that the representative of the church would bother to make it a point to meet and to talk with him, a non-Christian.

We had a thought provoking talk. The mere fact that I had devoted my life to a ministry to people like him, sailing on board of ships, impressed him. They were the people who would set sail again on Thursday morning or Friday night and would be unable to come to the Sunday service in my Centre. So what did I get out of it? He wondered, "What kind of benefit does this have for you?" I told him, "The point is what benefit will God get out of it? In fact not out of it, but out of you, when you give your life in dedication to Him."

"So it's about me and him?" he asked. I came back and said, "No, it's about him and you. You attend the Sunday service, courteously and respectfully the captain tells me. For this I make you my compliment. But God is saying, "Give me your heart.""

We had become friends. Regretfully I lost contact with him, but I am curious if he got through to *him*.

At noon I read the Bible, as suggested by the master. I encouraged the crew in their faith. I informed them, that it inspired and even surprised others that they wished to adhere to biblical principles. Their profession made some people refocus on God.

Late in the day, I drove through the city to my home. At the traffic light where I had to stop I looked around and saw the advertisement of the dry cleaner, informing me that he could do my shirts in one hour, even on Sundays, since he was open on Sundays. The dry cleaner has lined himself up with the majority of store keepers. The Government, which has brought in legislation, that allows anyone to open up his business on Sundays, curiously keeps all its own offices and services closed. The steady dislodging of the directives of the LORD has not enhanced our lives.

It is fascinating that on this ship—and on eight others as well—where the operation is a twenty-four-hour a day pattern, the message of the

Scriptures to respect the commandment of God about the maintenance of the holiness of his day, is carefully observed. Interesting, because of all the commandments, this one seems to be the easiest one to disrespect.

I reported to the Control Center and gave a detailed account of what I had heard and seen. It became a witness about the application of faith to the reality of life. The officer in the Control Center is still recovering, but he made one remark that reminded me that deep down in the heart of man there is still that call of the LORD to respect his principles of rest when he said: "I wish they would apply that kind of standard to this office."

PURIFICATION
CEREMONIES

I got a phone call, "Reverend, this is Matthew. I used to work for a shipping company, as you know. Well, I have now decided to open up my own agency. I have set up an office in one of the suites in a building downtown. I redecorated the whole place, new carpet, new furniture, the lot. I am planning to open up tomorrow. I am wondering: 'Do you do any Purification Ceremonies?'"

In my denomination we have a manual for ecclesiastical ceremonies. Somehow I did not feel a need to consult it. If I would have checked the index under the letter P, I would not have found anything that might even remotely resemble the subject of "Purification Ceremonies." It is not done in Reformed or Presbyterian circles. I have no recollection of any lectures on the subject in seminary. In my first eight years as a pastor in two congregations, I was never confronted with it, so, in a sense, I was at a loss.

But the Holy Spirit gave immediate insight, where the church manual was silent, "Matthew in the shipping business is calling you. He has never called you as long as you have been in Montreal. He has set up his own agency and is ready to start rolling tomorrow, but before he does he calls you. Why would he call you? He senses that he is beginning a totally new chapter in his life. He sees you repeatedly on the waterfront. He knows that somehow you bring the dimension of God into the lives of people. Deep down in his soul, maybe because he went to church as a child, he senses that it would be appropriate to bring that dimension of God into his new business. He hasn't thought it through, but he is actually asking that well known question, 'Reverend, what does God have to say in my business?' He knows you have the answer to that. Moreover, his 'language' is found in the Bible, in that tiny letter of Paul to his assistant Titus, where reference is made to purification... 'We wait for the glorious appearing of our great God and Savior Jesus Christ, who gave himself for us to redeem us from all wickedness and *to purify* for himself a people that are his very own' (Titus 2:13). There you have it, set in flowering language, so do your job in response to Matthew's call."

"Yes, Matthew," I said, "I do Purification Ceremonies. What time would be convenient? Three thirty this afternoon? Very well, I'll be there."

In preparation, I purchased a Bible in the language of today and a small distinguished bronze cross. I assembled hammer and nails, my Bible, and vestments.

By 3:15 p.m. I found Matthew, formally dressed in a three-piece suit with tie, in his brand new office. It was a beautiful place. It was freshly painted, had a new carpet, a sophisticated, highly polished desk and chairs, the latest technical equipment, and tasteful wall decorations. Physically it couldn't become more purified than it looked. But both Matthew and I knew that the Spirit of God was aiming for something else, something deeper, something spiritual.

After I had dressed myself in my vestments, I asked Matthew to stand at one side of his desk, while I stood at the other side. After all, his desk would be the central place in his office. From it, all business would be conducted. So I began, while explaining my every action, by placing the Bible on the table.

I proceeded behind the desk and in a strategic place I nailed the cross to the wall, so that everyone, who would come in, would immediately notice the cross. Returning to my place in front of the desk, I preached a brief sermon, based on Colossians 3:17; "Whatever you do, whether in word or deed, do it all in the name of the LORD Jesus, giving thanks to God the Father through him..." I stated that if justice and righteousness would prevail in all his dealings, it would bear God's approval.

If the fundamental principles of the Bible on his desk, telling us to seek the glory and honor of God in our business, would be applied, the blessing of the LORD would be assured. That was the heart of my sermon.

We knelt and prayed that God would inspire Matthew to measure up to his expectations. We asked God to bless the business, which would be done in his office.

In an industrialized ministry, one of the key issues is to be able to interpret the "language" of the people one meets. At the same time, one must constantly remain open to the guidance and subtle instructions of the Spirit of God. One should also realize, that the person who asks us the question, ought to be taken seriously and answered appropriately.

A Colombian engineer invited me into his cabin and almost immediately stated that a painful problem was on his mind, which he needed to share with me. He felt he needed to talk about this, because he wanted to get his mind cleared. I listened to his story. It sounded so familiar. It had to do with the education of his children and with inadequacy on his part, because he was away at sea for extended periods of time.

It was the kind of perplexity many a seafarer runs into: When he comes home he has a tendency to apply all sorts of rules and regulations. As a result, he gets into conflict not only with his children, but even with his wife.

During his absence she has to fulfill, of course, the role of father and mother. Wives of seafarers have to deal with adjusting to suddenly being in charge. Their husbands will have to make distinct adjustments upon coming home for vacation. She has set the tone. She had done the job well during her husband's four-month absences. He is now called upon to tread carefully and graciously. To speak bluntly, he should keep his nose out of a "well-oiled operation" managed by his wife. So when he comes home on vacation, he has to realize that he should calmly and quietly bond with his family by acting with consideration.

What happens to many seafarers is what happened to him: He immediately switched to his position as the head of the household. This turned into total frustration for the entire family. His frustration was increased by the fact that his few months of vacation should have been another "honeymoon." It wasn't. Now he was back on the ship, where in his isolated office, his prison as he called it, he reflected on his time at home. He was filled with unpleasant memories, frustration, and remorse.

It is, of course, an unnatural life to be married and to be a father, yet to live three quarters of your life away from home and family. You sense that you are out of touch with your social environment, your spiritual climate, and the setting you call home. In all of this, you also wrestle with that key phrase that was used in your wedding ceremony: "…with the gracious help of God we shall love and honor one another in good times and in bad times and…never forsake each other so long as we both shall live…"

She is always alone at home, with or without children. In her social contact she comes into touch not only with family, but also with friends. She may attend social gatherings. She may be part of the church community, but at home she is alone. She may be influenced by the morality of today: "Satisfy yourself and do as you please." She is not to give in to this.

Can he avoid temptation? He is a married man. He has physical and emotional needs. There are countless girls, who are willing to "meet" him. In that respect, both she and he are "in the same boat."

So they both must maintain the proper course and stay on an even keel. Otherwise their marriage becomes a foundering ship.

For officers, the time away from home is about three or four months in succession. For crew members, many of them married and with children, it is worse. They are contracted for six to nine months. When they come home, their own children may run away from them because they don't know this stranger who suddenly appears and seems to dominate the scene at home. While he is at sea, they can communicate with their father only via the telephone or by e-mail, often at high costs.

This was the frustration the Columbian engineer expressed. He let his coffee get cold, because he talked uninterruptedly for almost half an hour. Ten days ago he had boarded the ship again after his vacation. I could sense that he was weighed down with misery. Some people may call it stress. Irrespective of the name, it was visible pain.

I took the time to help him get relieved from his burden. I suggested a letter to his wife and some cards to the children, and a telephone call in the next port. I proposed that he speak to God about it and share with his wife, that he asked God for forgiveness. I furthermore suggested that he apologize to his wife, assuring her, that he had learned a lesson, maybe more than one, and that things would be looking very well four months from now, when he would be home again.

We were both exhausted. Putting down his cigarette, he stood up and suggested what I was going to suggest: The prayer with a blessing, not the kind of blessing, as in a ceremonial activity. This was a call for cleansing, for purification, for forgiveness, for restitution, which we all need regularly, when we go through our crises.

He was burdened with guilt. It was my privilege to absolve him in the name of the LORD. The whole drama at home, the contact with his children, or rather the lack thereof, the misunderstanding with his wife, the language he may have used, the frustration he displayed, in short his entire distorted vacation, and the resulting guilt needed to be forgiven. That was why I had to be on this ship at this time. In his presence I asked God to forgive him in the name of Jesus Christ. Such a prayer is always answered!

This type of ministry is so appreciated by many seafarers, who struggle with similar stress. When I walked up the gangway of a large cargo ship, I was greeted by one of the English sailors. He sported a huge hammer in one hand and an enormous wrench in the other. He greeted me by saying: "Have you come to bless the tools, Father?" Blessing tools was not part of my experience, but I liked the question.

Is there not a sentence in one of our table prayers that goes like this, "LORD, bless this food to our bodies and us to Thy service?" So that might extend to the hammer and the wrench, but I wanted him to understand it biblically. I also wanted to strip away any possible magical connotation of the blessing.

I told him, "Yes, I came to bless you, as well as your tools, not the tools alone, but as you use them with your talents and service. That is how the LORD will receive glory and honor through *you*, using hammer, wrench and all the other tools you have hidden down below. Those are included in this blessing."

That kind of reaction strips away the whole idea of what sounds like a flippant request for a magic ceremony and gives it body and substance through a serious reaction. For deep down in the hearts of us all, there is a genuine desire to be inspired and encouraged by the presence of God. We all need *purification* in the most common things we do. To give that kind of spiritual dimension to our daily routine is part of our ministry.

TABLE MANNERS AND
TABLE PRAYERS

My mother has taught me table manners as well as table prayers. I managed to retain them both. On board of ships, you will find excellent table manners almost without exception. However, table prayers are found sporadically.

When I am invited to stay for lunch or dinner on board of a ship, I feel that the agreement I have with our LORD, to honor him and to express to him my thanks before I eat, should not be cancelled. I may sit down with people who do not have such an agreement with our LORD, yet I should maintain my commitment. Christ has set the tone for this in Matthew 14:19: "And he directed the people to sit down on the grass. Taking the five loaves and the two fish and looking up to heaven, he gave thanks and broke the loaves. Then he gave them to the disciples, and the disciples gave them to the people."

When I started my career as a chaplain to seafarers, I thought it appropriate to speak quietly to God before the meal, out of respect for others at the table, who would not necessarily agree with my spiritual convictions. I know of people who, in such a situation, find a more comfortable way out. They just do not say Grace, or if they do, they do it unobtrusively. It is of course, somewhat embarrassing.

One occasion I remember vividly: After we sat down with the officers I asked for a moment of silence, so I could speak quietly to the

Lord. When I had concluded my prayer, all eyes were on me. For a few moments the atmosphere around the table was very tense. But then the Lord provided an absolutely magnificent and permanent solution:

During the morning I had been in conversation with the captain and I had discovered that his attitude towards God and religion was, to put it mildly, rather negative. He thought it was very nice of me to talk about it, but in his opinion, religion is only for people who are weak, or old, or unable to take care of things themselves.

Moreover, when I tried to get to the heart of the matter, he found it preposterous to believe that God would have any involvement with people. Life's philosophy boiled down to the simple statement: You make the best of it yourself, under your own steam, in your own strength. To believe, that God would even care about us, he considered to be ridiculous. It was very nice that I would bring up the Christian religion, but I should only speak to people who felt a real "need." He acknowledged that indeed there were "weak" characters in our society and they needed people like me. But he brushed it all off as worthless for himself, as he told me in no uncertain terms. However, he concluded his remarks with a jovial word of farewell, "Maybe some people on board might like to hear what you have to say, the chief engineer perhaps. He is a little bit more sensitive to that sort of thing. I think he goes to church once in a while, but you are wasting your time on me." He rose to his feet, shook my hand and said, "Join us for lunch later today. We have an excellent cook."

The idea of an excellent cook appealed to me. But to be quite frank, to sit down at lunch with someone who had as negative an approach to the Christian faith as this captain did not inspire me. I have had extensive training from the Spirit of God, who got me into all kinds of jams, for no other reason than to take hold of the challenges, in order to bring people to Christ. So I decided to stay on board for lunch.

I went to visit the chief engineer, a pleasant person, who indeed did belong to a church. Because of his profession, he was at sea for extended periods of time, so he did not darken the church door that often. "But," he told me, "When I am at home I go to church with my wife."

Was it merely to go along with his wife in order to maintain a good relationship with her, or was his heart committed to the LORD? Did he genuinely desire to be fed by the proclamation of the Word of God? These were the questions we examined in our talk together. He admitted he was on the level of merely "going along." He sincerely respected my efforts to get him on what he called "a higher level."

I visited a number of other people on board as well. Then it was time for lunch. I went up to the captain's cabin with mixed feelings, but was convinced that the LORD had a purpose. We went to the officer's dining room and sat down at the staff table, with the captain directly in front of me, the smiling chief engineer on my left, and a chief officer, whom I had not met, on my right. He seemed quite preoccupied with the business of the ship, but remained courteous.

I asked for a moment of silence to quietly offer a prayer. When I concluded my prayer, all eyes were upon me. For a few moments, the atmosphere was tense. Then, the captain fired a question at me: "What did you pray?"

I was taken by surprise. Then I answered, "I prayed for you, sir, for the chief engineer, the chief officer, the dining room steward, and of course, for your excellent cook. I also prayed for the crew and their families at home."

There was a moment of silence. Then the master said, "Well, that is interesting. Perhaps you might be kind enough to do it again, but now out loud, so we can all hear it." I did. It flashed through my mind that the LORD used this captain to "preach a sermon" to me! It was a priceless lesson. It fortunately happened at the start of my ministry to seafarers. I have never forgotten it, and I have never again prayed silently on board.

For years, I have been inspired by this experience. After all, the LORD Jesus prayed before he fed the five thousand people with five loaves and two fish, and again when he fed the four thousand. So did Paul, with or without handcuffs, on board a combination cargo and cruise vessel. He encouraged the two hundred and seventy-six passengers on board and prayed out loud as they sat down to eat in the midst of a hurricane at sea. I was impressed by the frank approach of this captain.

A cargo ship was thrown on the shore in a severe storm. The papers were filled with pictures. Hundreds of sightseers came to see it, causing traffic jams miles long. The ship was scheduled to come to port. Who knows from where it had come? Who knows what kind of needs the seafarers might have? Who knows if someone on board was perhaps sick?

There it was, on shore, slightly leaning over to starboard. How could I be of help? So, I telephoned the ship. "I am a chaplain to seafarers. It is my profession to minister to the strangers in the gate. This includes those who are stuck on a ship."

One of the officers answered my call. "So kind of you, Reverend, to contact us. No, we do not have any real needs. We are all in good shape. We will just have to wait until the ship is pulled free, after we have unloaded part of the fuel oil, so as to prevent possible pollution. We soon expect to be in port, where an examination will tell us if there is any damage done to the hull of the ship. So come and see us as soon as we are docked." This was encouraging.

After about two weeks, when the ship had been dragged into port, I boarded her. The officer met me, as I came up the gangway. He said, "I knew it was you. I recognized your voice on the phone. Do you remember me? I was in your Seafarers Centre two years ago. It was on a Sunday. You invited us to come upstairs to the chapel, where you were going to make prayers to God. We were impressed. At the close of your service, you offered a copy of the Bible to anyone who wanted it. You gave me one, too." He raced upstairs to his cabin and returned with the Bible in his hand. "Here it is," he said, as he showed it to me, "with your inscription and instructions in it. It is fascinating."

I was invited to stay for lunch. They proposed that I offer a prayer of thanks to God for keeping everyone safe. In spite of the accident, all on board were well. I rose to my feet and everybody followed suit. I gave thanks to God and remembered their families as well. During the next few days, I would stop by this ship and once or twice again I was invited to join them for lunch. They always asked me to offer prayer. Muslim officers asking me for prayers! What an honor! I gladly obliged.

I came on board again on one of the last days that the ship was in port. It was right after lunch. Officers and crew were still seated comfortably in the lounge, drinking tea. They expressed their dismay that I had come so late, unable to join them for the lunch, but they immediately asked, "Will you have tea with us?" I consented and tea was served.

I picked up my cup and was bringing it to my mouth, when one of the officers, seated next to me, grabbed my arm, preventing the cup from reaching my mouth and with a look of utter amazement asked, "No prayers today?" My coming on board was to them not merely a matter of associating with them during lunch. As a man of God, as a pastor of the people in the confinement of their ship, which is their office and home combined, they expected me to minister to them spiritually. On most ships they do not say this in so many words, although I have often noticed it expressed in subtle remarks. Here they did! It was straightforward: "You as our spiritual guide, representing the highest Authority, should bring us in line with him." I have never forgotten this.

It is significant, because it tells us something: Our "congregational" members on board or in the Seafarers Centers are looking at us as we ought to be looked at—as pastors and preachers. Some people suggest that we should be there for the seafarers only to provide a listening ear, a welcoming hand, and a readiness to be available to them. This pastoral need is unquestionably significant, but seafarers essentially expect from us more than that. They see us as their "Spiritual Guides."

On the fourth Sunday in Advent, a number of the officers and crew from this ship asked if they could come to my church. That Sunday I preached about the birth of Christ, who is the only Savior of the world. I preached in simple language, because not all of them were fluent in English and the material was foreign to them. Characteristically for seafarers, who are not familiar with the church service, they sat close to the front so as not to miss anything.

Four of the gentlemen approached me after the worship service and expressed their amazement, that the congregation had recited the LORD's Prayer. They inquired if they had learned it in church and if it was recorded somewhere in what they called "The Book." I showed them Matthew 6 in the Bible. Two of them were so intrigued they wondered if they were allowed to take a copy of "The Book" with them to the ship because as one of them said, "I want to learn this prayer."

Ahmed, from Morocco, is a man with flair and enthusiasm for his job. As Maitre d' in charge of one hundred and seventy-five dining room stewards on board of a huge cruise ship, he was in the habit of assembling all of his stewards in the main dining room every other day, shortly before dinner. He gave them last minute instructions. I was intrigued. We were seated in the main dining room in the very center, at a table for twelve people, underneath a global ceiling, displaying the stars in the sky. When I said Grace at that table many dining room guests could hear it, because of the way the ceiling was shaped. People, four or five seats away, would come up to me and express their appreciation for the Grace I had said.

Ahmed came to our table almost every night. As a man, who took pride in his work, he wanted to be assured that the guests were pleased. I approached him one day and asked if I could come to his meeting to speak briefly to the stewards and to offer prayers for them. Ahmed was impressed by the request and invited me to be there the very next day. I spoke to all the stewards and, to their amazement, offered prayers. The reaction of our own table steward expressed it all: As he came to our table that evening he said, in the hearing of all the guests, "This is a good day! We went to church and Father prayed for us." None of the guests understood what he meant. Since it was a port day, one of the guests asked, "Oh, did your Father come on board?" Our steward explained, "No, this Father right here!" pointing at me. I then explained what had happened just before dinner.

Judging from the reaction, I discovered that a number of guests at our table suddenly "saw" their Jamaican steward, not merely as a man who took their orders and brought them their dinners, but as a person also in need of prayer and spiritual food.

When I am asked to say Grace at the table, I always include those who stand in our service. I learned this while on my honeymoon. We had visited New York City and were returning home. We stopped early in the morning at a diner where we ordered the special: orange juice, bacon and eggs, toast, and coffee.

We got the orange juice and assumed we would have to wait a while for the rest of the order, so we prayed silently. To our amazement, the moment we opened our eyes, our charming Afro-American waitress was standing next to us, balancing half a dozen plates on one arm, ready to serve us. She asked Trudy, "Did you pray for me too, honey?" Trudy, who is extremely honest replied, "No, I didn't, but I will," and she did.

In fact, I do not see many people, in restaurants or dining rooms, saying "Grace." Twice in my life I did, once at Wendy's a family of six offered prayer while holding hands. The father prayed out loud. Trudy and I were just exiting. I went back in. I slapped the father on his back while congratulating him for saying grace out loud. He just about choked on the first bite of hamburger, but he thanked me for my remarks.

The second one happened at the Miami Airport. Waiting for a flight to Singapore, we sat quietly at a little table in one of the waiting areas. The place was packed. Two charming, hip-looking girls had just picked up their juice and were opening their homemade lunch packets. Before they took a bite they bowed their heads, folded their hands and prayed. It was a great sight to see right there in this packed airport! I wrote my compliments on my business card, got up and handed it to them, wishing them "bon appetite" and a blessed trip.

For several years, we sailed just about every other week on a cruise ship from Quebec City to Montreal and back. I had informed the Maitre d' that we would be willing to be seated with any guest, with whom they had a problem. One day, when we entered the dining room, the Maitre d' approached us with a combination of enthusiasm and panic. "You are just the people I am looking for, for we are desperate about these people," he said, ushering us to a table for six. He disappeared immediately. A very nice and well mannered couple was already seated. He was a professor of archeology at some university in the South; his wife had a job in administration at the same university. Two seats remained empty as yet.

I offered to say Grace. It was greeted with genuine appreciation by the professor and his wife. In fact, he admitted that they were in the habit of doing that at home as well. I did commit to the LORD's care any other guests who might join us at the table. Just before I came to the close of my prayer, a lady said, "Thank you" and pulled out a chair for a gentleman, who seemed to be rather unstable due to his health. She shoved his chair in next to Trudy, and then took the seat across from him. In less than ten seconds, we had sized up the situation, for she summoned the steward and the head steward demanding a dish for the gentleman, which did not appear on the menu.

An argument ensued and she demanded that the Maitre d' appear before her, to give account of why the selection, she thought her gentleman friend needed, was not on the menu. She felt she got abominable service, and gave voice to it in front of the stewards and the Maitre d,' to the embarrassment of all of us at the table. It was a noisy scene. The waiter rushed out to get what she wanted and the staff returned to their duties. Now we knew why the Maitre d' had brought us to this table.

Trudy had just met that very same lady earlier on deck, as we left Quebec City. In a discussion, as to what Centigrade was in comparison to Fahrenheit, the lady had again dominated the scene, but she got her facts mixed up. Trudy calmly gave her the solution for converting centigrade to Fahrenheit. She had appreciated that. At the table, however, another type of conversion was badly needed.

I started the conversation by saying, "Madame, I think you are one of the nicest ladies I have met today." That took her by surprise. Trudy smiled approvingly at her. Rather softly the lady asked, "Why do you say that?" I responded, "Do you remember that I was in the middle of saying Grace, asking God to bless those who would join us? Well, you said 'Thank you' and I was impressed."

She answered, "Thank you, but I do not believe in God." Then she revealed what really bothered her: She had lost her son in an accident, her only son, and they had been very close. Her husband too had died some years ago, and her son's death hurt her deeply. It was unfair of God to have taken such a young man with such a brilliant future in the prime of his life.

She was Jewish and felt that since God had not prevented the death of her son, it proved that he really did not care for anyone. I suggested that something very unusual had happened. I said: "Think of it. Trudy and I just came on board and the Maitre d' assigned us to this table. Now, what a unique occasion! You tell us that you are angry with God, because of the death of your son and you feel that it makes sense to talk about it, because by my attire you see that I am a minister. So, I think that the Maitre d' has been used by God to place us together at this table. Of course you are angry. Of course you feel bereft. A great emptiness has come about in your life. So, let's talk about it. That's why Trudy and I are here.

Do you remember this man called Job? He was stripped of all his children, not just of one son. He had seven sons. All of them died; a gruesome story in the Old Testament. Then Job made this miraculous statement: 'The LORD gave, and the LORD has taken away.' (Job 1:21). We can't disagree with that, but it's the next sentence he said that is absolutely incredible: 'May the name of the LORD be praised.'

So, sit tight; there are inscrutable dramas that occur in our lives and yet we are reminded by the Bible, that in these totally incomprehensible situations, God is to be praised. I cannot tell you why your son was taken out of this life at such a young age, but God himself, who does not give you an answer to that question either, is the only One who can provide you with the comfort and consolation you need. God's love for you is expressed in the death of his Son on the cross. That is the mystery of God's care for us. Do you have a Bible?" "I told you I am Jewish," she replied, "I don't have a Bible." I said, "Maybe I should get you one." She ignored my statement and continued, "I don't go to the synagogue any more." There was silence and then she said: "But perhaps I should return." "And get a Bible," Trudy said, "in which you can read about Job, and other remarkable events."

Two weeks later we were again on board of the same ship. At dinner, the Maitre d' exclaimed, "Reverend! Sit anywhere today. Do you remember that lady of two weeks ago? Well, you won't believe this, but during the entire return trip to New York, she was a changed person! What did you do to her?" I answered; "I think perhaps she returned not only to New York, but to the LORD."

A Finnish physician happened to be the medical officer on board of another cruise ship. His wife and children were with him. He had lived in the USA for quite some time, but for the sake of the children, had returned to Finland. We were seated at the same table for dinner. He had a real sense of humor and was very direct and open in conversation. There were about half a dozen other passengers at the table as well. So, we looked forward every day to this time of relaxation.

Their children were seated somewhere else, for they had made contact with young people on board. Our table discussions frequently went rather deep. One night the doctor volunteered that his son, who was fifteen, wanted to be confirmed in the Lutheran church and was receiving instruction. He had received a Bible and was actually reading it. The doctor and his wife were not attending church, but they found it quite intriguing that their son showed a sudden interest in the church.

Trudy said, "You ought to go to church with your son. It is important for him that you go as a family." "Oh no," he replied, "The church is out of touch. I get nothing out of it." "But your son needs your support," she continued. "Have you read the Bible?" "No," he said, "the language is outdated." "Not at all," we exclaimed, "There are new translations in today's language."

Every evening the doctor ordered a bottle of wine, which he shared with his tablemates. Every evening he proposed a toast to some person or to a significant cause. In many instances it was appropriate, but at others, it was totally ridiculous. However, those occasions gave us a good laugh.

One night the doctor confided, that one of his patients was in such a serious condition, he did not expect him to survive the night. So in my prayer I asked the LORD to save his life.

The next day at dinner, the doctor exclaimed, "We didn't lose him! In fact, his condition has improved. I have no explanation, but he's taken a turn for the better! The bleeding has stopped." We rejoiced with the doctor and I thanked the LORD for this miracle. As soon as the glasses were filled, the doctor raised his glass. We all were expecting another humorous toast. Instead he gave one of the best toasts I have ever heard, saying, "Since my patient survived, I bring out a toast to the LORD!" All ten of us at the table said in chorus, "To the LORD!"

Before we left the ship, we presented the doctor with a Bible in today's language. He was pleasantly surprised and gladly accepted our gift.

When we were seated with a charming Jewish couple during a world cruise, which lasted almost three and a half months, we were joined by a Jewish gentleman from Australia and his friend from Scotland. Our discussion often dealt with God's involvement in our lives. The Australian gentleman had lost his entire family during the holocaust. We delicately tried to articulate, that God does call out to his people and that the call is motivated by his love for them. This God is the God of Abraham, Isaac, and Jacob. He is the God we, the Gentiles, have come to acknowledge in the Messiah, but he is also the God of the very people, with whom we now sat at the table.

We expressed some of this in our prayer as well and remembered specifically the spiritual and physical suffering of our friend, who had lost his entire family. Every now and then, even before we offered prayer, they asked us to remember the needs of people they had come into contact with on board. So once again we experienced that the ceremony of saying Grace opened the door for being a witness to the Messiah.

A young couple on their honeymoon, another couple also fairly young, and a well-to-do Jewish couple with two children of about ten and eleven years of age, were all seated at one table. We were assigned to sit with them.

When I offered to say Grace, the Jewish gentleman rather firmly said, "We are Jewish," He said it in a tone which conveyed, "You are out of our ball park." So, I remarked, "In that case, I'll say it in Hebrew." I did and it broke the ice. An amicable conversation resulted. I thought we were off to a good start.

On the last day of the cruise our Jewish friend said, "I'll say grace tonight, but in English, because my Hebrew is not as good as yours." After he had given thanks to God he looked at us and said, "I have had more religion during this week than I have had in my entire life!"

CAPTAINS ALSO
NEED MINISTRY

"Good morning; you must be the priest or something like that," said the master of a Dutch freighter as he shook my hand. I sensed his attempt to keep distance between us, so I answered, "I am 'something like that.'"

He felt comfortable with my answer and ushered me to a seat in his large cabin but, before I sat down, he once again grabbed my hand, pulled me slightly towards him and said, "You are very welcome on my ship, but keep in mind that with *me* you do not talk religion." I responded, "Agreed." So we sat down and talked about the weather, the ship's voyage, his family, and the places both of us were familiar with in the Netherlands. The coffee, served by his private steward, was superior and the fifteen-minute get- together ended pleasantly. As I rose to leave, I even got a word of encouragement when he said, "Talk to anyone you want to here on board, and if you are still here at lunch time, be sure to join me for lunch."

About three months later, the ship was again in port and surprisingly, there was a sister ship of the same company berthed right behind it. I first boarded the ship I was acquainted with, out of respect for the master. I knocked on the open door of his cabin, as is the custom on board of ships.

I was invited in and when I met the captain again, he introduced me to a guest in his cabin saying, "This is Captain Cooke. He is the master of the sister ship, berthed directly behind our ship. Please sit down." Captain Cooke and I sat down in the social area of the cabin while the master sat down behind his desk to do some paper work.

I mentioned that an Old Testament professor I was acquainted with had the same name, and I asked if he, by any chance, was related to him. It turned out he was, very distantly, so we briefly talked about this Old Testament professor and then I steered the conversation into the direction of the Old Testament.

We briefly talked about the days of creation. We ended up with Genesis 3, "the fall into sin," the cause of the perplexity and trouble we face today. It is a peculiar account of the devil, in the form of a serpent, talking in a subtle way to Adam and Eve in opposition to God. That's how sin entered into the world.

While we were discussing this nasty subject, the host captain— seated at his desk with his back towards us—had obviously been listening in, because he suddenly turned around and without any introduction said: "Yes, Reverend, doesn't that have something to do with a snake who talked?" I do not know what made me react the way I did, and I was shocked at my own remarks, but I said: "Sir, with all due respect, I was under the impression that you and I were not supposed to talk about religion."

He responded, "Oh yes, you are right," whereupon he turned back to his paper work, while Captain Cooke and I talked about sin and salvation.

We didn't get there all the way, but we were going in the right direction. After about half an hour, I decided to leave. It had been an exhausting, but very meaningful conversation. I silently prayed that it would bear fruit. Both masters rose to their feet. I shook Captain Cooke's hand first. When our host captain shook my hand, he held it about three seconds longer than usual and said, "It would be nice if you could come back some other time, Reverend, because I *do* want to know whether or not that snake talked."

I did come back. He discovered that the snake did talk, but God had the last word. Here was a captain, who had closed his mind to the dynamic message of the Christian religion. Yet now, mysteriously, he tried to wedge his way in via the record of the devil's initial destructive operation. Was this the work of the Holy Spirit? We talked extensively about "religion"...

Protocol on board of freighters demands that the first person one goes to see is the captain, as one of them appropriately explained to me, "This is my ship. I am in charge and responsible for the ship, its staff, and its cargo. I have authority over who comes on board and who does not. I wish to be acknowledged as the master of this ship."

It is not merely a matter of being covered against possible lawsuits when one should slip on the deck or bump one's head on the low overhang at the entrance. It is also a matter of courtesy. This is a foreign ship. It sports the flag of another nation. So, as visitors, we should remember that we stay within the grace of the captain or, in the event he is resting, since some of them have to sail in the dead of night, of his second in command, the chief officer.

There is another reason: chaplains, who visit crew members on cargo ships, may have a tendency to forget about the captain, who also needs to be ministered to. He is the man who is in a sense totally isolated on board of the ship because he is at the very top. He functions as the master, and in a sense, also as the pastor of the ship. On the freighter, he has some thirty charges under him, all people who have left their homes to work at sea, all with their own personal concerns. They are expected to interact with the other seafarers on board; to work with them and to tolerate them. The captain has to stand above and, at the same, time next to his people. It behooves us to encourage him in every possible way.

When I came on board of a huge cargo ship late one morning and contacted the master, he was extremely upset. I asked him what his problem was. "I cannot talk to you," he said, "because I have to go to the shore office and make an overseas call to immediately get another cook. We cannot even get our lunch, which is in one hour. I have twenty-seven people on this ship. How do I feed them?"

I realized this was indeed rather upsetting. In my mind, I toyed around with getting twenty-seven orders of cheeseburgers at McDonalds. I wondered how the girl at the counter would react to that. I asked the captain a few questions. "Is your cook sick? Does he have to go home for an emergency? Did he abandon the ship? Why do you need another cook?"

He told me, "Half an hour ago the cook came into my office and said, 'I am not making any lunch today. I quit. I do not want to stay on board. I am sick and tired of this ship.' He gave me no reason. He just walked out of my office, dove into his cabin and locked the door. And here I sit. What time is it?" He looked at the watch. "In an hour twenty-seven people are coming in to eat. What am I going to say to them?"

I asked the captain, "Why did he throw in the towel? Was there an argument? Did you or anyone else complain about the food?"

"No," he said. "I told you already he gave me no reason. There was no argument. I never talked to him. I never complained. No one complained about the food. He is the best cook we have ever had. He prepares excellent meals every day. So I have no idea what got into his head. I am totally dumbfounded." He paced the floor in his office and slammed his hand on the desk in frustration.

Here was the man in authority about to cave in because one link of the chain broke. A ship, irrespective of its size, is dependent on the cooperative efforts of all those who signed on. They have their individual positions and each one is a vital link in the chain. The ship must sail; the show must go on.

In my heart, I thanked God that of all the ships in port, I had chosen this one at this time where the captain was all upset. I can cook, but not for twenty-seven people at such short notice, so I could only function as the person to whom the captain could let it all out. I listened and expressed my agreement with his furious reaction. I did make one suggestion, "Let me go down and see the cook. Do not

at times may forget the relationships with the members of their staff on board. But this is a dimension which is absolutely vital.

I talked about this after the master had recovered from his shock. I said, "In a sense you are the pastor of the twenty-seven people here on board. They look to you not merely as the master, the man in charge of the operation, bringing them safely through awful storms, and furious seas. I am not telling you anything you do not know, because you are in the same boat. Your crew does not merely work here, they live here, and they wrestle with their problems here. They struggle with their frustrations of being far from their families. All of what you suffer, they suffer. They need to be able, once in a while, to express that. They need to hear that they are doing a good job. A word of encouragement and appreciation is so needed by all.

"You are the one in charge of all staff and crew. They look to you for that word of inspiration every now and then. They cannot talk to their immediate superiors about their personal problems for the simple reason that they stand in a direct work relationship with them. You are above that because you, as the master of them all, can exert pastoral care."

"I am here to run this ship. That's my responsibility. We have orders to go from one place to the other with cargo that needs to be delivered properly and in time. Now are you asking me to also be a preacher like you?" he asked.

I responded, "Leave the preaching to me, that's my job, but yes, the similarity between the two of us comes closer when I suggest you are also a pastor. Look at the story in Luke 15. It talks about a person who is looking after his sheep. Your ship operates because of your 'sheep.' You said so yourself. '*We* have orders to go from one place to the other.' You are in it together, so your pastoral care for the sheep in the ship, all twenty-seven of them, contributes profoundly to the effective operation of the ship. That's clearly stated in Luke 15: The shepherd is concerned that the *whole* flock is in shape. Not one of them should bail out. When one did he went after it, found it, and carried it back on his own shoulders. He organized a party to celebrate the restoration of his flock."

I waited a few seconds, expecting the captain to come up with a reaction of some kind. Then I suggested, "Shall I go down and get the cook?"

"Okay," he said. I ushered the cook upstairs to the captain's cabin. It was sort of awkward.

The cook did not quite know what to say or even how to conduct himself. He had his worries, which he expressed to me, as we were walking up the stairs. "Will the captain hold this against me? Do I get demerit points if I stay on board? Shouldn't I get off this ship anyway? What if he gets angry and starts shouting?" I did not respond.

We arrived at the captain's cabin. I knocked on the open door to announce our arrival. "Come in," we both heard him say. I entered first. The cook came in right behind me but stayed in the door opening. He stood there somewhat forlorn. It was indeed most awkward.

The captain, it appeared, had picked up something from the sermon. He did not summon the cook to come to his desk, as he would have done with anyone else, who would come in with a message or on business. Instead he got up from behind his desk—imagine the captain getting up for the cook—and walked towards the door with an out stretched arm to shake hands with him. He said, "You are a good cook, everyone on board says so too." He couldn't get out another word. He is not the type of person, who can easily establish a relationship and make the other party feel at ease, but I thought it was a huge accomplishment for this captain to express such praise. The cook did not acknowledge the statement, but at least he heard it. He responded with, "I am sorry for this morning…Shall I get back to the job?" "Please," said the captain and off went the cook.

Lunch was served half an hour late. The captain entered the dining room at half past the hour. All the officers sat at their tables talking, in anticipation of the lunch to be served. I followed the captain. Before he sat down, he made what I thought was an incredibly clever statement. He said, "Today lunch is served late, as you have noticed. That's because I had some business to discuss with the preacher here. Enjoy your meal!"

I complimented him for sailing this narrow channel so smoothly, that all of his people considered me the cause of the delay. He had covered for the cook magnificently! Obviously he had picked up more from the discussion about relationships than I had dared to hope.

"Maybe it's your 'sheep' stuff," he said to me. I ventured it might have been the "sheep's staff of the shepherd" that had touched him.

On a huge bulk carrier there existed a peculiar situation. Most of the officers and crew members were from Korea, but the captain was from Japan. Reflecting on the political relationship between these two countries, I was rather surprised, but I had discovered on a number of other occasions that politics do not determine business operations.

I met the captain, who upon learning that I represented the Ministry to Seafarers, asked me if I could get him a copy of the Bible. Whenever a request like that is made of me, I am excited because obviously there is an interest of some kind.

In his case, it was due to the second officer, who always took his Bible along with him to the bridge whenever he was on duty. Not that he constantly read it, he had his responsibilities, but there were quiet times at sea. Besides, he was always accompanied on his watch by a quartermaster or an able-bodied seaman since at least two people have to stay on watch on the bridge. The second officer would then take some time out to briefly read a section of the Bible. It is interesting that this subdued witness of a Korean officer inspired the captain. He never talked about it, he simply read his Bible.

The captain related it to me and told me that it inspired him to take a look at the Bible. After all, why would the intelligent second officer on his ship take such an interest in the Bible? So he repeated his request, ascertaining that I would get him one in Japanese, even though he could speak Korean. I returned to my station wagon on the dock to pick up a Japanese Bible. It was a beautiful edition, and after I had presented it to him, I sat down to write a "prescription" of what he should read first of all. He started to page through the Bible.

When I come into contact with people who have absolutely no knowledge of the Word of God, I feel it is helpful if they get some kind of guideline as to where to start reading. In many cases, I present that humorously, so as not to embarrass them. I tell them that when they visit a medical doctor, he will examine them and write a prescription. "But," I say, "The problem with the doctor's prescription is that you cannot read it, and you cannot keep it. You have to give it to the pharmacist. My prescription is far better. You can read it and you can keep it."

I write my prescriptions on the back of my calling cards. Rarely do I omit this. Throughout the years, I have discovered the enormous value of it. Most people do not know where to start reading the Bible or how to read it. For many it is a matter of searching through the index to find the suggested passages. They are not familiar with the names of the Bible books.

Many do not understand the language we use when we mention a section of the Bible. For example, 1 Peter 4:1–2 needs to be passed on as "First Peter, chapter four, verses one and two." The word "verse" is particularly confusing, so I explain: "Two times in the index you will find the name Peter. That's because he wrote two short letters. So I suggest you read the First Letter of this Peter, chapter four, lines one and two."

When I give out a New Testament, I am especially insistent to present specific instructions. I would like to see them get to the very heart of the message of salvation and admittedly, I also fear that should they open the New Testament, like any other book, and start with Matthew chapter one, it means that they have to plow through seventeen verses, with mostly Hebrew names, of the genealogy of Jesus. That might turn them off to the point that they close the Bible at verse five or six never to open it again.

Fortunately, the LORD at times overrides my good intentions. That happened to a very nice Pakistani seaman whom I had presented with a copy of the New Testament in his language, Urduh. He came back to the Seafarers Centre the following day to express his appreciation and his joy. In fact, he was ecstatic.

"This is a very good book," he said. I wondered why he said that, but he exclaimed, "I read about Abraham, Isaac, and Jacob! They are my brothers!" He had started with Matthew 1, so I thanked the LORD that I had kept my mouth shut at that time.

In my contact with the Japanese captain, I did my best to write my "prescription," but the Japanese captain ignored it as well and started at Genesis 1. Now I admit that is good stuff. It introduces us to paradise, beauty, glory, peace, excellent relationships, God, man, and beast in total harmony. Then comes the cave in, mysteriously followed by God's groundbreaking ceremonies for restoration.

Some six weeks later, I met my Japanese captain again when his ship had returned to the port of Montreal. I inquired if my suggested passages had been of help. In fact, I hoped that he had met the Savior through them. But it turned out that I was in too much of a hurry. "I am in the second section of this book. It is called Exit I believe." I left it to him to find out the correct name.

His enthusiasm got the better of him as he excitedly said, "There I found the best section. It is called 'The Ten Commandments.'" He picked up the Bible, which was placed on his desk, and started to search for the Ten Commandments. When he had found them, he looked up at me. "Beautiful," he said, "absolutely beautiful." With that kind of approval, I was prompted to ask him only one question.

"Did you decide to follow them?"

His immediate response was "No."

I asked "Why not?" and he answered, "I will start following them when I am retired." That, to me, was an intriguing reply, so I asked, "Why wait 'til you are retired?"

He answered, "Because it is impossible to put them into practice when you are in my position. In some ports, I have to deal with nasty situations every now and then. It just is not possible to follow these commandments while you are at work." It struck me that here is a man who, for the first time in his life, is coming into contact with the biblical line of thinking and he sees the demands so clearly as being beyond his capability.

"To walk with the LORD, in the light of His Word...?" Try to do that, irrespective of your position, *before you are retired.* I remembered the discussions during the crossing.

On cruise ships, it is not easy to approach the master of the ship when you are visiting the ship in port. The ship comes in early in the morning. The master has been on the bridge during part of the night to supervise a safe docking, so he is most likely in a state of exhaustion. Late in the afternoon of the same day, he is scheduled to be back on the bridge to guide the ship out of the port.

In the course of the day, there may be special meetings, or parties for people from the shore, which demand his presence. The maintenance of a strict program of rest is a matter of priority. Therefore, when I visit a cruise ship, I first pay my respects to a senior staff member, the staff captain, or the first officer, alerting them that I am on board. In this way, I do not have to prevail on the schedule of the master.

With ships manned by over a thousand crew members the time flies by. Most ships come in at seven in the morning and depart at five o'clock. In my schedule of visiting, it happens now and then that, although I may be in touch with all kinds of people on board, I have passed by the master.

As a pastor of seafarers, I have of course a pastoral responsibility for the master. I feel guilty, every now and then, when I have spent a whole day on a particular ship and did not visit the person in charge of the ship who carries the awesome responsibility of supervising the enormous vessel with her nearly three thousand passengers and close to one thousand and three hundred members of staff. On this particular ship, it had happened again.

I had been visiting everywhere and the time of departure was approaching. But it was as if the Spirit of the LORD prompted me to conclude the day by going to the captain's cabin. It was a very luxurious ship. I had to pass through the passageway of the penthouses before I approached the door marked "For Staff Only." Behind that door were the cabins of the senior officers.

The largest one near the front of the ship is ordinarily the master's cabin. Some of the senior staff members on the ship were Greeks. Almost always on any ship I experience a very cordial welcome, but especially from Greek officers. I am somewhat familiar with the language since I studied Greek in college and in seminary in order to be able to read the New Testament in Greek, its original language.

When I was very close to the captain's cabin, I found myself suddenly confronted by the staff captain, who had only one question: "What do you want?" The manner, the face and the tone indicated to me, that I was not standing in front of one of the most happy persons on this ship. In fact, I sensed a spirit of displeasure. It flashed through my mind that perhaps I had made the wrong choice to come here. Maybe I should not have come to pay my respect to the captain. But here I was, and I had to deal with the situation at hand.

So, in the most cheerful tone I could muster, I answered: "I am on my way to the captain." "The captain is busy and cannot see you," he responded. It sounded like a justified remark, but I thought I should press the matter just a bit further, so I replied, "I am aware of that, but I need to see him for only thirty-seven seconds." I figured even this staff captain could not object to my seeing the master for only thirty-seven seconds. However, my remark accomplished nothing. "The captain is busy and cannot see you at this time," he repeated, as he stood blocking the open-door entrance to the master's cabin.

At that moment the master himself came out of his cabin, presumably because he had heard our discussion. Upon seeing me in my clerical shirt, he simply said, "Oh Pappas (the Greek word for pastor), it is you; please come in." I walked past the staff captain and entered the huge cabin of the master.

"I came for only one reason, Sir," I said. "I am aware that you are a very busy man. I have visited many of the members of your staff throughout the day. I thank you for that opportunity. You are the person in charge of all of them as well as of the passengers. You have to negotiate this vessel out of port and sail in good or bad weather. You have the final responsibility, so I believe you stand in need of the grace of our LORD, and I have come here to extend his blessings to you." The master was quiet for a moment. He then looked at me and said, "No one has ever said this to me. I am impressed. Thank you." I pronounced the blessing!

The thirty-seven seconds had come to an end. I shook hands, turned around and left. The staff captain stood at the door as I passed by. I looked at him, nodded politely and headed for the passageway of the penthouses to disembark. I felt justified to have pressed the issue, irrespective of the staff captain's insistence that I stay away.

He was justified as well. After all, it is part of his job to protect the schedule of the master in every way. I respected his decision. I may not have liked the staff captain's determination, but that was my problem. He was doing his job. I had just started to open the door leading out of the short hallway when to my utter surprise, the staff captain suddenly shot ahead of me, blocking my exit and said, "You bless him, and you do not bless me? Come into my office!" With that he opened a door nearby which led to his office. It flashed through my mind that I should have included him in the blessing of the captain. Why didn't I?

He walked behind his desk, where he started to pace the floor. I stood in front of it. I was not offered a chair because his heart was overflowing with what seemed to me justified frustration. He gave vent to his fury, not with me, but with God.

"My mother just died," he said. "My mother and I were very close. Now she is dead. If God does exist, could he not have prevented this? He didn't prevent it. He has failed her, but she was too young to die, and now he has failed me as well. My mother was very religious. She always went to church. You couldn't find fault with her. Now she is gone. What did it help her to be so religious? What kind of a God is this, who lets this sort of thing happen? Who can believe in a God who does this?" He had spat it out. This was rough stuff! But I could sense his sorrow and his frustration.

Quite understandably, the question about the involvement and justification of God is raised. When we are faced with death, we not only wrestle with our own loss but with the involvement of the "Giver of life." In many instances, His time schedule does not correspond with ours. To come to the point of acceptance of his schedule is a matter that is reflected in the LORD's Prayer where it says "Your will be done." But that also is rough stuff.

Who am I that I could justify the actions of the Almighty? To get through to the staff captain I identified myself with him. I said, "My own father died at the age of fifty-six. In my judgment, that is too young to die, but I have discovered that God has his own agenda with each and every person. He has his own building and construction plans for this world and for the next one. Mysteriously, he has slotted all of us in, without asking us, if we are in agreement. How could I be in agreement with losing my father at fifty-six?

We have to look to the future. Your Mother has died, and that is the end of her life here on earth. In the Bible God speaks about the resurrection of *His* Son and of *your* Mother and of *my father*. It says, 'We believe, that Jesus died and rose again. And so we believe, that God will bring with Jesus, *those who have fallen asleep* in Him' (1Thes.4:14). It does not lessen the pain of the loss, which is incredible, but there *is* the resurrection. Hang on to it!" I then prayed with him and gave him the blessing.

The gangway was about to be removed. I was the last person to disembark. When I came home, Trudy wrote a deeply moving letter to this staff captain with an exceptional message of encouragement. I later presented it to him, together with a copy of the New Testament, in the very language in which it was originally written:

Greek. He was a busy man when I saw him again. He thanked me warmly and left me with just one remark: "If ever you have trouble getting on board, tell whoever blocks your path to contact me!" I thanked him and thought, *"What a fitting remark!"*

It reminded me of the message of our LORD, who tells us: "If you ever have difficulty solving your troubles, or someone is blocking your path, *contact me.*"

JESUS EST SEUL
NOTRE SAUVEUR

Al Handra is an officer fluent in Arabic and French. My Arabic is very limited and there is something else about that language. I have often wrestled with the peculiar "spiritual" aura around certain words. I would be reminded every now and then that I could use certain words easily in terms of the language per se, but as a Christian I should perhaps refrain from some of them and use other words.

"Inshallah" is an example. Some people felt that this well known frequently used Arabic expression meaning "God willing" could as easily be used by Christians as by Muslims. Others felt that I, as a Christian, should not say this. The same holds for the ordinary greeting and the traditional prayer of blessing used not merely to "bless the food" but used for every significant action in life. So, one has to tread cautiously.

With Al Handra, I spoke French. He had been hospitalized along with thirty-nine other seafarers from around the world. They were all in one hospital. They were properly taken care of. Insurance paid the bills. There was no one who came to visit them. They had no family here and their ship had sailed away, so their colleagues were gone.

As chaplain-Director of the Seafarers Centre, I had my task cut out. I had all sorts of reading material with me especially copies of the Bible in every language. So, I distributed liberally what I had.

TV was not hooked up in the wards. CDs and DVDs did not exist as yet. Aside from the literature, cassettes and tape recorders were the most modern and only way of sharing music or the spoken messages. But what was particularly valued by these seafarers is what is valued everywhere: The personal human contact with someone who is there for no other reason than to visit you. Though very appreciative of the excellent hospital care, they needed human contact and communication.

Some of them could hardly believe I came just for them. They would ask me if my father was in the hospital or if my visit to them was because I had to be in the hospital anyway. Once we talked, their isolation became more apparent with each minute: They didn't know where they were. What was the name of the hospital they were in? Their biggest concern was: Had their families been informed?

In many instances seafaring people do not wish their families to know that they are in the hospital. The word hospital in many countries and languages is a word that has a "death-bell" ring. So they would not wish to make contact with home at this time for their families would worry…"Why is my husband in the hospital? For how long? With what kind of illness?" Most of these questions they could not even answer themselves. Their being in the hospital might well create anxiety in their home, so they preferred to keep their stay in the hospital to themselves.

They did not understand why most of the people in this hospital did not speak English. In Al Handra's case that was no problem since he spoke French. Other seafarers did not speak French at all. They were wondering where their personal belongings were. Did their ship leave the port and if so, where did it go? Could they rejoin the ship? Their discussion with the physicians was in many instances frustrating.

Physicians ordinarily do not say too much. This makes sense.

My second Father was the chief medical physician of the Netherlands. He always made it clear that he was only the physician. He would not be in a position to give complete assurance of the precise development of any illness. Only the LORD would be able to do that. Certain procedures would be followed and the physicians would then wait to see if those procedures had the right effects. So my father would not say too much.

The language barrier, as well as the unfamiliarity with the medical terms and procedures certainly did not contribute to a feeling at ease after the physician's visit with the seafarers. In many instances they asked me if I could explain why they had to remain in the hospital. They were feeling fine by this time. Since I had worked in hospitals, I knew my way around and had easy access to the staff. They realized that I was the pastor for Seafarers. I could give spiritual care as well as some medical information to the patients.

Al Handra was hospitalized because of an appendectomy. His ship had left port. I told him that his stay would be brief, a few days at the most. We talked about the nature of his illness. We talked about his family. They had not been contacted, which caused one burden to fall off his shoulders. We talked about the fact that God, at times, brought us to a point that we had to sit on the sideline. God was not in the habit of explaining His actions. But we agreed that an appendectomy right here in port, enabling him to be hospitalized, was far better than an appendectomy eight hundred miles out in the Atlantic Ocean. I said that I would like to offer prayers for him.

In my hospital visits I have experienced that when I make a suggestion like that, the patient would sometimes attempt to get out of bed and stand next to me or we both would kneel at the bedside. Al Handra stayed in bed. He listened as I carefully phrased my French prayer. I gave him a few copies of the National Geographic Magazine, which he appreciated. I also had with me a copy of the New Testament in Arabic. "Arabic!" he exclaimed, "How wonderful! That's my real language." I told him that this was an exceptional book and I suggested that he should read only the gospel of John.

I did say that it would take him three weeks to read it if he would read one chapter per day. But I proposed that he do it in nine weeks. He asked me why. I told him: "If you read all twenty-one chapters once it will take you three weeks. Then you read it again for another three weeks. Finally you go through it for the third time. Altogether that will take nine weeks."

He asked, "Why should I read it three times?" I said: "If you would read it only once, you might at the end of the three weeks say, 'Well, that was that. So what?' If you would read it a second time, at the end of the six weeks, you might say, 'This is an interesting book. I think I begin to get the drift of it.' Now sit tight, because what I am going to say next is something very unusual: If you read it for the third time, the Holy Spirit might well touch your heart. Before you come to the end, you will suddenly realize who Jesus Christ is. Guaranteed! Nine weeks, Al Handra, only nine."

Two days later I visited the hospital again. Al Handra had just left for the airport. He was on his way home. As happens with so many of my seafaring friends, once they leave, you lose contact. They get transferred to another ship owned by a different company. Or they are employed by a company that sails only in the Far East. Or they have to await the ship on which they are scheduled to sail. Sometimes they decide not to return to sea.

A card, a letter, nowadays an e-mail, or upon occasion a phone call are the snippets of contact that remain. Distance is a devastating element since it is breaking bonds. That is why it is so significant that they have facilities like the Seafarers Centers and the opportunity there to be regularly in contact with their families.

I recall one seaman who sat outside one of a Seafarers Centers sunning himself while talking to his wife in New Zealand. "Imagine," he said to me as I passed by when he had come to the end of his conversation, "When I am at home, my wife and I talk most of the time for just a few minutes. When I am away from home, I sit down to phone and we talk for an hour and a half without interruption. I do that for only twenty dollars with this phone card. To talk for an hour and a half to my wife is unbelievable."

Forty-one weeks later, I received a letter from Paris. It was written in French:

> Cher Monsieur,
>
> It is with pleasure and with great joy that I am writing you this little letter to give you news about myself and to tell you how happy I am.
>
> Dear Sir, I do not know how to thank you for all that you have done for me; Oh Father, you have saved my soul. You have brought me onto the right path. You have opened my eyes to reality by recommending that I read the Bible to learn to recognize who Christ really is. Today I know that Jesus is indeed the Son of God.
>
> *Jesus est seul notre Sauveur!—Jesus alone is our Savior!*
>
> May the Almighty God help me to love him day after day!
>
> Respectfully yours,
> Al Handra

…"My Word…will accomplish what I desire and achieve the purpose for which I sent it" (Is. 55:11).

THE FIRST CATECHISM
CLASS OF
AN ESTONIAN MASTER

Although it was of course an astounding matter, the Christian community quickly got used to it: Thousands of Bibles and New Testaments were being distributed in countries formerly under communist control. Suddenly everyone got into the act; agencies and individuals, both bona fide and spurious ones, raced through hastily opened borders with the Word of God in hand. On board of ships, some people became "collectors of Bibles," which had been offered to them in different ports.

I used to worry about that. I suspected some seafarers were hording Bibles in order to sell them on the black market at a handsome profit. Imagine, Bibles, paid for by the hard earned dollars of loyal ministry supporters, sold for ten times their cost on the black market! But then I figured, "Who knows; they might get read in the process." And didn't Paul say, "If some preach Christ out of envy and some out of goodwill, what does it matter? The important thing is that Christ is preached" (Phil1:15–18). Good common sense!

But here is something else which is found not only in former communist countries. It is a far more general malaise. It is the fact that the Bible is often not used as a guide in a life with Christ as Lord and Savior. Instead, it is used only as a symbol, a relic, an icon, not as the Word of God, addressing people in their deepest need. Yet, this is where the teaching of the church can be of help. We have something called "The Catechism." It is a good Reformed, and for that matter, also Roman Catholic word. Webster defines it simply as "oral instruction."

Along with the extensive programs of Bible distribution, we should ascertain their interpretation through "catechetical" training. The Spirit's directive to Philip to catechize the Ethiopian Eunuch is a case in point (Acts 8:29).

I ran into a similar case myself: On my way to the master's quarters on an Estonian freighter, I noticed obvious preparations being made for a noon day luncheon party for ship's agents and shore officials. Apologizing for interrupting his busy schedule, I entered the master's cabin and indicated that I had only come to greet him and to shake his hand. Though he was in the process of signing documents for the ship's chandler, who was seated across from him at his desk, the captain urged me to take a seat in the lounge area of his cabin. Somewhat reluctantly I sat down.

I had spent the entire morning with different officers and crew members on this vessel already and, to be quite candid, I had spotted another ship about a mile up river from this Estonian bulk carrier. It was a Dutch ship. The noon-hour on a Dutch ship can be a unique time for a challenging presentation of the gospel, since the officers always observe an almost "sacred" tradition of getting together for a drink before lunch.

Often I had been able to speak openly and extensively about the claims of Christ in precisely that sort of setting. So I really wanted to get to that ship. As I rose to follow my desire to leave and head for the Dutch ship, the master waved from his desk and almost ordered me to remain seated, so I sat down again, being aware that I should listen more carefully to the "hints" of the Holy Spirit in my ministry.

When the ship's chandler had finished his business, the master came away from behind his desk, sat down across from me and without so much as an introduction began to trace his spiritual history. It was fraught with perplexity, pain, and frustration. Deep down in the very bones of many people, who lived under communism, there had always been awareness that there is more between heaven and earth than meets the eye.

Some twenty years ago, the master wanted his son to be baptized, not out of biblical, covenantal conviction, but purely out of superstition. The child was sickly, listless and growing very poorly. Who knows but that baptism might turn this around, so he decided to have his child baptized.

The decision was against his own father's advice. He feared that his son would imperil his position and promotion as a young naval officer. As a member of the communist party and as a junior officer at that time, he was well aware that he had to proceed with extreme caution and in strict secrecy. His father's advice was not without foundation.

So he took the child with his mother and his mother-in-law on a two day journey into a mountainous region where he knew of a monastery. In an adjacent village he settled down for the night in the only hotel. As he went for a morning stroll the following day, he ran into—of all people—his very own neighbor, who happened to be vacationing in the area.

He decided to stay behind and to let his wife and her mother go to the monastery with the child for fear that his own presence might be reported by his neighbor. That would have disastrous consequences. The child was baptized. Curiously it picked up dramatically. He grew strong and healthy and developed into a very capable young man. Then the master with joy and excitement told me: "Today my healthy son attends church—on his own."

But the captain still felt the pain of the dilemma he faced more than twenty years ago: He could not go to the monastery himself. In an attempt to find some consolation and also to understand his son's spiritual development, he started to read the Bible, a very old Bible, "in fact so old," he said, "it was used in the days of King James I."

He had found it in some Seafarers Center just a few weeks ago. "Do you wish to see it?" He went into his bedroom and returned with it. As I examined it, he continued: "I do not understand it too well, but then, I have just started and am still reading in the 'history of the world' section." He had reached Genesis 21. Can you blame him? Doesn't everyone read a book, any book, from beginning to end? True, everyone does, but with the Word of God there is a difference. That made him curious.

Since he spoke Russian fluently we now examined together the Index of a Russian Bible, which I had brought along. With great care, armed with pen and marker, we noted the individuality of the books of the Old Testament and their prophetic account. Then we looked into the New Testament, witnessing to the Christ, his birth, suffering, death, and resurrection. So we briefly covered the history and plan of salvation revealed in the Scriptures.

He was absolutely fascinated. He kept asking questions which made us dig deeper. Somehow it flashed through my mind that the very thought of a noon-hour discussion on board of the Dutch vessel had been swallowed up by the immediate circumstances in the quarters of this Estonian master, which took precedence.

Here I was ushering someone into the mystery of God's love in Christ Jesus via a Russian Bible. If you didn't grow up with this, it is of course a miraculous story. Even if you did grow up with it, it never ceases to amaze you. But through the fervent activity of the Holy Spirit, it enters into the hearts of some people, many people, all kinds of people everywhere. That's another *miracle*...

I noticed that another engagement had become affected by our discussion. Three times someone knocked and entered the master's quarters, first the chief steward, then the chief engineer, and finally someone from the shipping agency. They all had the same message: The luncheon party was in progress, the visitors had all arrived. Could the master please come down and assume his role as host?

Ever so politely, yet firmly, the master responded three times in a row that he would be slightly delayed since he had "some very important business" to attend to before he could come down. I thought it inspiring that his first "Catechism class" took precedence over the luncheon party.

The current captain, whom he had served faithfully for three and a half months, told him that he was just following the policy of the company. "They should have told you so," he said. That caused Gabriel to run in despair to my colleague. He heard his story and drove him back to the ship, hoping to be able to speak to the captain, but the ship's engines had been started and they were scheduled to sail almost immediately. Time was not in their favor.

That's why I got the telephone call, advising me that three days later the ship would be thirty miles from our Seafarers Centre in Montreal. I asked for more details. I got the name of the ship and the name of the captain. I also learned that it concerned a total of fifty-five hundred US dollars, which constituted the total wages plus over-time Gabriel was due to receive. He was told that he would receive fifteen hundred dollars upon leaving. The remaining four thousand would be sent to his home from the office, according to the captain. In the course of time, he had collected already some twenty-five hundred dollars, which he had diligently sent home, keeping only a few dollars for his immediate needs while on board. Eight thousand dollars US were his total wages for two years of labor.

For Gabriel, it was an acceptable sum. He had never asked for more, but he could not understand that he would now leave the ship with only fifteen hundred dollars. My diligent colleague had also managed to obtain a copy of Gabriel's contract, deciphered it, and searched out the Maritime laws applicable to the situation. He informed me that Gabriel should be receiving his total wages, and whatever increments were applicable, upon disembarking the ship. So the captain, with all due respect, was obscuring the truth to the tune of four thousand dollars. Was it with "malice and forethought," as my lawyer friend would say?

At the time, the ship was scheduled to arrive early in the morning. I was there duly armed with all the information supplied. I sought out Gabriel who had been informed by my colleague that I would come on board. I asked him for his contract, to ascertain the facts and then reviewed with him the situation. He told me that he had approached the captain twice, while the ship was sailing down the St. Lawrence River, requesting him to change his mind and to pay him the full fifty-five hundred dollars. Twice he had received a negative reply.

He was now in the process of packing his belongings because he was informed that he would be picked up by the agent at four o'clock to go to the airport in Montreal to fly to Sri Lanka. He was extremely nervous and agitated. Someone from the crew told me he wasn't the same Gabriel. His anxiety was compounded because the captain had said that the agent might come earlier and he would have to be ready to leave immediately upon his arrival.

I felt sick at heart about the situation. This Sri Lankan steward, who had such an outstanding reputation, would finish his career on this ship in such a dreadful manner. I gave him two aspirins to help calm him down. I suggested that we pray to God for strength, hope, and help. I finally told him, that no matter what would happen, he should not get off the ship, neither with nor without the agent, until I had talked to him again. I also suggested that he continue his duties, which he did.

I mounted the three flights of stairs to the captain's cabin, who figured I was coming to pay a courtesy call. His faithful steward stood right behind me with two cups of coffee explaining that since the master obviously had a visitor, it would be appropriate to serve the captain's guest coffee as well. The time was eight thirty in the morning.

The captain, who had just returned from his breakfast, sat down, motioned me to the couch and lit a cigarette, kindly offering me one as well. I declined. We exchanged courtesies and then it was time to deal with the situation. I sort of liked him.

I complimented the attentiveness of his steward, prompting the captain to confirm that Gabriel was indeed a model steward, whose services had been enjoyed by the previous captains as well. He alluded to the qualities of Gabriel and seemed very positive. So Gabriel had no faults, nor any record of misconduct, causing a reduction in payment. He then bewailed the fact that the company had decided to eliminate the position of a captain's steward, which he felt was a real discomfort.

He even went so far as to say that his steward would leave today from Montreal and was scheduled to be picked up by the agent in the course of the day. I carefully asked if he would pay him off as he was leaving. The captain informed me, that according to the policy of the company, the bulk of his earnings would be shipped to his home by the office.

In my heart, I heard the Spirit of the LORD say, "It seems he is not telling the truth." I asked the captain if he had informed Gabriel of this to which he replied that he had. I asked if Gabriel was happy with that, to which he responded, "Not really, but that's the way it is. Policies are policies and I have instructions from the company to pay him only a limited amount upon leaving." I said, "Less than one third?" I noticed a slight surprise in his eyes. The companies at times are in collusion with captains, or an individual captain, through a type of terrorization of the very people on whom they are dependent, in order to fatten their own pockets.

My kind coffee-drinking captain began to sense that there was a different wind beginning to blow. I opened up the can of worms by saying, "I understand you intend to give him fifteen hundred dollars and to have the office ship four thousand dollars to his home in Sri Lanka. Isn't that correct? He lives in a village, in the sticks, so to speak. You and your predecessors had an excellent man making your bed, serving your meals, cleaning your cabin, running your errands, jumping at your every whim, and doing one thousand things in your service. After two years of faithful labor, you ship him off with a mere fifteen hundred dollars, while he is entitled to fifty-five hundred dollars? Now he is sent away with a promise that the company will send four thousand dollars to his home? You know very well, Sir, that the company will not do that.

"Maritime law, as I understand it, and in fact the very contract the man has in his hands, but cannot read, because of the language in which it is written, states I believe: 'Anyone who has been without demerit points and has faithfully fulfilled his job shall be paid off upon dismissal in toto.' In your steward's case, that amounts to fifty-five hundred dollars. Isn't that correct?

"You know this, because you know the law, and you are able to read the contract, and you are thoroughly acquainted with the fact that when a man, any man, leaves the ship, contractually and justly, he leaves with his full pay. I have been on board of many ships and I think I know what happens at times and what ought to happen. So, may I propose that you exercise justice towards your steward and that you go about it in a righteous way? That would be pleasing to God.

"Your steward is on the verge of a nervous breakdown, because you told him that he would go home with less than one third of his pay. But I suspect you have the money, Sir, in your safe right here in this cabin. May I suggest you pay him out completely?"

It pained my soul to have to preach this "sermon," but there was no other way. The captain made another effort to bail out of this predicament by suggesting that the agent would confirm his version. I knew very well that the agent would be capable of doing that. I responded that, irrespective of what the agent would say, the steward might not leave the ship without his full pay. Then I thought to myself, *neither will I leave this ship.*

I settled back in my seat as the steward came again to bring us another coffee. It was now coffee time, ten o'clock in the morning, and I regretted that I could not go down and meet the other members of the crew, but I felt I could not abandon my station.

The captain went about his business. He signed papers for the ship's chandler who had come in. He talked to the chief engineer who came up to participate in the coffee time. I joined the conversation about a great variety of subjects. The chief engineer, unaware of what had transpired, questioned me as to the denomination I belonged to, if I could get married as a clergyman, where I lived, and how long I had been a chaplain to Seafarers. After the amicable coffee-hour the chief engineer got up, as did I to shake his hand. Then I sat down again.

The captain continued to fumble about with his papers and his telephone while I studied the pictures in his cabin and considered what would happen and how this whole thing would end up. Would I be ushered out of his cabin by four strong officers or crew members? Would he issue orders for me to vacate his cabin? How would I react? Since he seemed to remain rather calm and friendly I did not get excited, nor was I worried. I figured the LORD would bring about the solution. So I just prayed that I might remain calm, cool, and collected.

After nearly two hours, the captain rose and said that it was time for lunch. He asked me if I would care to come down with him for lunch. I was absolutely flabbergasted, but then I figured, *He is inviting me, so why not?* We went down with the chief officer. The chief engineer remarked as he approached the table, "You are still here?" Gabriel served us. He was tense. I could not exchange a word with him. That would have been inappropriate, but I thanked him politely for his services, as did the others.

After the meal, we returned to the captain's cabin and once again I sat down, figuring that by now the agent would soon show up. He didn't, so I quietly picked up a nautical magazine and spent the time reading uninterrupted by the captain. After another hour had passed, I began to wonder if I would sail along with the ship.

A knock on the open door changed the scenery. The agent came in with a bag of mail and all sorts of weighty papers. We greeted each other. I happened to know him. His only statement to me, as he looked at his watch was, "Well, Padre, you are here? This ship is about to sail, or are you planning to sail along?" I declined to inform him that it happened to be the very thought in my own mind.

I watched the captain and the agent interacting, exchanging papers, and discussing the time of departure as well as a host of other technicalities and finally the destination of the ship which was somewhere in the Middle East.

I had watched the captain in the process of trying to take advantage of one of his crew members. I remembered the crew member, with knots in his stomach, riddled by worry. But, suddenly I saw the Spirit of God take over: The captain rose to his feet, moved from behind his desk and approached me on the couch. The agent was still seated in his chair. The captain stood there for just a few seconds. I suspected he would now explode to scare me away. Instead he extended his hand, causing me to rise, and made an absolutely incredible statement in the very presence of his own agent, saying, "Reverend, I want to be a Christian. Would you be kind enough to ask my steward to come up here to collect his pay?" He then marched to his safe in the wall. I could not believe my own ears.

The captain had said, "I want to *be* a Christian." He did not say I want to *become* a Christian, so he obviously, as a Christian, understood quite well, that he had to fall in line with Christ's teaching about justice.

I went down and summoned Gabriel. I assured him, before he went upstairs, that the LORD had paved the way and that the captain would pay him his entire wages. The captain did pay Gabriel fifty-five hundred dollars. He counted them out in the presence of the three of us, in one hundred dollar bills. I had never seen so much cash piled up.

At my request, we received an hour to go to the bank to certify the one hundred dollar bills and to transfer the money to a bank in Sri Lanka. I then returned with Gabriel and said to the captain, "Thank you for having acted like a Christian. I have been encouraged by the way in which you have acted. May God bless you as you sail!"

MANY ARE CALLED

I saw a large cargo ship in port with a flag from Liberia. Many cargo ships are sailing under the Liberian flag which seems to be due to the favorable tax terms the country offers. A flag does not give any indication about the nationalities of the crew on board.

Almost always, I receive a most cordial and courteous welcome on board of cargo ships as well as on cruise ships. The Seafarers Ministry has the reputation of a "Bona Fide" organization. Representatives are heartily welcomed. They are in many ways a source of information about the location of the Seafarers Centers and its facilities as well as about the city and what it has to offer.

Once in a big while, I board a ship where I am frozen out. There may be serious problems with the cargo or the crew may be under great stress. As a "ship-visitor," you are unable to gage the mood before you board. You step out "in faith." When you board a ship, you are completely dependent on God.

When I came on board, I discovered the crew was like the United Nations: A German captain, Croatian and English officers, a Dutch radio officer, and crew members from Pakistan, Bangladesh, Morocco and Algeria. The cook came from Brazil and the stewards from India. One steward came from Algeria. He was serving in the officers' dining room and lounge. His name was Abdul. During the morning coffee break, the officers met in the officers' lounge. The crew met in the crew mess room. What a challenge to meet such a variety of people on board of the same ship!

I had visions of testifying to this mixed assembly. Fortunately, I had some material in my brief case in Croatian, English, and even in Dutch. I started in the officers' lounge since the captain was there. Out came a few New Testaments in English and one in Dutch, which I carefully put on the table between a few copies of the National Geographic Magazine. There is almost always an interest in a copy in the Word of God for different reasons.

A Bangladesh engineer on one of the ships picked up a copy, which had been placed on the table in the lounge of his ship by some ship visitors. When I met him he said to me, "I saw it there and I thought, let me take it to my cabin and find out what the message of that book is. We have our sacred books, but it might broaden my mind if I could find out in which way the Holy Book of the Christians differs from ours."

I always "set the table" decoratively and tastefully when I come on board with reading material. I attempt to put the Word of God in a prominent place. I learned this lesson through an interesting, but indirect "hint" from an Indian on another ship. I had been invited into his cabin and we were involved in a very serious talk about the faith. He was genuinely interested and we explored some passages of the Bible in detail.

During our conversation a member of a sect passed through the hallway of the ship. He had copies of a magazine with him for distribution. Finding the door to the cabin of this Indian gentleman closed, he shoved a copy of the magazine underneath the door into the cabin. We both saw it being shoved in. I said nothing, but the Indian engineer made a remark that has stayed with me. He said, "A man does not think much of his religion when he shoves it under a door!" It reminded me again that form and manners do matter particularly when you present the Word of God.

As I "set the table" with what I had in my briefcase, I noticed that the English officers picked up some National Geographic Magazines. The Bibles remained untouched. The radio officer picked up the Dutch New Testament, looked at it and then threw it back down. A subtle defiant smile was visible on the faces of some officers. The others just sat there enjoying their coffee.

Rarely have I visited a ship where the atmosphere was so reserved, almost unfriendly, but this one seemed to top the list. No one paid any attention to my presence. No one offered me a cup of coffee except the Algerian steward. "Would you like some coffee?" he asked me. None of the "formal" hosts in the lounge made this offer, so it was a bit embarrassing to accept the offer from the steward.

I would have liked to get out of this "climate of rejection" in the officers' lounge and escape to the mess room of the crew. Protocol demanded that I stay. The Spirit of God was of the same opinion, but he didn't let me know it just yet. So, I responded: "Yes, I would like to have a cup of coffee"

The Croatians talked in their own language. The English ignored me. The Dutch radio officer obviously felt that I was the kind of person you should be very careful with. His only question was, "Are you a priest?" When I said, "I am a Protestant pastor," he remarked, "I don't care for any priests or pastors." I simply answered, "Thank you."

Courtesy is at all times a vital key. The British are good at that. When I visited a British cargo vessel there was no one in any of the public areas, but next to the officers' lounge was a notice board with a few numbers on it. So I wrote on it: "God bless you all."

When I returned the following day I expected that this blessing would have been erased. It hadn't been. Underneath, in clear letters, was written, "Thank you!"

So there I sat. Outside the window I could see the cold storage elevator. Some of the freezing cold air of that place had apparently blown into this ship.

These are the moments that your "old nature" starts to whisper in your ear, "Would it not be nice to be the pastor in a lovely, well-built church with a carpeted office, white telephones, and a perfumed secretary?" Sometimes the "old nature" is more blatant and says: "Don't you think God is letting you waste your time on ships where they really are not interested in what you have to say? Face it man. They are not interested." I have learned, however, to listen to the Spirit of the LORD while I minister on board. The Spirit of God moves mysteriously and in his own way. It is always fascinating to discover how he operates.

The coffee hour was finished and I felt I should "clean up" the table. Why leave Bibles and New Testaments on board of a ship where there seemed to be no interest? I put some reading materials back into my briefcase, but then I changed my mind, turned my briefcase upside down again and "reset" the table. That Bangladesh engineer on that other ship picked up a Bible from a pile of them lying on an unattended table.

Everyone left the lounge since their break had come to an end. I noticed that on this table there were two small bottles. The one contained salad dressing. On the back of it I read "Made in the USA." The other bottle had some bright, dark green pickles in it. They were of a slightly unusual shape. When I picked it up out of pure curiosity I read, "Made in the Islamic Republic of Pakistan." It struck me that *that* country puts its religion even on pickle bottles. I felt that the table was now fittingly set: A half empty bottle of Islamic country pickles stood next to the Word of God, which shall not return empty.

Abdul came in again to clear the tables of cups. He asked if I needed more space to display my literature. When I declined his kind offer, he asked, "Are you in a hurry to get off the ship?" I answered, "No, I have lots of time." He then asked, "Are you willing to see me in my cabin?" I replied, "I am willing." He continued to clear the tables and when he was finished, he passed me by and with an almost imperceptible head movement he motioned for me to follow him.

On board of ships there are at times people who wish to talk to you, but they may not want others on board to know about it. That is normal. The chaplain is seen as the person with whom strictly religious matters can and perhaps even should be discussed. I followed him through the narrow hallway to his cabin. He ushered me in and interestingly locked the door. He pulled out the only chair for me, while he sat on the bed. He didn't waste any time with a lengthy introduction, but laid the burden of his heart in clear language before me.

He was a Muslim, but he was disappointed with the Islamic faith. So he had become curious about the Christian faith. What was it all about? Where did it come from? Who was the final Authority in it? What does it have to say to him? If he would get inspired by it, what is the procedure to become a Christian? What are the obligations?

Well aware that he might have to return to his duties shortly, I made an immediate arrangement to meet him later in the day during his "off hour" in the afternoon. He was very happy about that. For the next ten minutes I gave a most concise description of the Christian religion.

Later that day Abdul and I talked. It was amazing to discover his keen observations and his concern to get to the very heart of the matter: The Unity in the Trinity, as reflected in the Hebrew word "echod" he understood since he spoke Arabic, the miraculous birth of Christ, the call of the Messiah to acknowledge him, he drank it all in like a parched land receiving a thorough shower.

I supplied him with a copy of the New Testament in his language and gave specific instructions about what to read first. I do not force the issue on anyone. It is profoundly significant that the person comes to this awareness on the basis of the testimony of the Scriptures and the promptings of his own heart.

I have always been a bit concerned about people who in their inter-action with foreign seafarers, especially Asiatic ones, seek a speedy "commitment" from them to Christ the LORD. Eastern people are reluctant to display a negative reaction. Out of pure courtesy they might say that they are willing to accept Christ as LORD and Savior because you have asked them to do so, but it is not the testimony of their heart. It is only the testimony of their mouth, but genuine commitment to Christ is a matter of the heart.

The ship stayed in port longer than a few days. Every day I dropped by and discovered that Abdul was making significant prog-ress in his study of the Word of God. On the last day of the ship's stay, Abdul came to me with the declaration, that Jesus Christ is the risen Savior. He had also discovered and read the story of Acts chap-ter 8 about the baptism of the Ethiopian eunuch. It prompted him to say that he would like to be an "Ethiopian," because he wanted to be baptized. He saw baptism as an inextricable link-up with the Savior.

I praised God for this commitment and we arranged for the cer-emony at a suitable time later that day. He asked me to pick him up. He was very much concerned that he be baptized in the chapel of the Seafarers Centre. He did not want me to invite any of his "friends" on board to join us for the ceremony. He wished to have a distinctly "private" baptism.

When I arrived by car, he came down the gangway in a three piece suit with tie and white shirt. Only one man, who worked on deck, saw him come down. Looking at his apparel, and at me pick-ing him up, he jokingly bellowed, as he came down the gangway, "Is the Priest taking you along, because you are going to get married?" Little did that person know that in some sense, he hit the nail on the head. In fact, the relationship between God and his people is often compared by God to a marriage.

At the Seafarers Centre, Abdul asked if he would be allowed to be in the chapel for a few minutes totally alone with God. He then came to my office adjacent to the chapel and said, "I am ready!" In a moving ceremony in the presence of God, with only the two of us present in the chapel, Abdul knelt down in front of the altar and was baptized in the name of the Father, the Son, and the Holy Spirit.

With the directives and guidelines of the Word of God, we briefly reflected on the marvelous incorporation of him into the Christian fold. We then observed a few moments of silence and I concluded with the blessing of God. When we came out of the chapel, Abdul walked directly to the gift shop. It was locked and when I had unlocked it, he went in and picked up the one chain with a cross attached to it that was still on display.

He offered to pay for it. I said, "Consider it a gift for the occasion." Abdul insisted that he should pay and he did. He then turned around and loosened his tie, unbuttoned the top of his shirt, kissed the cross on the chain, hung it around his neck, and said with a smile: "I am a living servant of Christ. I will serve him all my life, but on board of the ship I do not want to become a dead servant of Him. If they see my cross, they will kill me." Then he looked me straight in the eye and made this disturbing statement: "I am now no longer a member of my own family. A Christian will not be accepted by them."

Matthew 10:37 suddenly flashed through my mind, "Anyone who loves his Father or Mother more than me is not worthy of me." This is a stunning statement, which I had often read, but when I became a pastor in the Ministry to Seafarers and came into contact with Buddhists, Hindus, and Muslims, Matthew 10:37 suddenly took on a far more serious dimension.

Abdul returned to his ship in the fullest sense of the word as a different man. He said, "I feel I am on top of the world!" About six months later, I received a letter from him. He was scheduled to be transferred to another ship of the same company, so he spent some time in Istanbul in the Ararat Hotel. As I read the letter, it struck me that he ended up in a hotel named after a high mountain. Abdul had been "on top of the world," and his letter reflected he was still there.

"My dear Uittenbosch,

I am well here and hope you will be well there. I extremely sorry that such a very long time later I am writing you this short letter just to know that you are all right. I can not forget you till I am alive. Because you, just you, *identificationed* me Jesus Christ.

Still I remember your words which you wrote me in your first letter: 'Do not despair, I am sure that all things will work together for good. Stay in line with word of God.' So I am following your these words,

Your friend,
Abdul"

His English made the message more meaningful. There is theological strength and beauty in his description of what really happened: *He became identified with Jesus Christ.*

COMMUNICATING
IN CHINESE?

On the Chinese calendar, the year 2006 was the "year of the dog." For reasons not clear to me, every year in China is named after a particular animal. When I met the charming chief dancer of the cast on one of the cruise ships, the "year of the dog" had just started. So I congratulated her and in fact, immediately wrote her a New Year's card, expressing my best wishes for the entire "year of the dog." Then I added, "If you spell the last word backwards and capitalize it, it will be altogether an exciting year for you!"

She was so delighted with that suggestion, that she took my card to the telephone and read it right there in my presence, to her mother in Shanghai in Chinese.

I have always had a great fondness for Chinese people. When we were married, we had two Chinese bridesmaids. They had been adopted by a Chinese friend of Trudy. As babies in China, they had been left at the door of this wealthy Chinese friend, who took them in with the many other baby girls left at her door. Eventually the Chinese allowed her to keep only two of those little girls, while they took all the others away.

When this friend came to America with the two little girls, accompanied by a missionary through whom she had become a Christian, they were prevented from returning to China due to the war. The girls grew up in the USA and eventually were our lovely bridesmaids. So, full of enthusiasm, I went to visit a Chinese Communist ship, but it all turned out quite differently from what I had expected.

It was one of the ships from mainland China that came into port in the days of the full reign of communism. The ship was scheduled to take on a load of grain, so it was located near the grain elevator.

I am able to greet people in Chinese. Armed with a box full of New Testaments in Chinese, fittingly covered with a red cover, as well as with information about the city and with all kinds of maps, I boarded the vessel.

There was no guard at the gangway. That surprised me. I saw no one on the outside deck and when I came in, I saw no one inside either. Not knowing if they would have a "Political Commissar" on board, I decided not to visit the captain first, but to simply put some material down in the large empty crew mess room. On my way there I passed the officer's dining room and through a small window I noticed that the entire crew was being lectured. They all sat very sedately while someone "preached" to them in a rather firm voice. That explained why I hadn't seen anyone on deck or in the hallways.

Going to the mess room of the crew had a double benefit. By the time anyone would show up, I would have displayed the contents of my box. Secondly, I did not have to carry that heavy box with me to the top floor, where the captain would have his quarters.

I "set" the table, as is my custom, and encircled two stacks of New Testaments in Chinese with piles of booklets, maps, and information about the city. The New Testaments, fittingly with red covers, I put upside down. It contained admittedly a different message from Mao's red book, but, I figured the color red should help. I was proud of the way the table looked.

After a few minutes, some Chinese crew members walked in and looked at me as if I was a curiosity. Although I repeated my Chinese greeting and words of welcome a couple of times, they just stared at me without a response. I suspected this was due to my Chinese accent. Maybe they didn't understand what I was saying. I was of course a curiosity. My six feet two inches, my blue clerical garb, interestingly of the same color as their uniforms, and my materials were all intriguing to them. As more came in, some of them took a map and opened it up. It was interesting to see how almost the entire person disappeared behind these huge city and country maps. Copying each other, they all aimed for the maps.

Unable to do anything beyond what I had done, I just stood there, looking at this fascinating display of about a dozen Chinese seafarers all hidden behind maps. I prayed that they would fold them up again and turn to the one pile that had real value: *The Word of God.* That at least was a map that would get them to the right place, the safe haven, the real port.

Suddenly the Political Commissar came rushing in. Interestingly he did not touch a single brochure or map. He dove, as it were, directly into the pile of New Testaments in the center. He picked up the top copy, turned it around, looked at it for two seconds, then went around the entire circle, pulling the maps out of everyone's hands and dumping them on the floor. There they all stood, duly terrorized by the regime.

They now became witnesses to the continuation of the Political Commissar's power display. He walked around the table twice for some reason. Through my own mind flashed the thought that he was doing exactly what a lot of Western people are doing. They are walking around the Word of God instead of walking with the Word of God.

He then raced up to me, stopped in front of me, raised the New Testament which he still had in his hand, and holding it right before my face shouted at the top of his voice, "This no good. We not believe in God!" He grabbed the two piles of Bibles and threw them into my box, with enormous force, together with whatever else was on the table. He shouted some furious words in Chinese, shoved the box into my stomach and yelled at me, "Out!"

Thirty-five Chinese officers and crew members suddenly came rushing in and surrounded me. They all escorted me to the gangway.

Remaining calm, I kept greeting everyone in Chinese, until I had reached the gangway. Somehow it was a bit of an exhilarating feeling to have been escorted, albeit off the ship, by such a large group of people.

There I stood ashore on solid ground. Suddenly two guards materialized at the gangway. The rest of them returned to their duties. I looked around. The elevator, directly next to the ship, had a passage way through which the trains would pass. Anyone who wanted to go into the city had to pass through this passageway as well. I noticed there was a three feet high ridge on one side. It looked almost like a table.

I thought, "For years I have been at this elevator, I have walked through this passageway hundreds of times, yet I have never seen this *table*." So I again "set the table" figuring that anyone going into town would have a chance to take whatever he wished to take. It would give him the chance to determine if the Political Commissar was correct, when he shouted, "This no good!" If he would carefully scrutinize the book, he might shout, "This very good. This book the best!"

I returned later to check the table. All of the Bibles and materials were gone. I checked all the garbage containers near the ship as well. There was nothing in them that I recognized. Strict pollution laws would prevent dumping the lot into the water. Only the LORD knows what happened to those Bibles. Never mind the maps.

RINGING THE BELL
OF THE GOSPEL

The ship was scheduled to stay over Sunday. It turned out to be the only ship in port. Whenever there is a possibility to sail before the Sunday, ships will sail. The cost of staying in port without loading or unloading, which must be done by longshoremen, is very high.

I proposed to the master that I come on board and conduct a brief worship service for the officers and members of the crew. He agreed and the time was set. The lounge was filled with people and I preached about the insistence of God to get his reluctant representative, the Rev. Jonah to "turn to" and "to be on deck." Instead of handing him his resignation, because of his failure to follow God's command to ring his bell over the heads of the people in Nineveh, God pursued him on the ship and even into the water to get the job done. It's fascinating stuff. You can read it in the four short chapters of the book of Jonah.

The audience judged the message to be encouraging, because it obviously included the preacher. But there were other naval elements. Three things surfaced: First, God is in charge of the wind force and the sea swell. Secondly, there are times that the "storms" raging outside, or even in our lives, are caused by us, because we are not in line with him. Thirdly, the master of the ship calls the preacher to get up and pray. The "World" is calling the "Christian" to pray for them! How about that?

Looking at the captain, I noticed that he seemed moved. In fact, I was surprised when I detected that he was wiping his eyes. At the end of the worship service he stood up and gave instructions to the engineering department to take down the ship's bell from the front watch station of the ship. He told the carpenters to make a proper frame for the bell to hang in. We then sat down for coffee and refreshments.

I thought it was a rather odd reaction of the master. I realized that by and large the bell, located at the very front of the ship, is no longer in proper function. In former days, a sailor as look-out would be stationed at the front of the ship next to the bell, during heavy fog. He would ring the bell when another ship was approaching, thereby warning the people on the bridge to take action in order to avoid a collision. With the introduction of radar and the far more sophisticated equipment on ships, the bell is primarily decorative and is not used anymore. Most ships leave them hang.

The master asked us to return the following day for lunch. At the conclusion of the luncheon, he expressed his profound appreciation for the worship service I had conducted the previous day. He then ushered us off the ship to the gangway. There, to our amazement, stood the entire engineering department supported by a number of people from the deck department as well as the carpenters. In front of them stood the genuine copper bell with the name of the ship inscribed in it graciously mounted in a teakwood frame.

The master said: "In acknowledgement of what you preached about yesterday on this ship, we, the entire crew, would like to give you this bell, as a reminder for you to keep ringing the bell of the Gospel of God over the heads of the seafarers as long as he enables you…" I studied for the ministry, because I was "called." I was ordained. I was formally installed as a chaplain to Seafarers, but on that day, I felt anew the depth of my *calling* to the very people to whom I have now been ministering for almost half a century, *those who sail the seas.*

When one starts a totally new ministry, one is apt to make some mistakes due to ignorance, as happened to me on an English ship. The radio officer introduced himself to me by saying, "I am Sparks." Here was a name easy to pronounce. I wished I had a name like that.

The next day I boarded another ship, and in the course of the morning someone greeting me said, "I am Sparks." I exclaimed, "Well, that is a coincidence! Yesterday on board of that other ship I met your brother." He looked at me in surprise and said, "Sir, I have no brother."

"But, yesterday on that other English ship I met a chap by the name of Sparks." He laughed and said, "Sir, that is the nickname for the radio officer on board of ships."

We learn as we go along.

When I walked onto a Pakistani freighter, I hardly had a chance to enter the recreation room where crew members relaxed for a brief respite from their duties. One of them came up to me with a broad smile, and an out stretched hand, saying, "I am Jalal Massih." I responded, "I am Reverend Uittenbosch." "Yes, I know," he said. I was surprised; "Do you know me?" He pointed to my clerical collar, "That shows you are a Reverend."

Just then another smiling person came up to me and introduced himself; "I am Ramin Massih." I looked from one to the other and thought, "Yes, they do look somewhat alike, they might be brothers," but I was not convinced. Just then a third deckhand came in, also smiling, and on seeing me talking to those two men, he immediately stuck out his hand to shake mine. I beat him to the introduction by saying, "I am Reverend Uittenbosch." He responded, "Yes, we are so happy to have you come on board. I am Wasir Massih."

That floored me. He didn't look at all like the other two. Three brothers on the same ship? It could happen … I decided to find out. "Are the three of you brothers?"

"No, Sir, why would you think that?"

"You all have the same name." That made them all smile broadly again. Ramin asked, "Don't you understand?"

I confessed that I didn't understand. "Then we'll explain, because as a reverend, you should know. On board of this Muslim ship, we are the only three Christians. As a Christian in Pakistan, you take the title of the Messiah and use it as your last name. Messiah is Massih in the Urduh language."

When I returned the following morning, I asked the chief steward, "Where can I find Ramin?" He responded by saying, "You mean the Massih?" When I confirmed this, he directed me to the area where I could find him.

I have often used this story to explain to people that it is meaningful to identify yourself as belonging to the Messiah, the Christ. In a Muslim country this identification is significant.

Muslims on board frequently ask me if all of us in the Western Hemisphere are Christians. They like to see that expressed by proper dress, language, and conduct in harmony with belonging to Christ. The Christian community expects this unconditionally

Didn't Abdul say: "As a Christian you are 'identificationed' with him?"

PHOTO GALLERY

With our children, from left: Selwyn, Marcel, Desiree, who gave much of their time and talents to Seafarers

Providing Polish Seafarers with a touch of home

Entertaining Russian Seafarers in our home

Our Seafarers Centre

Above: Entertaining Seafarers in our Centre.

Right: A baptism in our beautiful Chapel

A baptism near his ship

A Japanese wedding on board

Meet our Seafarers at the gangway!

A coffee break with the engineers

Fellowship with the cooks

Contact in the bar

With members of the cast

A personal chat

With the Chief Officer on the Bridge

Desiree translating Spanish for us

The Christian fellowship

With the Maitre d'

Sharing a joke with the Engineers

Conversation
with officers

Mr. Sung re-surfaced

With crewmembers in the mess room

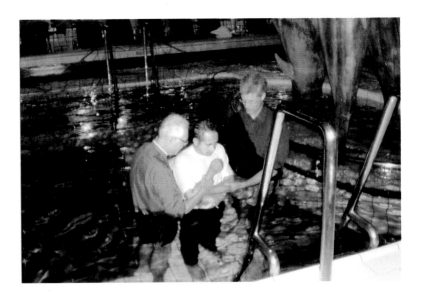

Baptism in the pool

A Formal Night
on Board

BETWEEN SHIP AND SHORE

Pakistani ships have always left a special impression. One of them was about to bring a load of grain to hungry people in Ethiopia and I had been asked to come out to "bless" the grain and the Pakistani crew who was in charge of transporting the grain.

A ship from Egypt left an altogether unusual impression. It was summer time and once again I was training some students from different Seminaries for a training period of about three months. I have trained many of them.

The student, whom I was training that summer, from a Seminary not of my denomination, was a very nice chap, but the Ministry of Seafarers turned out not to be his cup of tea. He had a real struggle with going on board and with talking freely to people who he felt were foreigners. He hit the nail on the head. They were foreigners. I admit that it is not always easy.

Many people wrestle with this. You walk into a dining room and you have to be able to deal with fifteen or eighteen pairs of eyes of foreigners staring at you as you enter. You have to develop a manner whereby you put everyone immediately at ease. You are to introduce yourself quickly, and in a subtle manner, bring to their attention your message in a short time, since the seafarers are usually pressed for time.

My friend struggled with this even though I had shown him repeatedly how to go about this and had pointed out the variations in this operation. Somehow I could not get him "started." He kept depending on me to take the lead.

I had learned there was an Egyptian vessel about sixty miles down the river. A Belgian vessel was also in that port. I proposed that we go together and he take the lead this time. I would follow him with less than ten feet between us. He was appropriately dressed in a clerical shirt. Shortly before mounting the gangway, I rehearsed the program:

- Talk to whoever you see.

- Notice carefully if they are on duty or not, or are unable to talk.

- Try to determine if they have had bad news from their families or are under stress because of pain, sickness, or difficulties on board or at home.

- Use your box with literature. Give freely and liberally.

- Under all circumstances, after half an hour you go on to the next person. You approach someone else.

- Trust the LORD to lead you.

In all my visits, I have discovered God has a lesson for us. Actually, on all roads in life he gives directions. He does that sometimes in an incomprehensible way. While alive here on earth, don't spend too much time trying to figure out why God acts as he does. He has his reasons. At times, he lets us come to closed doors to test us and to see if we are prepared to either open them or to walk around in order to try another door. We are to keep our goal in mind and to stay focused!

It was by now nine o'clock in the morning. Totally empty, the ship was very high on the water. The gangway, which was exceptionally steep, consisted of two sections, tied to each other halfway up. Each section had some twenty-five steps. I decided to be firm and said: "Go on up. You lead the way on this ship. I'll be right behind you."

With a box of Bibles under his arm, my student took step number one on the first tread of the gangway. The outfit moved slightly forward, because of the connection halfway up. My assistant obviously did not have a firm grip on the railing of the gangway, for, in front of my eyes, I saw the gangway sway and shake. My student lost his balance and fell between ship and shore.

Fortunately, a net had been put under the gangway! There in the net, ten feet below the shoreline, lay my student with Bibles all around him and tightly holding onto the net. As I started to pull up the net, it struck me that this was one time in my life, that I could meaningfully shout, "Hang in there!" I had literally become a "fisher of man."

In slightly less than ten minutes, he was back ashore and the Bibles were back in the box. He looked at me in the hope that I would abandon the visit, but I decided to maintain our focus. I counseled him to hang on very tightly to the railing of the gangway, particularly at the point where the two sections were somewhat sloppily joined. If we should fall we might not have as soft a landing as he had experienced, but instead start tumbling down all those steep steps first before we would reach the safety net.

We decided to step carefully. Halfway up the second section, about six or seven steps below the deck, we suddenly noticed the radio officer who stood at the very top of the gangway. One look at our clerical shirts prompted him to shout at my student: "Are you Christian?" I heard my assistant reply, "Yes, I am," whereupon the radio officer said, "I speak with you," and he immediately stepped aside to enable us to come on board.

I thought, *You couldn't get a better welcome than that. You board a ship full of Muslims and you get invited to talk because you are a Christian. You do not have to search out someone and ponder how to start the conversation. Here you get an invitation to talk with the radio officer.*

My student disappeared into the office of the radio officer, and I made my way up to the captain, who was Finnish. I knew him. We had met quite some time ago.

He was a very nice person, but he had an enormous problem. He wrestled with the bottle. I spent time with him because I realized that he wanted to be delivered from this. I have discovered that a number of people are imprisoned by different kinds of addictions. With the help of God, one is able to break away from them. He was delivered. The records do not tell the details. Regrettably, on the transatlantic voyage from Canada to the Mediterranean, he passed away. It still pains my soul. He was such a warmhearted man with a genuine love for his crew.

Unbeknownst to myself, I was the last person who had a chance to talk to him.

After my visit with him, which, because of the circumstances, lasted almost two hours, I visited the second officer, the chief engineer, and a sick seaman who was laid up in his cabin. The captain had asked me to pick him up for lunch at noon. I did. We entered the officers' dining room. On this ship, the captain sat at a table all by himself. So, we sat down together.

I did notice that my student was seated with the radio officer at another table, just the two of them. Protocol did not allow us to start a conversation. We greeted each other. I noticed his bright red face, presumably from the "hot" oriental dishes, and his attempt to put out the "fire" with water from a carafe. We lunched. The radio officer and my student left shortly after the captain and I had started our lunch.

After the luncheon, I went about visiting a number of other officers and members of the crew. Some of them had probing questions. The seafarers were eager to talk.

In John 14, 16 and 17, reference is made to the coming of the Counselor. One of the seafarers, with whom I was in discussion, suggested that this is a reference to the prophet Mohammed. I responded, "The Counselor our Lord has sent us is *The Holy Spirit,* not Mohammed. In the Scriptures no mention is made at all of Mohammed. We have to focus on the Triune God and not on anyone else. The Trinity is of course a mystery, but it is unique to discover that God has come to us in Christ Jesus and has taken his residence in us with the Holy Spirit."

The afternoon had slipped by faster than I thought. I felt we should still visit that Belgian ship. After all, it had taken us nearly two hours to drive down from Montreal, so I decided to hunt up my student. I asked the steward who was just passing by: "Have you seen the young chaplain with whom I came on board?" He replied, "Yes, he is in the office of the radio officer." By then it was 3:30 p.m. I thought, *That is impossible,* but the stewards on board of ships usually know what is going on.

I approached the radio officer's office located on the top deck. There sat my exhausted student next to his box of Bibles. He had not visited anyone else. He had been dominated by the radio officer before, during, and after lunch. I suggested, "Let's go. We have to get to the Belgian ship." I greeted the radio officer, who said that he would like to talk to my student upon his return to Montreal in about seven weeks. We left and reached the gangway, which had become less steep since the ship had taken on an enormous supply of grain.

As my friend was about to step onto the gangway with his box under his arm, he turned around, looked at me, and said: "Lucky thing you came to get me. If you would have come half an hour later, I would have become a Muslim." I made the recommendation that he might wish to reconsider returning to the seminary. He felt that the summer experience had become an excellent lesson for him. He had discovered that his talents did not come to fruition in the ministry. He was a wise man and resigned from the Seminary. He then developed a brilliant career in the Spirit's gift he had been entrusted with: The world of electronics.

SMUGGLING BIBLES
ON BOARD SOVIET SHIPS

At least twelve years before the collapse of Soviet communism we had contact with crew members of cargo vessels from the USSR. They came to the Port of Montreal and often picked up cowhides which were stacked in a salt preparation on open skids on the water-front and produced an odor which many people did not appreciate. Personally I sort of liked it. When some of us, with the help of visiting college or senior high school students, invited the seafarers on Sundays to join us at the Seafarers Centre for an evening of worship and fellowship, the students always asked us why these hides were there. We tried to sell them the story that "extensive Soviet research had discovered that, due to the extremely low temperatures in the Soviet Union, an extra coat was needed for cattle to improve their milk production." Unbelievably, some of them bought the story lock, stock, and barrel.

To come on board with the overt presentation of the gospel was, of course, anathema. Each ship had a political commissar called the "first officer"—in Russian: *pervij pomoschnik*, or "Pompolit." No one could come on board for any kind of business without first checking with him. He would then assign an escort to go with the visitor wherever he went. So the visitor was never alone with the person he needed to see. This regulation even applied to the captain.

There was a second political commissar on board, a secret one. In most instances, no one knew who that was, not even the chief officer. Once I met one of them. It was a strange experience. He pulled me into his cabin while I was alone for just a minute. Once inside his cabin he proudly showed me the files of the people on board. Every action of any significance was recorded. I did not understand how he dared to reveal his identity by showing me his records. When I asked him about it, he told me that there was a third political commissar as well. So people could never experience freedom from spying eyes. I suspect that's why on board of Soviet ships there was never a single person who smiled or showed any relaxation or displayed any joy.

Going ashore was possible for them only by going in groups of three. Two could make a covenant, three is a crowd. Despite subzero temperatures, they would never accept a ride in my car, in the van of the Seafarers Centre, or in the car of anyone else. They would never use public transportation, although that might have had something to do with the cost.

I noticed an attitude of rejection, especially in the way they looked at you, whenever I boarded their ships. I discovered that the same attitude prevailed toward everyone else who had to board the ship for technical or commercial purposes.

Ordinarily, I would have with me some large brown manila envelopes. In them were a few copies of the latest Time Magazine and the National Geographic Magazine as well as some copies of the entire New Testament in Russian in microprint. That was an edition, which looked like a standard business letter, but in reality was printed on thirty sheets of rice paper. Its weight was like that of a letter of less than thirty grams. I had a few of those.

As I developed my contacts on Soviet vessels, especially during the cold winters, and noticed that the guards were very heavily dressed to withstand the subzero temperatures, it became easier to give to the guards a copy of the micro-print New Testament.

Every ship had a medical doctor on board, yet once in a while we would find a Soviet seaman in the hospital. In most instances, they were too scared to receive even a copy of the National Geographic, let alone a copy of the Bible. But I recall one seaman who had a broken ankle and was in a cast, which reached up to his knees. I suspected that he might be interested in a copy of the Word of God. I had various copies with me.

I presented him of course with the complete Bible. I figured while he was in the hospital, he'd have time to read. He looked at it, seemed to like it, but gave it back to me. I concluded it was too bulky and too heavy. I then presented him with a New Testament. He liked that one even better, but he still felt he did not dare to accept it. I figured since he hadn't accepted what I had shown him he most likely would not accept anything.

I pulled out my last stop: The microprint edition of the New Testament. He opened it up and seemed pleased with it. He said, "I will take this." I had already pointed out that anything I gave him would be gratis, free of charge. Yet he said, "I do not want the other ones, I like this one." Ignorantly I once again tried to push the hard cover New Testament. But he demonstrated why he preferred the last one.

He pulled away the blankets from his leg with the cast. He then took the microprint New Testament, bent his leg somewhat, thereby creating an opening between his leg and the cast, and carefully slipped the entire microprint edition into the space he had created. It disappeared totally. He looked up at me and smiled. That was the most meaningful smile I had ever seen from a Soviet seaman.

The doctor who worked on another ship did not smile. He had received a copy of the New Testament with the orthodox cross on it. I had given it to him the first time I met him on his ship. It had made a profound impression on him and through his reading of the Word of God, he came to acknowledge Christ as his Savior.

When I met him again he did not smile but was instead close to tears. When I expressed my concern for his well-being, seeing that he looked so distressed, he asked me to come into his cabin. As we sat down, he explained to me that according to the Word of God we must follow His ways, yet on board there were several girls as stewardesses. A few of them had become intimately involved with some of the male crewmembers and had become pregnant.

As per the instructions of the company, it was his responsibility to perform abortions. When he had become a Christian, he could no longer do this. He realized that this could create problems for him. It could lead to his dismissal. That's why he was so distressed. We talked about it. There are times when we see water coming into the ship of our lives, threatening us with drowning.

He experienced one of those times on his ship. The threat of losing his job became bigger by the day. He believed that he could no longer kill a child in utero because he had come into contact with the LORD who had given the overt summons to obey his commandments. Peter, in his first letter, talks about this. "Do not be surprised at the painful trial you are suffering..." (1Peter 4:12). For us Christians, living in the free world, permitted in most instances to do as we please, we do not feel threatened by that sentence of Peter. We are not experiencing painful trials... *or are we?* The trials come about when we consistently and conscientiously practice our faith.

"Painful trial"—that's what it says in the Bible to Christians. When we stand up for Christ, life—that means our whole world of relationships, position, job, health, and welfare—can suddenly turn into a "painful trial." The doctor was in that boat on the level of his job. With a wife and a seven-year-old boy, his job became imperiled if he would consistently practice his faith. Painful trial! For these lovely girls the Word of God has a message about their relationships. If they accept that message, they also end up in a painful trial.

When a Political Commissar, who was called to come to the gangway, saw my large envelopes he would inquire, "What is in them?" I always responded with, "Something to read." He would then try to find out what kind of reading material it was. The Soviets were concerned that with their coming to North America, the seafarers would come into contact with either "Biblia or pornographia," with religion and morality. Did they want to protect themselves from either one? They were, by now, some seventy years removed from the influence of the church. In some instances, they were even unable to identify me as a representative of the church.

I always assured them that I would never have any "pornographia," but I would admit that I had materials that could indeed be classified as "biblia." In the course of time, I noticed that there was not always a direct opposition to the Bible, although I could not openly present one to any person.

I found that mysterious, but one day the supervisor of the Political Commissars of the Soviet ships came to Montreal on board of one of the ships. I had heard that he would be coming and I wanted to meet him, because I wanted to get his permission to come on board with a folk-singing group. I was carrying my four envelopes when we met. I got from him the same questions. I noticed his interesting reaction. He said, "If they do not wish to have what is in the envelope, what should they do with it?" I answered, "In that case they can destroy it or return it to me." I found it intriguing that he left it to the individual judgment of the recipients.

This director of the Political Commissars turned out to be a very nice person, and in my heart, I thought the LORD God selected this man to be where he was, because he became a channel for passing on the Word of God without knowing it himself. He did not get excited about my envelopes. He also approved our coming on board with our church's folk-singing group.

In those early days, the Soviet people were not permitted to come to a Seafarers Centre. The Political Commissar would not be able to control his people there. There would be seafarers present from other non-Soviet ships. There might be interaction, possibly an exchange of whatever it is that people wish to exchange.

To come on board would not interfere with the control of the Political Commissar over the people of his ship. So we came on board week after week. I functioned as the master of ceremonies.

The folk-singing group performed excellently every time we came on board. They were a group of dedicated volunteers from the church, gifted in singing. They became an inspiration to the people we ministered to. The Soviets would not allow a church service, but they were always impressed by the Christian songs this folk singing group presented.

At one time the Political Commissar asked us what the meaning was of the song "Sinner Man." The words "sin" (kreag in Russian) and "sinner" (kreashniy) had lost their meaning for these people, who, for seventy years had been weaned from the church. In our democratic society, we do understand this meaning and the LORD may well hold us accountable.

Our evenings on board were much appreciated, but as soon as the concert was finished, all seafarers filed out except the political commissar. He stayed with us while tea and cookies were served. We always left with a pin, or propaganda materials about the reign of Stalin, or some photos of a Russian city, such as Moscow or Leningrad. The unique aspect of our little concerts was of course that we could present him with a token of our appreciation. So we gave him some of our envelopes, and who knows what he did with those?

Eventually the Soviet people were allowed to come to our Seafarers Centre to attend the worship service there. I was then able to point out to them that the Christian gospel is more deeply embedded in the Russian language than in our secular English language: When we speak about the days of the week in English, we refer to the solar system. Monday refers to the moon. Thursday to thunder, Saturday to Saturn, Sunday to the sun. But in the Russian language, we detect a Judeo-Christian awareness. When they speak about Saturday, they say "Subota," which is like the Hebrew "Shabat," or "Sabbath." For Sunday, they say "Voskresenie," the day that Christ arose, which is the Christian orientation for the first day of the week. It reveals that in its history, the Christian gospel had deeply penetrated into the Russian language.

When a captain arrived in our Centre one Sunday evening with a few of his officers, he said, "Thank you for your invitation, but please tell us how to behave in church. Where do we sit? When do we stand? How do we hold our arms and hands: downward or across our chest?"

I responded, "Downward."

I also gave them the assurance that God is looking at the heart. Their physical conduct, though characterized by respect, would not be the most critical element. "We are here to worship God and to hear His Word. Feel free to copy what the others do."

They entered the chapel with hands clasped together and with bowed heads. They sat down in the front rows. They listened intently as I exerted myself to speak as clearly as I could to enable them to understand my message.

Some Russians had visited our country a number of times. They had taken pictures wherever they had traveled, in other countries as well as in Montreal, and they examined what they had seen in the light of their own philosophy or, if you will, in the light of their own "spiritual" convictions.

So, two of them, both engineers, came to me one Sunday evening after the church service while we were all relaxing with coffee and cake. He asked my opinion about some photos he had taken.

One represented an army marching in the street of some city. The army parade was headed by a heavily robed cleric looking like some sort of bishop or cardinal from the church. Two young attendants, one on each side, both carrying a cross, were marching along with him. He looked somber, almost sad. The acolytes had their characteristic innocent, non-committal look.

The second picture displayed a group of young people, all in white robes, standing behind one gentleman who was in charge. He was preaching in the street. An enormous crowd of curious people surrounded this group. The white robed group seemed to be from the Hara Krishna movement.

The third picture portrayed the entrance to a movie theater showing a large poster of Raquel Welch with her legs draped seductively. One leg had a black band around it with a twenty-dollar bill sticking out of it. The title of the film was, *The Oldest Profession.* Above the scene was a huge sign: "Restricted." Underneath it said: "To persons eighteen years of age or over."

The last photo he showed was the entrance, somewhere in North America, to a topless bar and in case you would not know what that meant, they had written underneath: "no pasties." Underneath were three signs reading: "New, Daring, Revealing." There were two pictures of some girls, nude above the waist.

The Spirit alerted me: "Two reflections about religion, two about morality. Didn't they ask you about Biblia and Pornographia?"

The engineer explained, "These pictures I have taken in Western democratic countries. Is it the business of the Christian church to head an army parade? Should it not parade for peace? A non-Christian sect, publicly preaching in a Christian country? How do you explain that? Prostitution in the film-entertainment world? A bar where you can get a drink and look at girls cavorting around without pasties, and that in a 'Christian' country? Where are your principles?"

In the eyes of many Asiatic, Muslim, and Soviet people particularly, North America is viewed as a Christian country. Our heritage does have distinct Christian roots, but the spirit of secularization has been influencing our society. It is coupled with an increasing tolerance of the religious orientation of our immigrants. We have become reluctant to uphold our distinct Christian principles.

It would have been out of step for me to emphasize the atrocities of a communist controlled society under people like Stalin. It would have been senseless for me to explain that the democratic West is not predominantly Christian. Judging by our historic development, that is of course a lame excuse. So I focused on the Christ of the Scriptures and on obedient service to him in our religious and moral lives. About this theme, we talked for the better part of the evening for this was the only theme that really mattered.

The incongruity between our religious conviction and our practice in a country, which is perceived to be a Christian nation, is of course most perplexing.

I had been tipped off. On board of one Ukrainian passenger ship, the sports director asked me, "Are you aware of the need of the senior officer on board that other Ukrainian cruise ship here in port?" I wasn't, even though I had just sailed along with that vessel the previous days. She had come from Germany and Greenland with some six hundred and fifty passengers on board. We had been asked to board her in Quebec City and to conduct an Ecumenical Worship Service in the German language. The service would take place in "The Tchaikovsky Bar."

The senior officer had been on duty and, though we did exchange courtesies in the course of the journey, he obviously had not dared to express his need. That's why the LORD arranged to have his closest friend become his spokesman.

Inspired by this challenge, we immediately returned to the other ship in search of the senior officer. To our surprise, at the very moment we boarded it, he was standing by the gangway. When we approached him he took us into his office and apologized for not being a Christian. That was his opening sentence. It also explained his hesitancy to speak to us the previous day.

I encouraged him to express what was on his mind. So he said, "My wife in Odessa has joined a group of sixteen Ukrainian people who desire to examine the Christian faith, but they have no Bibles." We thanked God for that group of sixteen, which included his wife. He had been asked to try and obtain sixteen Ukrainian Bibles for them together with some study materials. He, the non-Christian, was willing to provide courier service. "Can you possibly help?" So the non-Christian became a "missionary" to the group of sixteen.

We mustered not sixteen, but twenty Bibles, as well as an adequate stock of Catechetical and study materials, and put them all in a sealed box. We left one Bible out of the box, together with some study materials for the senior officer's own examination. He was delighted and assured us, "I shall carefully study all of this."

Thank God that he sent the sports director on our path to be of help to his friend. The intricate trails we all travel to get to the program of Christ.

Shortly before I started to visit Soviet vessels, I approached one of my Russian friends, seeking his counsel and wisdom. He gave sound advice when he said, "Do not learn Russian at this time. Keep in mind that you are 'tagged' by now. Do not hand out your calling card to them, because they would add the card's details to their file. Do not report that you have come to see me."

In this world of intrigue, one had to be extremely sensitive. There is profound value in Christ's message to his disciples when he sent them out to preach the gospel: "…be as shrewd as snakes and as innocent as doves" (Matt. 10:16).

LUNCH WITH
A POLITICAL COMMISSAR

When I received a telephone call from the agency, I was surprised: "Would I be kind enough to visit a Soviet vessel at Berth 67? They would like me to come for lunch at 2:00 p.m." The surprise was due to the timing they gave me. On Soviet vessels people always eat at noon, not at 2:00 p.m.

Although we trusted the LORD in his guidance, every now and then we were shaken in that trust. Once in a while, Trudy and I talked about it especially in connection with my visits to the Soviet freighters. I went on board regularly, but they were Soviet Communists cargo ships. I had New Testaments with me in Russian. It may have been an old fashioned translation, but it was in Russian. We knew their "concern" about the Biblia. They were against the distribution of the Word of God among their people.

I would be going on board alone. They might feed me some kind of drug. It was possible that they would quietly dump me overboard. There was an eight and a half mile an hour current in the St. Lawrence River. I would be in Quebec City before I knew it. Lunch at 2:00 p.m.? Was that a set up for one of the above mentioned scenarios?

The Spirit of the LORD challenged me. "What's the matter with your trust? Why are you so suspicious? You have been in touch with these people for years. Has anything untoward happened? If today is going to be your last meal, like your old nature seems to be suggesting to you, look at it spiritually: Where do you end up? In Quebec City? Can't you look beyond Quebec City?

Leaving your wife and children behind is your concern? Could that not be addressed by me? You are on the job here on the waterfront. They are calling you to come to their ship. Have you ever had a call from a Soviet ship? No? So this is the first time. You are suspicious about a 2:00 p.m. lunch? Enjoy the lunch. Do not worry about the time."

I decided to go. After all, lunch was an involvement of many people. That thought comforted me, but the timing just seemed so odd. In my ministry on the waterfront, I had picked up some Russian. I could speak about fifteen words. If I juggled them around I could make it forty-five.

On a number of occasions, I had heard from some Soviet people that they suspected I was fooling them when I said I did not speak Russian. Judging by my accent, they said, they were convinced I spoke it fluently, but I just tried to appear ignorant. So they suspected me of being a possible double agent.

I wondered how they could make that judgment on the basis of my limited Russian vocabulary. I discovered that it had to do with my having been born in the Netherlands. The few words I spoke in Russian sounded fluent to a Russian because of my Dutch background.

I had been on this ship some time ago but because I met every day, different people on many ships, I tend to forget that I have met some people at an earlier stage. The space between the times of meeting the same person is often very long. It may be months or even years.

The guard at the top of the gangway embraced me in the Russian tradition. He did not ask me what I wanted or if I wanted to see the Political Commissar. He just went to the telephone, shouted some Russian into it and simply told me, "Sash minute"—"Wait a minute."

Almost immediately the Political Commissar appeared, with a slight smile, which surprised me, and he fired off in Russian at high speed, after he had shaken my hand. His manner seemed rather friendly, so my fears subsided, although the timing of the lunch still bothered me.

Strange that in the process of "trust" as we know it, there is every now and then "doubt" that pops up. That is an irritable disease. Matthew 11:3 commiserated with me and encouraged me. Here is John the Baptist, the forerunner of Christ. He was the one who called everyone to repentance, because the Savior was right behind him and His Kingdom was about to come.

He was the one who baptized Jesus with his own hands and stood by, to hear with his own ears, God Almighty speaking in audible Hebrew, saying, "This is my Son, whom I love; with him I am well pleased (Matthew 3:17)."

That same John the Baptist later, while he sat in jail biting his nails, came up with the question: "Are you the one who was to come, or should we expect someone else?" That is doubt in "optima forma."

Was God teaching me a lesson? The Political Commissar put me on the little bench in his cabin and served me a drink. It had no color, so there were my suspicions again, but he poured himself a glass as well out of the same bottle and drank it.

I heard the Spirit of God whisper: "You are looking at his glass and at his actions. Don't trust in what you see. Trust in God!"

A dish of tasty Russian sausages was shoved at me and then he sat down, continuously talking in Russian, at break-neck speed. I thought, "There is no point in explaining that I do not speak Russian. His entire attitude displays that he would not believe that." So, I decided to swing over and pretend I did understand him.

Listening carefully I agreed with him when it would seem that his most recent spiel could be supported by a Dah—yes. But there were times while I was studying his facial expressions, that I felt I should go into the negative direction and insert a Nyet—no. It seemed to work. He was pleased and cheerfully carried on after we had one more drink, which I discovered had no effect on me.

Then, interrupting his own speech, he rose and said we should go down for lunch. The time was exactly 2:00 p.m. We walked down the stairs, squeezed ourselves through the narrow hallways, and ended up in the officers' dining room.

Three stewardesses stood ready, one at the table and two in the adjoining pantry. The table was set with an empty bowl for the soup, a dish of salad, the condiments, some rough Russian bread and a pitcher as well as a glass of water. The table was nicely set with flowers, somewhat bedraggled, but nevertheless real flowers, in the center of the table.

There was just one thing that was extremely intriguing: The table was set for one person, not for the two of us! Two thoughts raced through my mind: Didn't Trudy and I discuss precisely this type of thing? "They'll feed you something and then they'll throw you overboard." The second thought was: "One place setting, so you'll eat alone. If it is your last meal, you may as well enjoy it! The LORD can protect you no matter what." That is of course the biblical attitude we are summoned to display at all times!

So, I offered thanks out loud, while the Political Commissar sat across from me and the one stewardess stood still in the middle of the room, with a bowl of soup in her hands. Then I was ready to start, encouraged by the Political Commissar's good wishes: "Priatnova Appetita" (Enjoy your meal).

The food was tasty, typical Russian, but I like all sorts of cuisines. While I enjoyed the meal, the Political Commissar kept talking, uninterruptedly. Eating enthusiastically, I was mercifully delivered from having to comment with yes or no in response. I figured, "You keep talking, and I'll keep eating."

When I was finished with the dessert, I walked into the pantry and thanked the ladies for the excellent food and services. That produced a shy smile. I needed about five words for that, and I thought that proves again to our friend, who is standing at the door waiting for me, that I do speak Russian.

I followed him upstairs. On board of a Soviet ship you do not move about alone. You are always escorted. I sensed no ill effects from the meal; actually, I felt quite good. Moreover, the railing was at a safe distance from where we were walking.

So back in the cabin of the Political Commissar, I was again ushered to the bench for another drink. As he was preparing the drinks, I spotted between a few books in his tiny library a copy of a calendar of a Missionary organization. I recalled that I had presented those calendars to all kinds of Soviet ships. The pictures showed beautiful Canadian scenery. And a calendar is essentially for taking note of the date. This one also had an encouraging Bible verse underneath each picture.

His calendar was closed and stood between the books. I figured he had put it there to possibly take it home. To have a "Christian" calendar with Bible verses hanging on the wall would be problematic for a man in his position. The ship had all kinds of spies, so he could well be reported if he would have had a Christian testimony hanging on his wall; irrespective of the Canadian scenery.

We had the drink. There were a few pieces of sausage left, so he urged me to help myself. Out of courtesy I decided I should have a small piece. As I picked it up, I wondered what I was doing here. I had not invited myself. I had spent almost an hour and a half with someone, who has rattled on incessantly in a foreign language. I had no idea what he had said or what he was saying. I was asking myself how and where this would come to an end. Just at that moment the answer was provided.

The Political Commissar stood up, went to his door and locked it. He then changed his position and took the seat behind his desk. He pulled open the right top drawer with a firm swing. In went his hand and out it came with a copy of the New Testament in Russian, the kind I had been handing out to people on Soviet ships in a very unobtrusive way.

I thought, "Where did he get this?" I could not recall if I had given it to him, but there it was. I did not pursue the thought because the scenery changed rapidly. He took the New Testament in both hands and kissed it enthusiastically in front of me. Then, as rapidly as it had come out, he stuffed it back into the drawer and covered it up with some papers and a writing pad.

He slammed the drawer shut, took one more sip from his glass, as if to fortify himself. Then he stood up and extended his hand to me so as to get me to my feet. He went to the door, and just before he unlocked it, he kissed me on both cheeks in Soviet fashion.

He now changed his vivacious attitude and returned to the formality of his office by seriously thanking me. For what? Till this day, I don't know. With the customary straight face of a man in his position he delivered me into the hands of the guard at the gangway.

The guard obediently showed me the way down. The Political Commissar had disappeared into the ship. Ashore, at the foot of the gangway, I turned around and noticed that the guard, who had escorted me down the gangway without a word, was on his way up, back to his position, and it all looked as if nothing at all had happened on this ship.

Something had happened, but to this day I have not found out what it was. I had not understood what the Political Commissar told me in his lengthy speeches. I have not understood why I had to drink what he served me and to eat the sausages he offered me, nor why I should sit at a luncheon all by myself and be served by three stewardesses.

I suspect that at one time I had given him that copy of the New Testament and that calendar. Never mind the calendar, but with his action behind locked doors, he must have said something like, "I have come to appreciate the Word of God. In fact, the Christ of the Scriptures has become dear to me." Is that why he kissed the Bible so fervently?

I was simply the courier and since he was not able to stand up in a church and profess his faith, and rejoice in what he had found, he obviously was expressing to me his joy and thanks. I was the closest link he had to Christ.

I regretted that in my reactions to his speech I had introduced a few nyets. Had I known the outcome of all this, I would have only used the word dah (yes). Never mind, I believe the Political Commissar has said "dah" to Christ and that's what it is all about!

KEEP YOUR FOCUS
ON YOUR CALLING

It all started quite some time ago. For more than a year already, we had noticed that along with our seafarers attending the festive Sunday evening services at our seafarers' center, a number of Sri Lanka young people kept returning week after week.

We learned that they were refugees and resided in the city. What we did not know at the time that adjacent to the port we served stood a dilapidated former RC hospital, which had been turned into a refugee home with the intriguing name: L'Abri, the shelter.

To the more than sixty-five residents, all young people who had escaped from politically troubled countries, the place was simply known as: "The Camp." The residents had come from Afghanistan, Palestine, Middle America, South America, Poland, Ghana, and South Africa.

The place called "The Camp" was of course more than that. It provided shelter and food and functioned as a base for governmental organizations, which gave direction into the intricacies of the Canadian immigration laws. It also supplied information about schooling and reasonable living accommodations because the maximum period of time anyone was allowed to stay at The Camp was only two months.

The refugees were then on their own, with an allotment of $140.00 per month from the Provincial Government. This was to cover the cost of rent, food, clothing, furniture, and transportation.

But there was another dimension to their lives. It had to do with finding a "niche" in our society if you will.

It dealt with adjusting to a totally different kind of society. It was in the area of letting down roots spiritually and knowing oneself to belong somewhere. To put it plainly: Here were young people, who were looking for some parental guidance, fatherly advice, motherly love, and pastoral insight in this, to them, totally different world.

When we encountered a few "slow" Sundays among the seafarers, because many ships had left the port before the weekend, we decided to invite the few people who were spending Sunday afternoon in The Camp to join us in our festive worship service.

To our amazement, more than fifty people stood at the doorway of The Camp, when our twelve-passenger van pulled up to provide transportation to our Seafarers Centre shortly before seven o'clock in the evening. It turned out that the news of the invitation had traveled to a number of refugees who already had settled in different apartments throughout the city and who had come back to The Camp to visit. We in turn thought it might be of advantage to some of our seafarers. They might be able to communicate with each other in the language of either the refugees or of the seafarers.

So they trooped into our chapel utterly fascinated by the fact that they had been invited to join in for prayers. They listened breathlessly while in the simplest of terms, I articulated the gospel of our LORD and Savior. I then led them in prayer before the throne of God.

Following the worship service, which none of them left without expressing his sincerest thanks, they inspected our lounge, tasted our coffee, ate our donuts, played at our ping pong tables, and sniffed at the extensive variety of literature. They alerted us that there were no Scriptures in the languages of Iran or Afghanistan (Persian, Dari, or Pushtu).

Then we talked. We heard reports of their disenchantment with the Khomeini regime, their circuitous escape to Canada, and their initial adjustment to a new world. We detected their struggle with our language and discovered their need for even the bare essentials in apartment living. Not easily given to swallowing stories, Trudy suggested that we go on an inspection tour to some of the apartments.

It was worse than we expected: Bare mattresses lifted from box springs to enable the use of both. No blankets, no sheets, no pillows, no cutlery, no pots or pans, an occasional plastic cup, one fork for five people, an empty fridge, and a closet with some rags in it. All of them were headed into a Canadian winter with slush and snow and temperatures dropping to below zero.

In line with the directives of the book of Acts and the letter of James, we alerted the churches and Christian High School parents. We soon found ourselves deluged with an abundance of needed items with which God had blessed our congregations.

Part of our Seafarers Centre became a refugee donation area and the needs were gradually met. When Christmas approached we allowed the camp inhabitants to join our seafarers for Christmas dinner. We figured that by Christmas Day, most of the ships would have left port, enabling us to expand our energy on the refugees. But we had completely misjudged the situation. The weather deteriorated. Many ships could not leave. Refugees, living in the city, had gotten wind of our Christmas celebration and decided to join in. To our amazement some two-hundred-and-fifty people showed up. They poured out of the bus and metro stations.

Ships' chandlers, friends, church members, and people familiar with the Ministry to Seafarers had supplied us with large amounts of food, so we could feed everyone liberally. First we had our Christmas Service in which I preached the sermon about the Birth of Christ, the Son of God. It was based on the beautiful verses found in St. Luke, chapter two, where in seven verses the amazing plan of salvation is placed before us: The Word of God challenges us to acknowledge him who has come and continues to come. He presents himself to each one of us, irrespective of our schedule, accommodation, or convenience. We sang the beautiful Christmas Carols and I gave the Benediction to all present.

Then dinner was served, and we tried to bring joy into the lives of everyone present. But, when we finally began with the distribution of clothing, blankets, and utensils, complete bedlam broke out. We, our staff, volunteers, and premises, were all taxed to the very limit until deep into the night: *We had lost our focus.*

We realized we needed to give up working with refugees and return to our *calling,* which was the Ministry to Seafarers. So, we donated all the supplies of clothing, bedding, and household articles to the "Welcome Hall" Mission a few blocks away.

We made the Seafarers Centre a center exclusively for Seafarers again, but some refugees continued to attend our church services in the chapel. They wanted to know, if we had already received the Scriptures in their language. They were disenchanted with their religions because of the ruthless killings in their country in the name of religion.

Some of them asked for further instruction in the things concerning this Jesus. Bewildered by the confused picture of a nation, which in their judgment was Christian but in many ways seemed secular, they were really groping, searching for a new basis, for direction, for meaningful religion, for God in Christ.

It is interesting that for immigrants, as well as for refugees, who come to our nation we represent the motto on the American dollar: "In God we trust." The Western society in their minds is Christian. What distinguishes us to them is our faith in Christ, not our economic wealth. What foreigners always look for is what kind of spirit drives the nation. There is a fascination with our democratic society, but many people search for the deeper spiritual meaning that drives us. It is fascinating that this is the very opening statement of our Lord, according to Luke 4:4 where Jesus says, "Man does not live by bread alone."

When the communistic system began to collapse, a hunger for spiritual change and restoration was dominant. In our missionary outreach we continuously discover that it is on this level that people seek guidance, direction, vision, and encouragement. So, we can tell ourselves that, with respect to the refugees in our port area, to continue ministering to them isn't our job. Very well, whose job is it then ... ?

When on the Sunday after our decision to change our course, some fifty refugees walked into our chapel, many of whom had attended for more than six months; did I have the right to lock the door? In the course of time, however, as the refugees were absorbed by other churches, we steered our ministry back into the waters where we were "called" to sail.

One must keep the goal in mind. One can lose focus by becoming concentrated on non-essential aspects of one's ministry. One can also lose focus when one becomes involved in "another" ministry, which is closely related. That was our difficulty. To address it, we had to go through a painful period of saying goodbye to many people, who had become a part of our lives. The French expression says it well: "Partir, c'est mourir un peu."

One Sunday Mazyar approached my wife and asked if he could get a picture of our LORD. As a devout Bible teacher, Trudy gently hinted that the LORD did not express great favor in having pictures or images made of himself. She suggested that the LORD is worshipped in spirit and in truth and becomes visible in us as we do his will, stand in his service, and trust his word. So, she offered him a copy of the Bible, for it would give him the best portrait of Jesus.

Mazyar had begun to understand that Jesus is holy and awesome in power, so he asked, "May I then have a picture of the *shadow* of the LORD?"

In the Bible, there is a reflection of our emergency telephone number 911. It is found in Psalm 91:1. This is what it says: "He, who dwells in the shelter of the Most High, will rest in *the shadow* of the Almighty."

As the ministry to the refugees drifted out of our purview, we discovered that Mazyar, and for that matter Ramin, Mustafa, Ishmael, Elias, Hamid, Mahmoud, Hamzeh, Farhad, and several others, who had been in touch with the Light that shines in darkness, found rest in the *shadow* of that Light.

THE CALL
OF THE MASTER

It had happened too often and in too many ports. It was happening again in Montreal in the sixties. As I drove up to the gatehouse I could see the trouble from afar: The National Harbours Board police cruiser with flashing lights, standing so obviously in the middle of the road; a group of longshoremen, curious about what was happening; the gate-house guards, excitedly attempting to interpret the crisis that had come to their otherwise quiet post; and in their midst, a group of disheveled seamen, Filipinos, Greeks, Pakistani, a few Egyptians, one from Lebanon and some Indians, about fifteen in all.

They had obviously left their ship, only a stone's throw away, in a hurry, for I detected that some of them still had their working gloves on, but one ambitious Egyptian carried a suitcase. All the others were evidently dressed for work, if you can call it dressed: broken boots, flimsy raingear and rags wrapped around their necks and faces to keep out the bitter cold. Their coveralls, or rather what remained of them, were hardened with paint stains, rust and dirt. They looked overworked, underfed and some of them looked downright sick; in short, they presented a pitiable sight.

It was the National Harbours Board Police this time, and not the gate-house guard, who summoned me to a halt. When I got out of my car, they marched me right up to the seafarers who stood—half of them inside and half of them outside the guardhouse. "It's a job for you, Padre," they said. "You take it from here." They left me with the group and two gate-house guards, one of whom was rapidly working himself into a state of hysteria. He had reasons for it. He had, after all, already heard the story from the seamen. His wrath and fury got the better of him to the point that he started hitting his own guardhouse with such fury that he was liable to do damage to himself.

I grabbed him by his coat and asked him to control himself so that I could get the story as well. He fortunately responded by quieting down. So I got the story, not from him but from the men themselves, while our guard supported it with his exclamations of indignation and shock, couched in language that does not bear printing very well. A sorry story it was.

The M.V. Borboros had docked late the previous night after an almost five-week trip from the other side of the world. It had stopped in Montreal to get fitted out for entrance into the seaway and now, one day later, it was ready to sail again. The M.V. Borboros was in a hurry. She was headed for Chicago to unload a very expensive cargo and was then due to load grain at the Lake Head for delivery to, I believe it was, Cuba. All this had to be done before the closing of the St. Lawrence Seaway, which usually happens at about the middle of December.

Her owners had well prepared for the delivery of their costly cargo. Formalities were expedited. Notification of arrival had duly been given to the agents. A welding company stood ready upon arrival to fit the ship for seaway passage. Bunkers were taken on from a barge to save time. Telexes had been readied to order the cargo of grain. Customs were summoned to put down their signatures and straighten out the enormous bulk of paperwork associated with the shipping world. Linesmen were ordered, a pilot was notified, and tug-boats were called up. There was no time to lose.

But one thing had been forgotten: The M.V. Borboros sails by the grace of the people who have been hired to man her. In a world in which the demands of business and the need to make a profit are to be met, the human element and the needs of people are at times pushed into the background or not attended to at all. In our capitalistic structure, it is a continued struggle to maintain the dignity of humanity.

On the M.V. Borboros it came to a head.

Despite a full day in port after five solid weeks at sea, no mail had been forwarded to the ship's agents in Montreal. The very lifeline of the men with their families had been cut, because in the larger pattern of the M.V. Borboros and its heavily documented cargo, there had been no time to look after it.

Payment for the crew, enabling them to send money to their families, was not on the agenda. The Head Office overseas had sent enough to give everyone some cash to buy stamps and some cheap souvenirs, but the wages were kept safely stashed away in head office's safe. Moreover, no one on board could even get so much as an hour off, while in port.

Four men were visibly sick and had repeatedly asked to be sent to a medical facility immediately upon arrival, but in the context of the ship's busy schedule, there was no time for that either. Moreover the ship could not run the risk of losing men to a hospital ward while there was such a precious cargo in need of delivery to Chicago.

The heating system in the crew's department had broken down, but shore-repair crews would take too long to come to grips with the problem, so the matter was left for what it was. Broken pipes, flooded cabins, and freezing temperatures on board played no role of significance in comparison with that other aim: *To deliver safely and in time some of the costliest cargo Chicago ever stood to receive.*

For ships used to plow tropical waters, coming to Montreal in the beginning of December and then going up the seaway is no picnic. In fact, it can be disastrous. Some companies, aware of this part of the world and its fierce climate, coupled with a remnant of human concern, provide their entire crew with proper winter gear when their ships are sailing on the Great Lakes in the late fall and early winter. The human concern must indeed be an overriding factor. The provision of winter gear for a crew—consisting of some twenty-five people—might run as high as ten thousand dollars. Such an amount should not even be considered of any significance in comparison to a "costly cargo," running in the neighborhood of millions of dollars. Yet, it is not infrequently judged to be too much as an "extra" for the crew, even though it may have been part of their contract.

But then a Lebanese or a Pakistani can hardly be expected to understand what he is signing when he puts his name to a contract, written in a foreign language, and supported by promises and assurances of an agent or a master who is in need of a cheap crew. Furthermore the ship may be registered in Panama, the owners are perhaps in Greece, the charterers may live in New York, the agents in Montreal, and no one is really prepared to be bothered by hands that show signs of frostbite when those hands belong to a Filipino seaman or an Indian deckhand.

A master of a ship today has enough headaches with his owners, charterers, and agents, and can hardly be concerned with the dietary needs of some twelve or thirteen different nationalities on his ship.

Fair enough, but at least see to it then that there is enough food. On board the M.V. Borboros there was not. There was no proper food, no water, no heat, no facilities, and the ship was infested with rats and cockroaches. There was no mail and no money. Yet, the laborer is worthy of his hire irrespective of the amount. Some of the crewmembers had been on board for more than sixteen months. However, every time they asked for their wages they were pacified with a few ten-dollar bills and assurances that in the next port they would get their due. In every "next" port it was the same story, just as in every "next" port the ship would be fumigated and the crew would get medical attention and the mail would be brought on board. Except that the "next" port never seemed to come.

So the patience of an otherwise docile, yet tried, crew had come to an end. What triggered it was the human concern for each other. One of their four sick crew members, a fifty-nine year old Pakistani man, was no longer able to face up to the continuous strain that was put on his exhausted body, and so he let go of the will to live. Slumped near one of the exits on board, he was prepared to die from lack of medical attention, cold, frustration, exhaustion, and pure disgust.

That did it. As one man, the entire deck crew picked up their sick co-worker and marched off the ship straight to the gate-house and there verbalized what not only the guard, but any untrained eye could see: Human life was at stake.

We have a law in this city: The moment a foreign seaman steps outside the gate, which encloses the Federal Port Authority property, while unauthorized by his ship's master, he is considered to be entering Canada illegally.

Once, a group of Chinese seafarers, having sustained intolerable conditions on board their vessel, had had enough. They walked off their ship and sought refuge in a Seafarers Center where I was visiting. In less than five minutes, the police officers had them against the wall, searching through the crumpled contents of their pockets, consisting of half torn contracts, faded pictures of their family, broken worry beads, peppermints, and some worthless Vietnamese coins.

I still can't forget the sick sight of seeing these already degraded, stripped seamen who somehow still maintained their human dignity, treated by those officers as if they had just taken in the front line of the world's heroin pushers. And to top it off, the stripped lot was shipped off to the city jail, awaiting extradition.

So, when I had a chance to react to the plight, which the crew of the M.V. Borboros had placed before me, I suggested that they stay put inside the gate, while their Pakistani friend was brought to the Medical Clinic. It proved to be of value. In less than twenty minutes our Pakistani friend found himself in an oxygen tent in the hospital, where he stayed for thirty-seven days, with what was later diagnosed as tuberculosis.

I arranged for a small delegation to accompany me for an inspection tour to see for myself how bad it was on board. It was worse than I dreaded. As we slithered through half flooded, unimaginably dilapidated hallways, we entered the crew's mess room just in time to see a rat get itself caught in one of half a dozen rat traps, set up around the room—most unappetizing!

A brief walk through the galley confirmed what had been said. The officers' rations were of a different quality than the rations of the crew. The cabins were so infested by cockroaches that literally hundreds of them shot away in all directions when we opened the door. The place looked awful.

Even as I climbed higher, to the officers' quarters and finally to the captain's cabin, I could not get away from the conviction that I had entered some sort of a dungeon. That is strange about ships; some of them have the appearance of Hilton Hotel foyers, while others look like blighted inner-city apartments.

I had promised the crew that I would speak to the captain on their behalf, in an effort to resolve at least some of their problems. In a crisis of the sort I found myself in, it is always rather unpleasant to have to speak to the captain. After all, in almost all cases, he is the one who has precipitated the crisis, although our judgment should be garnished with mercy and grace. The man is in a tight spot. He is caught between his people on board and the owners for whom he works. But not infrequently the owners, in their relentless efforts to make as big a profit as possible, care little for the men on board.

At times, they find an ally in the captain, in their attempt to make an extra fast buck, at the expense of the crew. On board the M.V. Borboros, that appeared to be precisely the case. The company probably had made a deal with the captain to keep the "foreign" crew at bay, where it concerned their demands for wages. The captain was to pacify them with a few dollars in every port, but their pitiably poor wages should stay overseas in the office until their contract of ten to twelve months was finished. In that way, the interest would nicely accumulate. The company and the captain could split the frosting of this cake and the individual seaman would never know the difference.

The cake's frosting would be even thicker if savings could be achieved on repairs, on all the other extras, such as medical treatments, food, you name it. It would all be to the advantage of the company and of the captain. Fifty/fifty, or seventy/thirty for the captain would still provide him with a tidy little extra income, and the word *little* should be struck.

As the crookedness of the whole sordid situation came more and more into focus I approached the captain with the message of the prophet Malachi, who in the Bible, attacked some very corrupt situations. Somehow, it pained me that there were two distinguished representatives from the agency seated in the same cabin. The pilot was seated there as well, and his only remark, to my apology for the delay in sailing, was: "I could not care less; they'll pay me 'waiting time' at double-time wages." Of a truth, at that rate one does not care.

The linesmen, also paid by the hour, to throw a couple of lines loose could wait as well. The tug-boat, at a high cost, could also wait. Only the distinguished representatives were worried. A huge fine was attached for late delivery of the "special" cargo. In fact, they told me that every day's delay would cost the company thousands of dollars. It seemed of little concern to them that, without the delay of one day to bring about improvements in the horrifying conditions of the crew-quarters, serious illness or mental breakdown could conceivably result for the crew.

But then again, the captain is in charge. He decides to sail or not to sail. And even that is not altogether true. With fifteen deckhands and catering staff standing ashore, not even the master could declare his ship "safe" for sailing. So at least the captain gave me a hearing.

I approached him with God's instructions. The Spirit of God will take the lead in such encounters and it all comes out exactly the way it should come out. So, to my own rather shocking amazement,

I found myself raising my voice at this man who had kept his eyes closed to the dreadful conditions of his very own men. They are the people on whom his own safety at sea depended.

I continued to address the captain, while looking at the representatives of his company, whose only concern seemed to be the prevention of a huge fine. I informed him of the LORD's relentless summons to take up the plight of the stranger.

I pulled out my Bible and said: "This is what God says … 'Do not hold back the wages of a hired man overnight'" (Lev.9:13). I reminded them that they could not possibly expect to have this sort of thing go unpunished.

To be quite frank, I had expected that during my speech the captain would stand up and usher me to the door. Since he did not, I expected he would do so at the end of my remarks. But to my great amazement, after a short pause, he simply said: "Now, what do you suggest I should do?"

When I had recovered from my surprise to that reaction I said, "Please, get an order out to pick up anyone in need of medical attention for an appointment with the doctor. Kindly make arrangements to get an extra supply of food for Eastern people on board. Have the ship fumigated at the earliest opportunity. Get money from your office, every last cent to which your people are entitled, and allow me to muster twenty-seven winter coats from the Welcome Hall Mission. The company ought to supply additional winter gear for the entire crew."

It was suppertime and the banks were closed. In Europe, it was midnight and everyone was asleep. A huge fine hung over their heads. An expensive tug-boat stood by, idling a costly engine. The pilot and the linesmen continued to look through their rule book to see if they could get an extra buck out of it as well. There was no way in which these suggestions could be met without staying overnight and halfway through the following day.

The crew also needed the chance to send their pay home to their families in dire need, perhaps in distress. There were the unseen tears, the unheard mutterings, the curses, and cries of those who were suffering, because they were the victims of the sins of others.

The master gave in to "the call of the master" over the objections of the distinguished representatives from the office. What caused it? I still do not know. I like to think that it was the Spirit of God, who firmly grabbed this man in his soul and set him on a new course. I have reasons to believe that I was right about this:

The ship did stay overnight. The money appeared the following day. The crew received time to go to the banks. Twenty-seven coats were obtained and delivered. Three men stayed behind in the hospital, two of them with tuberculosis. Sacks of rice and an assortment of other supplies were brought on board. And so, the M.V. Borboros left for the Great Lakes to deliver a cargo of "great" value (I still don't know what it was) and next for the Lake Head to pick up a load of grain, which fortunately, always needs to be prefaced by fumigation.

The crew returned to work in oversized winter coats and stood by, night and day through one of the most grueling voyages on blizzard covered lakes and stifling cold channels. A most harrowing voyage it was!

We went by every ship in port the day before Christmas, in order to invite the seafarers to our Christmas Eve chapel service and celebration, in honor of the birth of our LORD. I was pleasantly surprised, when I vaguely could make out the contours of the M.V. "Borboros" returning from her voyage on the great Lakes fully eight days overtime. Carefully negotiating the harbor in a blinding snowstorm she tied up, again at suppertime, about two miles away from the Seafarers Centre. An invitation to the crew to come to our Christmas Eve Service was not necessary, because almost every one of them came rushing off the ship to attend. Roman Catholic Filipinos, Indian Hindus, Egyptian, and Pakistani Muslims, Orthodox Greeks, and some who knew no God, all streamed into the chapel. There we sang of the birth of the Savior and heard once again the ever thrilling story as told in Luke 2.

It was during the second lesson of Matthew 1, where it says: "…and you shall call his name Jesus for he shall save his people from their sins" (Matt.1:21), that the throng of people in our chapel was slightly disturbed. Two bent figures, huddled in heavy snow-covered overcoats, made their way to a seat in the back.

They were the captain and the chief engineer of the M.V. "Borboros" who had walked two miles through a blizzard to be in attendance at our Christmas Eve Service. They were the last two people on earth I expected to see in the Chapel.

After the service, the captain sat down among the large group of seafarers from the M.V. Borboros. The catering staff and deckhands were ready to enter into a new relationship with their master, a relationship of understanding and trust, which only the Spirit of Jesus Christ could have brought about. It was a long Christmas Eve, in which much was said, many hands were shaken and in which a new spirit started to reign. It was a moving scene: A new humanity had taken hold of a man, who had been driven by inhuman forces.

I stood by, observing that mysterious hierarchical relationship, that prevails on board of ships in which the master is the supreme commander, yet is meant to be at the same time a father for those under him, many of whom hail from countries where lines of authority are clearly understood. I noticed how this relationship was newly cemented on the basis of the directions of God. I had to think once again of the prophet Malachi who concluded the Old Testament with that beautiful sentence …"He will turn the hearts of the fathers to the children, and the hearts of the children to their fathers…" (Mal. 4:6).

CHRISTMAS PARCELS
FOR SEAFARERS

It seems to be the custom of many people to remember the less fortunate with a small gift around Christmas time. In churches there are "Angel trees" to remember the children of prisoners. Groups of motorcyclists make an impressive tour through certain cities to collect toys for the less fortunate children. Hospitalized people, young and old are remembered, as are the prisoners, and those who are homeless.

These expressions of love may well be rooted in the very essence of Christmas: God gave the gift of his own Son for the salvation of all those who come to him in faith. That is, of course, a miraculous display of love. In no other religion, except in Christianity, do we see God coming down to earth, in human form. All our expressions of love for the neighbor may well be a reflection of this divine display. Theologically, and in terms of faith in the Christ of Christmas, many people may be off track, but their sharing of gifts with others remains a beautiful display.

The Ministry to Seafarers has had the tradition of presenting Christmas parcels for nearly two hundred years. When we had set up our Seafarers Centre in Montreal, I continued that tradition. Primarily cargo ships came to the port at that time. The number of seafarers on them was limited to, at the most, sixty people. It was my conviction that we should utilize this program as a means to witness to the birth of Christ.

Churches, societies, youth groups, and individuals were mobilized to participate in preparing the Christmas parcels with at least one item of some value, such as after- shaving cream, a toque, or a pair of gloves, or a scarf. The winter season in and around the Great lakes, where most of the vessels had to go before Christmas, certainly demanded some warm clothing. Some ships might sail to cold ports in Northern Europe around that time. A few little items such as writing paper, candy, or some toilet articles were usually added and were most welcome since many seafarers were not able to go ashore to make purchases.

We suggested that people put their gifts in shoeboxes in order to equalize the size for each recipient. We asked them to include a card or a letter with a little message explaining the meaning of Christmas and how they celebrated it. People would be curious about our manner of celebrating. I also suggested that in their letter they might wish to say that they would offer prayers during Christmas for the recipient of the parcel, even though totally unknown to them, and for his family, from which the seafarers were separated, not only during Christmas, but for months on end.

It is significant for anyone to hear that you are saying prayers for him or her. In this way it is not threatening, since you are thousands of miles away, but you are reminding them, that geographical distance can easily be bridged with prayer. When I pray to God, He is right there. If I incorporate a distant "friend," he is also incorporated despite the distance separating me from him. That is an inspiration to the recipient.

It would also inspire the sender to become meaningfully involved with someone they had never met and most likely would never meet. I concluded my message by reminding them that they might wish to enclose their complete mailing address. The avenue for a "link-up" would then be open.

This of course was all in the days before the invention of e-mail. Many seafarers developed a contact with the people from whom they received a Christmas gift. That contact, in a number of instances, lasted for years. Only the LORD knows what kind of influence it has had on either party. Most ships have crew members from many different nations.

The master of the ship would customarily feel obliged to give a little Christmas speech and then hand out the gifts. I thought I could be of help in this, so I asked the master, "Is it true that you give a little speech at the Christmas dinner?" Several captains told me that having to give the speech was the worst part of the Christmas celebration. I would then say, "I can understand that. Your business is to run a ship, to give orders, and to maintain the safety of the vessel. That is what you were trained for, not for giving speeches." "Exactly, giving speeches is your business, not ours," they would answer. I construed that as one of the key openings to bring the gospel of our LORD Jesus Christ into this ceremony of giving out Christmas parcels.

I would say, "I understand, so may I offer some help in this?" They would always reply, "Thank you. That would be excellent." I then offered to write a brief speech which the captain could read with the simple introduction: "I have here a letter from the Padre you all met in Montreal. I would like to read it to you, before I hand out the parcels he has left for us." My brief one or two page letter told the Christmas story as recorded in Matthew chapters 1, 2, 3, and in Luke 2.

I figured that most people, who listened to my letter, would not have the foggiest notion what it says in either Matthew or in Luke. I therefore mentioned in the letter that they might wish to double check these sections in the Bible. For good measure, I would insert a couple of other significant passages, which would clarify salvation.

I made it a point to contact every master well before the ship sailed in order to obtain the exact nationalities of his crew members. I then bought Bibles or New Testaments in the language of every individual on board. I would ask the master to present these Bibles at the time of his speech, prior to his presentation of the Christmas parcels. These Bibles and New Testaments were, in many cases, an extremely welcome gift.

I will never forget the Egyptian Muslim engineer who returned to Montreal a few months later and reported, "I followed the procedure of the distribution of the Bibles carefully, figuring that it would not be so difficult to present an English Bible or a Spanish one or even a Dutch one, but I did not expect the captain to have an Arabic Bible. After all, that is in a totally different script. I was afraid I might be passed by, not only because of the script of an Arabic Bible, but also because I was the only Muslim on board. But then, the master handed me a Bible in Arabic. I couldn't believe my eyes, I was so surprised! The captain told us, that the letter was written by you. Do you still have a copy of it, because in that letter you mentioned some specific sections in the Bible?" The next day I brought him the letter.

On some ships the master, after having read the letter, posted it on the notice board. The wife of a British officer, whom I met later on a sister ship where the distribution of Christmas parcels came up in the conversation, expressed her great surprise. "Here we were in Montreal and you came on board with these parcels, prepared by people from all kinds of different cities in Canada. These people didn't know us from Adam, yet they had prepared such a lovely parcel. It was unbelievable."

On Polish and Soviet ships there were also girls in service. Some wives of officers might be on board as well, especially around Christmas time. Thus, we developed the strategy to add some parcels for women. We asked the people to clearly mark the wrapped parcels which were for the ladies. It did not always work out that way. One seaman told us he had received a very nice box with a pair of nylons and some facial powder as well as a tiny bottle of perfume. Fortunately, he was married, so he gave it to his wife, but when he opened the parcel at the Christmas party, the entire crew fell apart in hilarious laughter. Most people were aware of the spirit of this entire project.

We collected annually about two thousand Christmas parcels and started to distribute them in early November when we knew that during Christmas, the ship would be at sea. One master gave us a touching testimony in his letter in which he stated that they were in the Indian Ocean, in a totally desolate part of the world. His crew had become depressed. They felt utterly forsaken in this lonely and distant part of the ocean at Christmas time far away from their families.

They had a hard time being joyful, despite the hymn customarily sung at Christmas time: "Joyful all ye nations rise, join the triumph of the skies; with the angelic host proclaim: Christ is born in Bethlehem." But then each seaman received a parcel, lovingly prepared, especially for him. Someone cared! Their depression turned into joy!

The chief steward on an English ship was charged with the distribution of the parcels. He wrote:

> "I organized a raffle. I am very happy, not only did I receive a parcel, but most importantly, I knew that it had been prepared by people who have a good heart who gave their compassion, their prayers, and their time to care for us at sea. But the very best was the Bible, the Word of God—I will do my best to keep up reading the Bible and to pray. Thank you very much! More power to the Seafarers Centre. May God bless you always."

An Indonesian second officer put his appreciation in simple terms and wrote: "Thank you for the Christmas gift, the card, the letter, and especially the Indonesian Bible. In fact, the Bible was the most wonderful gift."

The captain of another huge freighter looked at it in a different way in his letter:

> "During the old days, the seamen did not belong to the possessive part of society, and therefore, for the well being of the people at sea, many charity funds were founded. Fortunately, these days are over, but another lack of feeling comfortable came into place. Nowadays the shipping industry is so tremendously capital intensive that the human parts in it are also used as purely capital good or tool. The industry needs your physical strength, your hands, sometimes your brain, *but is absolutely not interested in your spirit.* It is great to know that you recognize this and took a splendid initiative to do something about this problem, which belongs of course not only with the seamen. Thank you therefore so much and to greet you with a professional term: 'You are steady on good course.'"

One seaman, who did not identify his position on board, wrote: "We are sailing from storm into storm." Then he reacted to receiving the Christmas presents. "It is very nice to know that there are still some people on this planet, which is full of war, hunger and other terrible things, who are thinking of the lonely men at sea. Therefore, it was a great pleasure to receive your Christmas presents."

He continued, "I was especially pleased with the Bible, not because I am a religious man, but by reading it, it becomes easier to understand why people, who are religious, do the things they do and think the things they think. If all people would try to find out something of the backgrounds of other men's behavior, then there would be a lot more of understanding in this world, and there might be less hate and sadness. Therefore I would like to thank you very much and wish you a very Happy New Year and years thereafter."

The chief officer of an American freighter drove the importance of gift giving home to me in no uncertain terms. I recognized the ship, since it had been here the previous year at more or less the same time. It then had forty-five seafarers on board, all Americans, as well as twelve passengers. We had many Christmas presents and supplied this ship, including the passengers, with a Bible and a present.

Now, one year later, this ship was passing through Montreal again. A few seafarers were on board the previous year, but most of the others had been replaced by a relief crew. I visited the ship, but since we did not have too many parcels this year, and I was scheduled to supply a ship from Bangladesh located at the oil docks, I felt I should give priority to them, because they were living in a state of what could be called poverty on board.

Thus, I just visited the American freighter and briefly ministered to passengers and crew, but I did not mention Christmas presents to anyone. When I was ready to leave, I was caught. The chief officer spotted me, when I passed his window. He rushed out and called me in a loud voice yelling, "No Christmas presents, Padre?"

I responded apologetically with the weak statement, "I am running short of parcels, so I thought I'll pass you—rich Americans—by, and give preference to the ship from Bangladesh." I figured that would convince him that we sometimes have to set priorities, but I had misjudged him. He politely, but firmly, said: "Would you be kind enough to come into my office for a moment, Padre?"

I stepped inside and recognized his neat, well equipped office. But then it flashed through my mind. "I can see a difference, but of course this is an American freighter." I also recognized the place, because last year's Christmas parcels had then been deposited in this office.

The chief officer offered me a chair and then did something that made me think *there is something more serious going on here.* He closed his door. No chief officer on any ship ever closes his office door. He is the man who, day and night, is always approachable with an open door. Business could then be expedited conveniently. All kinds of people regularly walked in to settle whatever it was pertaining to the loading of the ship, inspectors, ships chandlers, merchants, or other officers. They had to be in contact with the key person on board: The chief officer.

After closing the door he walked behind his desk, sat down and said in a soft voice, "Did I hear you say, 'I passed by these rich Americans?'" I thought I had offended him. I said, "In comparison to the ship from Bangladesh, and in connection with the distribution of Christmas parcels, of which I have only a few left, I did say 'you rich Americans.' I apologize; I should not have said that."

He leaned back, looked me straight in the eye and said: "Padre, you supplied us with Christmas parcels last year, but you were not on board when we handed them out. I wish you would have been there. It was the first time that my crew and even the few passengers on board experienced this. They were overwhelmed. You should have seen their faces. I mean the crew. Some of these men are on board because they are escaping the land not because they like sailing on a freighter. Their marriage fell apart. They were rejected at home. They could not keep a job ashore. They have no relationship, no bond, no contact, and no fellowship with anyone."

He went on, "When some of them received their parcel, they just could not stay with the party. They started to choke up, trying to keep their tears back and disappeared into their cabin. When I saw them a bit later, I discovered they had opened up those lovely parcels of valuable and meaningful gifts, had spread them out on their little desks, including the Bible. They were sitting there stunned, wiping their faces with Kleenex. Grown men, Padre, with cropped up emotions because they looked at these gifts and were reminded of what is missing in their lives. They saw love in a bloody tube of toothpaste and in a box of peanuts. They had set up a card from somebody they had never heard of, the only card they would get for Christmas."

He concluded with the following, "And there was a Bible; imagine, what is it a ten-dollar Bible? Your people did not merely give them a Christmas parcel. They gave them their heart. So, Padre, I don't care how many other ships you must still serve, and I don't know if you have any presents left at all, but do me a pleasure: Go back to your place and get me forty-seven parcels for our ship. I don't care what you put in them. For my part you wrap up a toothpick! *But don't forget us.*"

Let me finish with this very special letter from a Korean captain...

"Dear Sir:

I, master of M.V. Kalato, Captain Kim Ton Man deeply appreciated to your kindness, for Christmas presents. We arrived in Barcelona, Spain, on the 21st Dec. and had the Christmas Eve at there.

I gave to all crew presents which you gave me at Montreal. Of cause, I kept the present boxes as it was, didn't opened myself before Christmas as your advices. When they receipt it at Christmas Eve, all crew surprised for beautiful box to each others, and many kind of precious, necessary goods for them.

But your presents were 21 boxes only for 22 crew, and I could not had your present.

I had received New Testament and I had read on board all.

This is a big event in my history, because it's first time for me.

I was impressed deeply by the Bible, and my brain-work will be effected by it very much.

So I would say to you 'Thank you very much.' Now we are coming to Japan, via Baltimore, Panama and Los Angeles with soybeans.

Will be arrive at Nagoya Japan on 22 March. In this chance many crew will be repatriated to home for vacation, me too.

Before leave M.V. Kalato I recalled your kindness and your friend ships.

Always we had a glumly Christmas but we had a delightful Christmas on 24 December of this year, and it was first time receiving Christmas presents.

All crew had a quiet night and listened history of Christmas by me. I said to crew: 'Now I give you a good Christmas presents for minister of the chaplain to seamen in Montreal, Canada' and explained all about history of Christmas and told them about that.

All crew listened to my speak devoutly.

My speech was done very smoothly and very good unusually, just like you coaching from my back.

We had a good and significant Christmas Eve. Therefore, I think, I will never for-get your kindness everylastingly on future Christmas, and all crew will be same to me.

Thank you very much,
Yours respectfully

Captain Kim Ton Man
Master of M.V. Kalato"

THE LAST RITES

In the Roman Catholic tradition, this expression refers to a formal ceremonial administration to a person nearing death. Rarely is this administration delivered well before death when people appear to be full of life.

The expression came to my attention when I approached a cargo ship located at the grain pier. The ship was almost filled to the brim with grain for some country in the Middle East. So it was headed on a mercy mission. Starving people were eagerly awaiting the arrival of food, be it ever so minimal, due to the enormous number of people in need. Nevertheless, even a small amount would be of help to thousands of people who would become the recipients of this ship's donation by a rich Western country.

The grain elevator was wrapped in a thick cloud of dust as it spouted the cargo vessel full with its riches. I had a hard time finding my way to the gang plank. As I was close to it I noticed one of the longshoreman seated on a short pillar. He had the job of adjusting the grain bins slightly left or right to ascertain that the grain would be evenly divided into the cargo hold of the ship. He had just made a little adjustment to one of the bins and now he sat relaxing on that little pillar as I approached the ship.

What struck me was his greeting. People often greet me with a little association of their anticipation of my duties…"Are you going to marry someone?" or "Do you have to bring a shocking announcement?" Sometimes they are a bit more mundane and ask, "Are you going to have lunch on the ship?" So I am used to an accompanying remark with their "Hello." But this chap used an expression that slightly startled me. He asked, "Are you going to administer the last rites on board?"

My first thought was, *Why did he ask that?* He provided the answer himself almost immediately, "Look at that ship; it is an old rusted crate. It will never make the crossing of the North Atlantic. I was on board earlier this morning, and I decided I would never want to sail on this one. So you better go on board and do something."

What I was scheduled to do, according to his opinion, had already been expressed…administer the last rites.

As I made my way through the clouds of dust and entered the area where staff and crew could be found, I somehow felt that the longshoreman had made a fairly accurate assessment. The ship was rusty, in ill repair, not maintained at all, and I found it to be exceptionally deep in the water, but who am I to make a judgment about the condition of the ship, of any ship for that matter. If it was seaworthy and approved by the authorities to sail, it would sail.

The captain was Eastern European, The Crew represented a variety of nationalities, mostly far Eastern, Indonesian, Thai, Philippine, Burmese, as well as some people from the Middle East from Iran and Egypt.

They were an exceptionally courteous and gracious group, headed by a very kind and affable captain.

After I had made the customary initial contact with the captain and with many of the Crew members, several of them including the captain, urged me to perform a short religious service with prayers. It was not a Sunday, neither was it a day of significance on the

Christian calendar. In this assembly, there were Roman Catholic, Eastern Orthodox, and Protestant Christians, besides some Hindu and Islamic people. Yet they all supported the request to have me offer prayers and conduct a brief service of worship.

In almost all instances on board *I* would be the one to suggest prayers or a Christian worship service. Here the tables were turned. *They* expressly asked *me*. I was reminded of the remark of the longshoreman, suggesting a service of the Last Rites, as I listened to the request of the master and Crew on board.

Why did they ask me? Did they have a premonition? Did they not trust their very own ship on which they all had spent many months sailing across the oceans? Were they now afraid? Why would they be afraid? What had happened? Had they recently experienced a wild ocean coming to port? I realized that I had better pay attention to their anxieties. They had approached me with a specific request … Offer prayers and conduct a Service of Worship.

So we scheduled the time at shortly before dinner when all of the crew could be in attendance. We gathered in the rather dilapidated crew mess-room with broken chairs and damaged tables. There were no decorations on the wall, no altar, no symbols of any liturgical association. We just sat there all together as human beings, as brothers, despite our religious backgrounds, customs, and orientations.

Strangely, I had never felt as close to my congregational members as on this day. There they sat in their shabby clothes. In their hasty attempts to make themselves a bit more presentable, they had not succeeded to remove all the dust out of their hair. But there they sat in utter silence and with undivided attention, thinking, *God in heaven, we don't even know why we want to pray, but we are doing it, because deep down in our bones we sense that we need you. And we might as well be frank about it … we are afraid.*

I sensed their fear and anxiety and in light of that I became aware that this should not be an ordinary Service of Worship. Somehow we were all aware that we were touching upon something that could not be defined or expressed, but was an awful reality. Who knows, but we might indeed not make it? Despite the fact that almost everyone around the tables was in the spring of their lives the thought of a sudden end to it could not be easily digested. So, they all kept smiling, be it ever so slightly.

I did not preach in the traditional sense. I spoke very personally to everyone present and encouraged each one with the assurance that in Christ Jesus, we have life everlasting. That is of course the very heart of the Christian religion and it is applicable to every human being who will acknowledge Jesus Christ as LORD and Savior. There is also a tremendous consolation in the fact that through Christ Jesus we become acceptable to God and as a result have therefore an undeniable hope both in life and in death.

I then offered prayers. Most of the audience remained seated, but two or three of them rose to their feet and I noticed one who sank to his knees.

It was a deeply emotional scene. In their very expression of respect they showed their awareness that we were in the presence of the living God.

So I expressed to God our anxiety and fears, our insecurities, our worries.

I rehearsed what everyone deep down in his heart already knew, that we had no idea how this trip would develop, but I asked for the presence and nearness of God to each one of us, and also for the protection of the ship in its mercy mission to the hungry.

I remembered their wives, their children, their families, wherever they would be, that they all might be encapsulated in the hand of God. I concluded with the acknowledgement that we were encouraged in the assurance that no matter what comes about in our lives we would be safe with our LORD God who had journeyed with us each and every day up to this very point.

I then concluded my prayer with the LORD's Prayer.

A few attendants joined me in English and some in their own language ever so softly. I extended the blessing of God to each person in the room. We all sensed the presence of God in our midst.

The master on behalf of the members of his crew expressed sincere thanks, and I returned through the heavily dust-clouded air to the gangway, fittingly waved out by a few crew members. The longshoreman was no longer on duty and only one bin in the very front of the ship was still spouting grain. The ship was just about totally filled. That same night she left. It takes about twenty-four hours for a ship to reach the open ocean.

> *Five days later she was overwhelmed by the fury of the seas and sank.*
> *The Master, every Officer and all members of the Crew drowned.*
> *No one survived.*

May God have mercy on them all! May God extend his grace and consolation to their wives, their children, their fathers and mothers, their entire families!

THE MIRACLE

It is undeniable that we are not always able to discern the workings of the Spirit of God. Why would some people be touched mysteriously and others not at all. That tells us that God is in charge in the lives of every one of us and at his time and according to his purpose, he touches people's hearts.

In that process others are frequently involved as his messengers.

Sun Kae Ton was a young engineer on a Korean cargo ship. The ship had a contract that brought her almost every year to the Great Lakes before going down to the Gulf area of the USA. When I visited the ship, one December day, I met most of the crew, but we met only briefly and Sun Kae did not stand out either in my mind or in appearance.

The ship was scheduled to be traveling to Europe. At Christmas, she could be expected to be wrestling with the North Atlantic, a rough ocean especially during the winter. I had prepared a set of Christmas parcels all nicely wrapped and I had added a copy of the Korean Bible for every person on board. As always, I had no idea who would be touched by that book and who would leave it untouched or possibly dispose of it.

A fourteen-year-old-girl from the neighborhood of Sarnia wrote me a note that she had prepared a Christmas parcel and had included a little booklet of prayers by Watchman Nee. Her parcel ended up in the hands of Sun Kae, the second engineer, who expressed his sincere thanks and proposed to meet her in the spring in Sarnia. When his ship returned in the spring, she was invited on board with her parents. There they met Sun Kae and following an elaborate Korean dinner, she received a beautiful Japanese-dressed doll in a glass case.

They were well received by the master and by the entire compliment of seafarers on board and were requested to explain the motivation of the distribution of Christmas parcels which most of the attendants had received. They had never experienced anything like it. What impressed them was the fact that this was a program of the Christian church. Some did not believe at all. Others adhered to some Buddhist form of belief.

What fascinated her was the enthusiasm of Sun Kae about both the Bible he had received and the booklet of Watchman Nee which she had included.

There were thirty-two Korean people on that ship, yet one of them got singled out to the point that we became witnesses to the miracle of the working of the Spirit of God in his heart. In fact, Sun Kae expressed that he had been so touched by the message of the Bible that he felt compelled to come to the acknowledgement of Jesus Christ as his LORD and Savior. That miraculous matter so frequently mentioned in the church and expressed by people whose heart the Spirit of God has touched brought about a total change in the life of Sun Kae.

Possibly others on that ship may have been touched in a similar manner, but it was not brought to our attention.

About half a year later, I had an international meeting of chaplains to Seafarers in Houston, TX. I fondly recall that visit since one of the Roman Catholic chaplains had asked me to speak at the Chapel of a large Catholic School. In fact, he had invited me to stay overnight at his residence, a huge structure, spacious with a great variety of rooms and halls. I felt as if I had ended up in a kind of palace. After I had addressed the school and had challenged the young people to commit their lives to Christ Jesus and to spend their lives in dedication and service to Him, I spoke to my friend, the Roman Catholic chaplain, thanking him for the opportunity to speak to the students.

I then expressed my surprise at the lavish residence, he as a Catholic had been supplied with, to which he simply replied, "You Protestants may have the better halves, but we have the better quarters."

In the port of Houston, I discovered, rather surprisingly, the very ship on which Sun Kae sailed. So I made it a point to visit that ship. When I met Sun Kae I was thrilled by what he told me. He assumed that I knew the girl who had prepared his Christmas gift. So he propelled me to the telephone, called her and told her that the pastor who had presented the Bibles to his ship was standing next to him. He then turned around and said, "Since I have found Jesus Christ I want you to know that I have made arrangements with a Christian pastor to baptize me on October 4, when I expect to be back home."

Korea is a far away country and a flight to Korea would be too expensive, preventing us from flying out to attend the ceremony. But once again the ceremony was characterized by Angels praising God for this officer who had come to acknowledge Jesus Christ as his LORD and Savior.

The Angels were on overtime, because seven months later I got a letter from Sun Kae informing me that he had been speaking to his brother about what he had experienced himself. That had touched his brother to the point that he also committed his life to the LORD Jesus Christ.

His parents were now the only ones who had not as yet come to a profession of faith. Yet Sun Kae was making it a point to speak to his parents, who were greatly impressed by the change that had come about in their son's life.

The Angels were celebrating again, this time for Sun Kae's brother. They stayed at attention, because Sun Kae wrote me that he had found a Christian girl whom he planned to marry.

But the letter had one additional sentence that was genuinely moving: He felt that since God had called him into his light and had brought him into contact with a Christian girl, he wanted to devote his life to the ministry and so he had applied to a Seminary.

Imagine, a Christmas package with a bottle of after-shave lotion, a toothbrush, a roll of candy, some writing paper, the Bible, and Watchman Nee's booklet about prayer, prepared by a young girl who did not know where her parcel would end up, brought about a miraculous change in the life of an Engineer.

"I tell you, open your eyes and look at the fields, they are ripe for harvest" (John 4:35).

HER MAJESTY'S YACHT

Security for Her Majesty's yacht Britannia was so tight that even the Marine Reporting Service had received instructions not to give out information on the precise location of the yacht as she steamed up the St. Lawrence River.

The yacht was occupied by Her Majesty and some members of the Royal Family who had come to attend the Olympic Games in Montreal. When the yacht did arrive and was about to berth at the pier, reserved for visiting foreign and Canadian vessels, patrolling RCMP officers immediately took to some rubber boats and kept circling the yacht and her escort destroyer. This would prevent anyone from approaching the yacht by water.

On land, a larger than normal area had been cordoned off. Even though the National Harbours Board Police took part in the control at the gate, the Royal Canadian Mounted Police were in charge. As a chaplain of the Port of Montreal, I felt it to be my duty to extend my services to this vessel as well as to any other vessel coming to the port.

About six months prior to the arrival of the yacht, I had come into contact with the RCMP. At that time I had come off one of the Soviet ships. Ever since they came to Canada, I considered it my task to visit them especially.

Their political orientation was, of course, of a totally different order from the one we have in our democratic society. My concern was to bring them into contact with the Christ in one way or another. At that time their minds had been closed for seventy years to any form of infiltration of the gospel or of the church.

So I limited myself to a methodology that historically breaks all barriers. I came on board with a small Folk-singing group from our church for a little folk concert on Sunday nights. Music crosses all borders and barriers. During the week I would then follow up to make arrangements for another concert or to thank them for having so courteously received us.

As they always overloaded us with communistic propaganda literature, I would feel justified to bring along what was close to our hearts, albeit duly covered up, since there was not only the Political Commissar on board, functioning as the spiritual police, but it was well known of course that there were all kinds of unidentified Commissars on every one of their ships.

One Tuesday, I had visited one of the Soviet ships and driven off. Before I exited the gate at the Harbor I noticed that a car was following me very closely. We all sped along on the eighteen kilometer waterfront which is actually a private road on Harbor property.

I noticed a car in front of me slowing down. The car from the back suddenly pulled up beside me, and the driver motioned me to stop. I had no idea who these people were, who had now boxed me in. In those days I had not been fed the current TV dramas to get any understanding of being "blocked in," although I did think that they might possibly be a group of robbers.

The thought did not bother me that much. I had hardly any money, but I could offer them a copy of the Bible. They could even take a box full of Bibles for distribution among other robbers. I would then suggest that they read 1 John 2:15–17. There you find a whole sermon containing sin, salvation, and service in three little sentences. In abbreviated form that would be SSS. I could suggest that might lead to SOS.

So I stopped, and four men came out and surrounded me when I got out of my car. They showed me their medallions, shiny identification badges. They all said almost in chorus, "We are from the RCMP." I felt good about this: The RCMP on my tail. I must be important. Having just come off a Soviet ship, however, I was a bit suspicious and attempted to examine them. They were very cooperative and answered all my questions. Then they said that they had watched me, visiting Soviet ships, for a number of months already. I was surprised that they had "spied" on me for such a long period of time.

They even indicated that they had seen us go on board with the folk singing group. Now they had just one favor to ask, "If I would see 'something unusual' would I be kind enough to inform them?" After all the safety of the country was their motivation, so they did their job well. As a Canadian Citizen, and proud of my country, I complied. Fortunately I never detected anything unusual.

I also had a question for them: Her Majesty's yacht would arrive some months later. Would they be kind enough to give me clearance to visit the yacht? After all, I am a padre on the waterfront. The port is my parish. I would want to visit the seafarers on every ship in my parish. That has been my philosophy during my entire ministry. God had put me in this particular port, so it is my assignment to do the job thoroughly.

The RCMP stated that they were not in a position to grant that request. They suggested I make my request known to the Chief of Staff at their Head Office in Montreal. The Chief of Staff appeared to be sensitive to the needs of the seafarers. He gave clearance.

When I arrived at the gate where the yacht was located one National Harbours Board Policeman was moved to extend to me, with a smile, words of apology and consolation. We knew each other. For years the police had been familiar with my roaming around on National Harbor property. "Padre," he said, "this time it is beyond our control. The RCMP is in charge here. If they would have left it to us I would have said, 'Of course, Padre, you are part of the National Harbours Board's 'furniture,' so get on board,' but we have no authority here."

I thanked him for his kind words. I reminded him that if I happen to be part of their "furniture" to be sure to make it a lectern or a pulpit, but not a chair or a couch. I want to preach. My friend came back with the simple answer, "Whenever you open your mouth you are preaching, but today your preaching won't help much. I cannot give you permission to get on the yacht." I suggested to him that in my preaching I always encourage my hearers to check "the records in the Book." "So please," I said, "be kind enough to check your book with the names of the people who are permitted by the RCMP to board."

Even though we had known each other for years, he had to ask my name. Throughout my life on board and in harbors, my difficult name has been a problem. So I have become known simply as "The Reverend," "Padre," or "Father."

I have always had to swallow when they use that last expression, even though I am well aware that it comes out of the Roman Catholic Church, but I remember what Jesus tells us in Matthew 23:9 when someone did use that term, "And do not call anyone on earth 'father' for you have one Father and he is in heaven." I realize that I could not say that to any seafarer, for he would look at me and at my clerical shirt and at my Bible, and he would think: What is the matter with you? Are you a man of God? Or are you representing some curious cult I should stay away from?

He checked the list, called on the junior RCMP officer to confirm it, returned to me, looking somewhat sheepish, and said, "You are on the list." He then opened the gate and I was free to drive to one of the world's most elegant and well-kept ships, her Majesty's yacht.

The royal yacht was actually a mini cruise ship with some very special features. I approached the admiral. The officers, staff, and crew were all British and I felt it would be appropriate to present every member of the staff with a copy of the Olympic edition of the New Testament, in the language of today.

I had discovered in my years on the waterfront that particularly many British people seemed to have been estranged from the Scriptures in the traditional King James Version. So a highly modernized translation could well function as a breath of fresh air. The Bible League had prepared a magnificent edition with a brief message on the back cover for all the visitors attending the Olympic Games. At my request they had shipped me one thousand copies. I had handed out hundreds of copies already. I thought I had about seventy-five copies left in my office which, in my estimation, would be sufficient for the staff of the yacht.

The admiral, whom I presented with a sample copy, greeted my offer most positively. He asked me to make arrangements of delivery with the coxswain. The coxswain, who had received the confirmation by telephone from the admiral, informed me that delivery should be made by 2:30 p.m. He said, "Her Majesty is punctual. So I do not mean 2:31p.m." His staff would be on standby. As I was about to leave, I suddenly turned around and asked him how many officers, staff, and crew members there were on board. He replied, "Three hundred and twenty-four." It blew me away. By now it was noon: Delivery of three hundred and twenty-four copies had to be made by 2:30 p.m. Where on earth would I get so many copies in such a short time?

As I drove back to my office, I recalled that the organization of Evangelicals had formed a cooperative body under the name "Aide Olympique." They wanted to make the witness and ministry of the Evangelical churches more effective without highlighting individual denominations. I thought one phone call would solve my problem.

They informed me that a French Evangelical Church had been set aside as the Literature Depot. Imagine, English New Testaments in a French church. That was already a step in the right direction for a province where the relationship between the French and English could certainly stand some biblical tolerance and acceptance of each other. So I called them.... no answer! The church was on the main street of Montreal, but all the way on the East side. I drove out there and discovered that the church was locked up. A little piece of paper on the door said, "Fermer jusqu'a a 1:15 p.m." So they were out for lunch. I caught myself surveying the church, the windows, the roof, the back alley. If I would break only one window I could get in. No, that wouldn't do.

Imagine the Gazette Newspaper reporting the next day, "The Reverend caught stealing Bibles from a church." I had to trust the LORD to help me out of my dilemma. He will open the door: "Ask for it!" I found it difficult to trust the LORD while under such pressure. I prayed that the door would open. The LORD let me wait for another ten minutes. Then one of the staff members came sauntering down the street in second gear. God was surely teaching me patience. Or, was he teaching me to keep my cool?

I managed to get half a dozen big boxes of the "Olympic edition" of the New Testament. That's what it said on the outside cover. I liked the inclusion: "Olympic edition." It reminds me of the remarks of Paul when he challenges us to "run the race" for Christ and reminded us that all of us are in that race and exhorts us to run for the prize (1 Corinthians 9:24–"Do you not know that in a race all the runners run, but only one gets the prize? Run in such a way as to get the prize.").

As soon as I had reached my office again, I composed a letter to the admiral in charge of the yacht, informing him that on the occasion of Her Majesty's visit to Montreal in connection with the Olympic Games, I was making this presentation to him and to every yachtsman on board. I would trust that this edition might contribute to their spiritual refreshment, as I had indicated in my brief encounter with him earlier in the day.

I was running out of time. But I am reluctant to give anyone a Bible or a New Testament without some sort of guideline or direction. The Canadian Bible Society came to my help. They had a little brochure called "Where to look in the Bible" which would help anyone to find suitable passages that have bearing on special circumstances such as anxiety, grief, temptation, happiness, failure, etc.

Since most people do not have the foggiest notion where to look for anything in the Bible, I thought this might be a good brochure. They had to be neatly inserted in every copy and every copy had to be examined to make sure that it was in absolutely perfect shape. Some of them always get damaged, when they are shipped out. When the church makes a presentation it should be of the highest quality, both as to its content and as to its appearance.

The clock kept ticking. I hoped that a few seamen would be in the lounge adjacent to my office, but during the afternoon, seamen are ordinarily at work on board.

When I came out of my office I noticed, to my surprise, that three young men were lounging in some chairs. They gave the impression they were tired, and justifiably so, for they were "Aide Olympique" workers from South Carolina, North Carolina, and Georgia. They had been working all morning in French Montreal, distributing literature for an Evangelistic rally to be held later that day and they were taking a break in the lounge of the Seafarers Center.

I explained to them the concerns on my mind and I concluded by saying that I was looking for three young men. All three rose to their feet and the one from Georgia said, "Praise the LORD, you've got your three men." It was an odd thought, but as I ushered them to the Bibles, I had to think of the first part of the last verse in Jonah 1, where it says: "But the LORD provided a great fish..." Here He provided "three small ones" by comparison, but they "saved" the day.

As we loaded the last box of twenty-four boxes into my car, I noticed it was 2:20 p.m. At breakneck speed I raced down the harbor road and arrived at 2:29 p.m. at the yacht. The coxswain stood on guard with six young deck-hands, who were immaculately dressed in white uniforms.

"Right Padre," he said. "You could work on the yacht, because you are on time. Give me your car keys and please go down to the Wardroom for a drink." As I mounted the gangway, I heard him give instructions to have a copy placed on the bunk of every yachtsman in every department without delay. The wardroom was a very convenient lounge with a bar. There were perhaps fifteen off-duty officers sitting in comfortable lounge chairs, all glued to the television to stay in touch with the Olympic Games.

I had been escorted to the wardroom by a young officer, who seemed to enjoy the idea of having a chat. He offered me a drink. So I accepted orange juice. The officer serving at the bar participated actively in the discussion and seemed quite informed about the church and the religious climate in the UK. We made a serious attempt to keep our voices down, so as not to disturb those who were watching the Olympic Games.

One of the officers watching the TV seemed to get increasingly restless. He even got up and started pacing the floor behind the two of us seated at the bar. I thought he was pacing the floor because he wanted one or the other party in the Games to be winning, so I didn't interrupt him. But the scene changed rather rapidly when he suddenly stopped behind me and sort of leaned into the space at the bar between the officer and me.

He then quite forcefully asked, "Excuse me, Padre, but are you a Roman Catholic Priest or a bloody Protestant?" Taken by surprise, I looked him straight in the eye and responded, "I am a bloody Protestant." He immediately spouted, "As a man of the church, as a man of God you preach that God is love and that he is good, don't you? But if he is really so good, why does he permit all that bloodshed in Northern Ireland? Was it God's love that the British Official to Ireland had to be ruthlessly murdered by a Protestant last week? Was that not done by people who pray and believe in a loving God? Can you justify this kind of conduct of 'Christians'?"

I could not! This drama does take place under the flags of "Protestants" and "Catholics." Both words refer to the "Christian church," to Christ, to God Himself in one way or another. That pains my heart and it puts me in an awkward position when I am summoned to "justify" those who are of either denomination. I told him, "I cannot justify anyone. On behalf of all the Protestants I apologize to you." I then told him that he should not measure Christianity by the conduct of Christians, but by the Christ. That was a lame excuse of course, because I felt he really did not know Christ. Those who do not know Christ are supposed to get a glimpse of Him precisely by looking at Christians, Catholics, or Protestants.

So, I asked him to acquaint himself with the manner in which we had been created good, perfect in fact, and what disaster we had brought on ourselves through our disobedience to God and the resulting fall into sin. I tried to make clear to him that one should not place the blame on God for the chaos his creatures had brought on themselves. After all, God had not created us as puppets, as marionettes, but as individual beings, responsible for our own actions. The chaos we created finds the solution in the gospel of the forgiveness of God. The uniqueness of God is displayed in this: However disastrous we have made our lives, he will forgive us, but he also says, "Sin no more!"

He said, "How do you know God is so forgiving, in fact how do you know he exists? Have you ever met him, or seen him? I wish I could see this God you talk about, or if I could see something special, that might convince me that he does exist, like if someone would get up out of the grave, or an Angel perhaps."

I said, "Are you suggesting a real Angel?" "Yes, that's what I am suggesting," he answered, "a real ephemeral being through whom I could put my hand as it were and who would speak to me in plain English." I looked at him and said, "Well, that could be arranged. It seems to me that the Bible suggests to us that we, as Christians, are the sons and daughters of the King. The Angels are his servants. That means that they stand in our service as well. So, if you insist on seeing an Angel, let's get a fairly well known one. I suggest Gabriel. He is known by name. He has been on a number of missions to ordinary people, so I personally do not see any difficulties. But, will it really convince you permanently?"

"Absolutely," he said pointedly, and then he added, "It would not only make me believe, but the rest of them here would believe as well." That "rest" I discovered had by now grown to about two dozen people whose interest for the Olympic Games had suddenly waned for they were all looking in our direction, half suspecting that we were going to pull it off. An Angel would appear in all reality and they were going to be in on it.

"Let's think this thing through before we start," I said. "We want to know exactly what we are doing. I request the appearance of an Angel. Where? Here in this wardroom? How many people can this room hold? Forty, fifty maybe? Where does that leave the rest of the crew? How many people are on board?" He didn't know the answer and just took a stab at it; "A hundred maybe. Perhaps a hundred and fifty."

I said, "I've got bad news for you. There are three hundred and twenty-four on board. You cannot get them into the wardroom. Are we going out there and report to them after we have had the appearance of the Angel? Would they believe what we told them? Something else, are you married?"

"Yes, I am," he replied.

I continued, "You'll be home in a few weeks and you'll report to your wife about your trip to Montreal and to the Olympic Games. You tell her that the Padre came on board with someone else: 'No, not with his wife. He came with the Angel Gabriel!'"

"How is she going to react to that? She is going to ask, 'He came with an Angel? The Padre was on board with whom?' And if you say it again, there is going to be a little smile around her lips. She isn't going to buy that one. She might even ask you if you have been in a pub after you came off the airplane."

I asked him, "What about you? If you would come back to Montreal in a few months, or in a year, perhaps on another ship and we should meet again, would you at that time still be convinced that you saw an Angel? I'll go a step further. Suppose you are facing some severe trials that rock your life, would a vision of an Angel now be of help then?"

I sensed that he was weakening. I hoped that the other two dozen people, who had been following this discussion from a distance, would also have become more uncertain. "You were convinced that God exists and that he is real because you saw that Angel in Montreal. Three years from now you might suddenly be kicked out of the Navy because they discovered you have cancer. Or you are down in South America and you receive some really bad news from your wife and you cannot even get off the ship. Do you then still believe in this God, in whom you had put your trust after you saw that Angel in Montreal? And that he would help you face up to the terrible blow in your life? Or will you come back with the same question, 'Is this the loving, merciful, and forgiving God who let me see a real Angel in Montreal to convince me?'"

I went on; "Face it! You need more than a one time vision. What you need is a continuous support, a steady assurance under all circumstances! Every time you cave in, you need to know that God has not abandoned you. Despite the overwhelming odds we see round about us, you want to see a light at the end of the tunnel. You want to know that there is hope. You cannot expect that Gabriel could start flying down to see you, every time you face a crisis. He'd be on overtime."

I could almost "see" him think and weigh the difficulties of convincing the people back home, the rest of the crew, and himself six months down the road. The "excitement" of seeing an angel seemed to slowly evaporate. It reminded me of the shepherds at the birth of Christ. "Not one shepherd said, 'I'd better go home first and tell my wife that I saw an angel. Will you look after my sheep for a while?' No, the shepherds reacted to *what* was said, not to the appearance of the Angel. Therefore God has put it in 'black and white' for everyone to read again and again."

My friend reacted; "What are you talking about, black and white? Oh, I get it; you are talking about the Bible, right?" I said, "Right on! No mistaken identity, always accessible, his own Word in plain English, to be applied to our individual situations." "I figured you would get around to the Bible, Padre, but that book is written in such a way that no one can understand it and it's not in plain

English. It would be nice if it had been written in a language I could understand."

I replied, "Listen, the Bible has been put into plain, straight forward English." He exclaimed, "It would be nice if I had a copy of it!" I responded, "I have good news for you: There is a copy lying on your bed in your cabin right now!" He laughed and said: "You are joking. You are saying this because you want me to believe the Bible, right?" "That above all," I replied, "but I am saying it because it is a fact. Check it out and see if I am speaking the truth."

He laughed again, a bit louder. Then he got up, and allowing room for a "miracle" in his own heart, as well as in his cabin, he walked out of the Wardroom. At the door, he turned around and said, "All right, Padre, I'll believe it when I see it!" A few minutes later he returned with the Bible in today's language in his hand, looking somewhat embarrassed. A spirited discussion followed!

OUR DESTINATION

Only once during the last twenty years since we have specialized our ministerial outreach to officers, staff, and crew of cruise ships, did I take a cruise without my wife Trudy. She is a former secondary school teacher and a gifted counselor. Her interaction with seafarers has, at all times, been highly effective and much appreciated.

I honored a request to go back to sea even though we had just taken an extended cruise together on another ship. The ship, which I sailed on without her, had a distinct charm and a significant history.

While standing in line in the port terminal with other members of staff scheduled to board, I struck up a conversation with a young girl who happened to be the manager of the casino. It was a new contract for her. She was somewhat surprised that I, as a clergy-man, would sail along. She had never met a clergyman during any previous voyages. I explained that on most ships, if there was a chaplain on board, he might have received instructions not to come into the casino.

I mentioned that on board, I functioned not merely as a chaplain for passengers but also for officers, staff, and crew since I am chap-lain of the International Ministry to Seafarers. I assured her that I would come into the casino. After all, there would be times when the attendants in the casino, although on duty, would have vacant time such as while passengers were attending the evening show in the Grand Lounge or theater. I added that I would come only if she gave me permission. I guess she liked that, because it prompted her to say, "Reverend, you are welcome any time." She was a South African girl, so I responded with "baye dankie" and we continued our conversation in her language.

We had a long wait. She raised a number of questions about the Christian religion. In distinction from many people in her city, she had not been brought up in the church. In fact she told me, "I am un-churched. I guess that is what you call it? You would probably say I am a heathen." I immediately extended my right hand and said, "Congratulations." Surprised at my reaction she asked, "Why do you say that?"

I replied, "An extremely old friend, called Malachi, who happens to have written the last book of the Old Testament of the Bible, once spoke on behalf of the LORD God Almighty. This is what he said, 'My name will be great among the heathens from the rising to the setting of the sun' (Mal.1:11). This tells us that the LORD God is interested in heathens; that includes you."

It seemed that the line, in which we were standing, was beginning to move. To my surprise, she invited me to join her for dinner later that day. She planned to have dinner in one of the special restaurants on board with four friends; three girls working in different departments and a young man, the manager of the stores. She added, "Two of my friends are also heathens." I thanked God for that invitation. I had not even boarded the ship and promising contact had already been made with the staff.

At the dinner, it turned out that one girl had an Anglican background. She was likewise from South Africa. The other two girls had no relationship with God, or with any church. The gentleman admitted that he had been an altar boy, long ago in England, but he did not now practice any religion.

The dinner was superb. The conversation was intriguing. It was fascinating to discover that they were curious why a clergyman involved himself with members of the staff. They had suspected that if there were a clergyman on board, he would be there exclusively for the passengers. They believed a clergyman is only summoned for marriage ceremonies, burial ceremonies, and of course for worship services. A personal contact with the members of the staff was an unknown concept to them.

But what inspired me was that we got around to talking about the God of the Scriptures who extends his care to us, especially to the heathens. In fact, in Romans 11, Paul says that the invitation to the heathens to live a life of praise to God might become a challenge to the Jews; imagine, the heathens becoming missionaries to the Jews, who according to the Bible, are the people of God. I am not sure if they got the point or understood the tone of what I said, but the store manager and one of the girls asked me if I could get them a Bible.

I mentioned that I had Bibles in my cabin and suggested that I could rise to the occasion immediately. I excused myself to get some. I brought back four of them. Upon my return I gave one to the store manager and one to the girl, who had asked me for a copy. Two Bibles were left at the center of the table next to the flowers.

Soon, a second girl picked one up, paged through it and then asked if she could keep it. The casino manager decided to pick up the last one. As per my tradition, I prepared a "prescription" for each of them. They compared their prescriptions and copied certain sections of each other's "prescription." The dessert and coffee time had become a "Bible study."

God has given me a constant desire to seek out and find those who are not as yet committed to Christ and are in need of being challenged with the gospel. As a result, I got deeply involved in a conversation with his friend. That's when the concierge walked in and asked me to step outside for a moment because there was a message for me.

I suspected that a passenger had become gravely ill or had possibly passed away, so I mentally prepared myself to visit the hospital on board. However, the concierge told me that my own wife had telephoned and requested that I return the call immediately. The reason? Her mother had passed away.

I suddenly realized that this was the second time in my life that I found myself on board of a ship when death came to our family. We were in the middle of the North Atlantic when my own mother had passed away, some years ago. At that time Trudy and I were on a British cargo ship. It was a horrible experience to be stuck in the middle of the ocean, unable to communicate with members of our family, unable to get off the ship, and unable to attend the funeral.

On board of ships, it is very difficult for seafarers to talk about death, because often they find it difficult to come up with any meaningful, consoling words in such circumstances. In my years on board, I have discovered that whenever a death has occurred in the family of any of the members of the crew, I am immediately notified by a fellow crew member. He will whisper in my ear that it would be a good thing if I went to see "so-and-so" in his work place—the galley, the print shop, the bridge, or wherever he might be at the time.

It's almost always an occasion for having a serious talk about life and death and the significance of it for ourselves. We need to get to the point of being sure that in life and in death, we belong to our LORD and Savior, Jesus Christ.

I often think of my Scottish Presbyterian friend who, as a minister, served three small congregations near the town where I had my congregation. He mentioned that the attendance in his churches was pitiful but he said, "At a funeral, and I have many of them, everyone from far and near comes out and the church is packed, so bear in mind that the caskets are the sounding boards of the gospel."

I have never forgotten that remark. I agree with him and at every funeral, I preach about the gift of Eternal Life, which we receive by believing that Jesus Christ is the Risen Son of God.

Now I was summoned to telephone my own wife who was of course terribly distressed by my absence at this difficult time of sorrow and death.

When the concierge had alerted me, I went up to the top deck where I hoped to find the radio officer still on duty because I needed to call home. But neither at his office nor at his cabin nearby, did I get any response. In the vicinity I heard people talking and laughing. I discovered that the noise came from the cabin of the captain. His door was wide open. There was obviously a party going on.

I knocked on the open door and was invited to come in. Twelve senior officers, seated around a huge table, suddenly became as quiet as a mouse. I addressed the captain and explained that I was actually looking for the radio officer, because I needed a telephone to call my wife in Canada since her Mother had passed away.

When I said that, the master and all twelve officers rose to their feet, extended their hand, and offered their condolences. The captain, whose cell phone was lying in front of him, picked it up, handed it to me, and pointed to his office, saying, "Use my office and call anyone you want to call, but be sure to come back because we need to talk."

About twenty minutes later I returned and joined the officers, who wished to hear not so much the details of Mother's death but what to believe about life after death.

Apprehension frequently overwhelms people when they talk about death, so we looked at John 14, where three things are mentioned.

> **First:** When we stand at the grave of a loved one and are moved to tears, Christ tells us in verse 1. "Don't

let your hearts be troubled." That is on the same wave length as I Thes.4:13 "Don't grieve as some, who have no hope."

Secondly: Trust in Jesus Christ, who is God. That is to be the heart of our reaction to the greatest crisis in life, the death of someone with whom we had a bond of love.

Thirdly: The testimony of Christ is that he has prepared a place for us *beyond death.*

When the discussion had come to a close the captain said, "It is a good thing you are here, because there is one more thing we ought to discuss. As you well know, it is my responsibility to welcome all passengers on the first night of the cruise. Now the office *could* say, 'Out of respect for the religious views of the passengers, who represent a variety of beliefs, we like to suggest that you end your welcoming remarks for the December holiday cruise with 'We wish you all Happy Holidays.' Kindly, do not use the expression 'Merry Christmas.' That could happen."

I reflected and thought, "How interesting and at the same time, how devious! They might say that of course. Some head offices are already saying it. Nothing bombastic, nothing big, or so it seems, just a small change in the wording except that it is another little push to the Christian religion to get back into its 'private' corner whereas the Christian faith is in reality a 'public' matter relating to every aspect of life. How have we come to the point that a crèche in the public square of a city is an infringement by the church on the territory of the state?"

More than a century ago there was no ice- control in the Port of Montreal. The ice piled up so dangerously high, that the entire community on the waterfront was in peril of being destroyed. The founder of the city publicly offered prayer. He then made an oath, that if his prayer would be favorably answered, he would bring a cross to the mountain top. The size of the cross would be similar to the one on which Christ had been crucified. A large illuminated cross has replaced it. There it stands today in a public place.

According to some head offices "Merry Christmas" ought no longer to be said in a pluralistic society. Yet, Christmas refers to Christ. As my friend Spyros wrote in his Christmas card to me, "In a world of so much war, pain, disease, agony and misery we are more than ever in need of love, peace, and sanctification. This is precisely what God in Christ gave to our sad world."

It is Christ's birthday we are celebrating and he, in the last analysis, is the only one who can make us genuinely happy. Some head offices are suggesting that to refer to any happiness or merriment is fine as long as we leave out the word "Christmas." We could attempt to create happiness with sales, bargains in stores, Christmas trees, which are now called "Holiday" trees, and with holiday parties, holiday vacations, and holiday visits to friends and families, but in the public squares of nations with a fundamental Christian heritage, the mere mention of "Christmas" has become problematic because it refers to Christ.

The captain continued, "I grew up with the celebration of Christmas as the birth of Christ, the Son of God. It sets the tone in my family and hometown. I believe that this annual event, though viewed and treated by the business world as a purely commercial enterprise, is about the birth of Christ. As master of the ship, I could be requested to no longer express my conviction that the 'joy of the season' is because of the birth of Christ?"

He added, "I do not preach like you, I do not give my personal testimony, but I would like to continue to use the expression 'Merry Christmas,' which has been part of our tradition forever. To stand before the passengers with a large part of my nine hundred members of staff and crew, and to say 'Happy Holidays' would be nonsense. For them it means extra time, overtime, and double time in terms of their work. They are unable to be with their families. They cannot go to church. They cannot join a choir to sing carols. They are stuck here on a ship. I could not possibly insult my crew by saying 'Happy Holidays.'"

The office is of course concerned with passengers, actually only with some passengers, because many of them, though they may not flock to the church, do believe in their hearts in the Christ of Christmas.

He added the following, "So what do I do when this type of instruction comes to my office? If I go by their suggestion there is no problem, but then I have bribed my belief. Yet you know what might happen if I should not follow their suggestion: Someone might well report it in a letter to the office. This isolated voice will be heard and my job might be on the line because of what one, or perhaps two people, would write. As master of this ship, I am totally in charge. I have full command in smooth sailing, in storms, in fire at sea, and in disaster. Whatever happens, I am responsible for and in charge of the passengers and crew alike. Every word I say becomes law. However, when it comes to welcoming passengers at what I believe to be the most glorious season of the year, the office could suggests to me what to say and what not to say, irrespective of what I believe and of the centuries-old tradition. So, what can I do when this happens to me?"

I said, "Sir, I compliment you on your conviction, on your allegiance to the Christ, whose coming into our world has made all the difference. I compliment you on your readiness to stand up for him and to risk your job. The Bible tells us in 1 Peter 4:14, 'If you are insulted because of the name of Christ, you are blessed.' So stand by!" "I thought you would say something like it," he responded. He rose to his feet, shook my hand and said, "Merry Christmas!" The date happened to be August 10.

A NEW DIMENSION

It was an older ship, but it hadn't lost its popularity. It didn't sail to any intriguing islands except to one. It took day cruises. One could enjoy the sun, the sea, the show, the games, and some excellent meals.

But on Sundays, the ship functioned as a ferry to one of the islands. About a thousand passengers boarded at 6:00 a.m. to sail to this lovely island and to stay there for a week. An additional thousand people, who had spent a week there, sailed back on that same Sunday to return around midnight.

At times, I had spent a few hours on it in order to contact the members of its multinational crew. I'd encourage them in the LORD and direct them to his Word. But the pressures of their duty, as the passengers were boarding and then sitting down for a lavish breakfast, restricted my access to countless staff members.

It had occurred to me that the officers and crew never had a chance to attend a church service; neither did the passengers have that chance since no church services were offered. But one Thursday, something happened: As I had concluded my visiting on board, shortly before the vessels' departure, I ran into a very distinguished looking gentleman immaculately dressed in a business suit, totally out of line with everyone else dressed in vacation attire. He came up the wide stairway inside the ship, as I was about to go down.

What made me address him I don't recall, but I extended my hand and said half-jokingly, "Good morning, Sir. You must be the President of the Company." To my stunning amazement, he responded with "I am."

The Spirit of God gave me direction, so I came back with the response; "Allow me to introduce myself. I am a chaplain to seafarers. I have visited your ship with the master's blessing. I have often thought about approaching you in your office, since it struck me that neither the crew nor the passengers seem to have an opportunity to worship God on Sundays while the ship sails. So I thought, perhaps I should offer my voluntary services to you?"

He listened quietly then took one of his business cards out of his pocket, handed it to me, and said, "Come and see me in my office whenever you have a chance." That was my second surprise.

I spent an exhausting day and did not have a chance to pursue this challenge until the next day. When I saw him in his office, I explained to him some of the spiritual needs on board. I was happy to discover his genuine interest and concern for both the crew and passengers. He seemed ready to pursue my suggestion. "In fact," he said, "you should see my assistant director, who is in charge of all programs on board. Tell him that I should like to have you and your wife board this Sunday. Can you make that? Then advise me how we can best address this matter in the future." I walked out of his office and praised the LORD.

The arrangements were made with the assistant director. The Conference Room on board was set aside for the worship service. There was a distinct hesitancy to use the Grand Lounge since a worship service was considered to be a bit "risky" in terms of popular appeal. But carte blanche was given for access to every area on board. To our delight, a lady with whom we had sailed on board of another ship the previous year, turned out to be the cruise director.

On Sunday morning, we set sail at seven o'clock with close to eleven hundred passengers and slightly over three hundred and fifty members of staff of every conceivable nationality: Spanish, Portuguese, Korean, American, Czech, Greek, Jamaican, the Philippines, Indonesia, and at least a dozen others.

It was an exhilarating day. The Conference Room turned out to be totally inadequate in accommodating all attendees for the worship service. Trudy, functioning as hostess and chief usher, managed to squeeze young and old into the corners and the open spaces of the room. The remainder of the crew and passengers were forced to stand in the hall. It was a blessing and an inspiration for our flexible cruise director, who immediately suggested that the Grand Lounge be set aside for the next time.

Following the worship service, we spent a fifteen-hour day contacting as many officers, staff, and crew members as possible at their stations, during their breaks, at their meal times, around their bar, and in their recreation room. We conducted another worship service at night for the staff. We encouraged them, witnessed to them, and inspired them in Christ, the Savior.

We challenged them to read the Scriptures and to find their directives in the specific instructions of our Lord. When we boarded, we took along three boxes of Bibles in a variety of languages. By the end of the day we had none left; yet there were still requests for more.

Upon returning home, we prepared a report for the President, who was so encouraged that he invited us to return every Sunday. For weeks on end we returned every Sunday.

Some Cruise ships have little Chapels mostly on the top floor. They are used frequently for the ceremony of weddings. The couple would be married and stay on board for a cruise while the family and friends would be just joining for the ceremony and for a reception on board.

Most people would assume that an Interdenominational Worship Service would be held in the Chapel on Sundays. The lack of space would not allow this as most chapels can seat only two dozen people.

Interdenominational Worship Services for passengers, if they are offered, are ordinarily conducted appropriately in one of the lounges. It is significant to take note of the fact that there is an increasing interest among passengers in Interdenominational

Christian worship services, as well as in meditations, or biblical teaching sessions on sea days.

The political, economic as well as natural climates in many nations are characterized by severe upheavals. It is witnessed in ethnic intolerance, unabated war and rebellion, earthquakes, floods, violent storms, volcanic explosions both on land and in the waters.

Personal, spiritual, and medical pressures likewise behoove pastoral care.

The Staff are represented ordinarily by seventy to eighty nationalities. They are on board for many months in succession. They have increasing stress when upheavals above referred to take place where they have their own homes and family.

Personal concerns, such as medical or spiritual problems in their homes, anxiety in marriage relationships, death of a very close relative are extremely stressful. The pastor, providing voluntary pastoral services for extended periods of time is esteemed of high value by the staff.

The presence of small Christian fellowships is an indication of the fact that there is a serious concern among staff members for the need to share each others' concerns and seek biblical counsel and direction. The need of the vast majority of personnel is most definitely demanding pastoral care by a professional pastor.

THE HAPPIEST DAY
IN MY LIFE

We were sailing in the Indian Ocean on a world cruise. The unique advantage of such a long cruise is that you become thoroughly acquainted with passengers and personnel. The opportunities for genuine ministry abound.

One of our responsibilities was to lead what was called "The chaplains Hour," a session for passengers, held every morning on sea-days. The Rabbi, the Roman Catholic Priest, and I, the Protestant chaplain, sat together in the lounge. The passengers joined us to discuss anything they wished to discuss. We, the clergy, were to facilitate the discussion. We were not to give answers unless we were specifically asked for our opinion on the subject. It was to be an interaction among passengers to stimulate them to talk freely.

We discovered that people of different religious orientation, as well as those who had no religious orientation at all, joined in and the sessions became extremely popular.

I remember a Jewish passenger who asked on the very first day, "What is Christianity all about?" His question was occasioned by the fact that one of his children had married outside of the Jewish faith. He referred to animosity in his native city between Christians and Jews and the resentment he experienced against Jews.

Trudy gave a ringing testimony to him by referring to the Scriptures where we learn that God himself chose the Jewish people as his own, and how his Son, Jesus Christ the Messiah, was a Jew. In the reformed tradition, one grows up with the knowledge of the Old Testament and through it, with the history of God's covenantal love. Anti-Semitism was unknown in our Christian experience in Holland.

Religious, as well as moral, issues came on the table: homosexual marriages, euthanasia, abortion, the relationship between different religions. The scheduled forty-five minute session usually lasted more than an hour. Each session had a different character. Thoughtful discussions prevailed.

One day the Rabbi was in charge. He felt that we should steer away from the continued emphasis on the religious aspect of every subject. So he said, "I suggest that we talk today about 'the happiest day in our life.'" We were all in for a surprise: A lovely British lady rose to her feet in response to this introduction and said, "*The happiest day in my life* was the day I accepted Jesus Christ as my LORD and Savior." She was genuinely excited about it and went into great detail to explain her continuing happiness in the LORD.

The Malaysian wife of one of the staff members attended those meetings as well. She listened carefully and got increasingly excited as we discussed the significance of a commitment to Christ, his grace in accepting us, and his assurance that in him, we have life everlasting: *A happy subject.* While sailing in the vicinity of countries with devastating floods and incredible death tolls, we were talking about life everlasting!

The moment the "chaplains Hour" was finished, the Malaysian mother came up to me and wanted confirmation about "life everlasting." I responded that in Christ we are assured. He is the bridge! She burst out in tears and said, "I have constantly wrestled with the concept, that upon death, I and my three-year-old-child would cease to exist or possibly come back as an animal. Now you are telling me about life hereafter. This is incredible. I am a Buddhist. I do not see personal life after death in Buddhism. I need Christ."

The following day I presented her with a copy of the Bible in her language. She was again moved to tears and happily embraced me. *It was the happiest day of her life!*

Every month, we had a fundraising session on board for an orphanage. One of the ways in which we raised funds was by inviting passengers who passed by the area where we were seated to have their blood pressure taken for five dollars. A retired professor from New York took the blood pressure. The Roman Catholic priest advertised the fundraising session in the lounges. The rabbi hung up ads everywhere.

I sat next to the professor and wrote on a piece of paper the result of the blood pressure tests while talking to "the patients" and sometimes quieting their anxieties and giving serious or humorous little talks depending on the result of their test.

One gentleman told us that he had not seen his doctor for two years. We took his blood pressure and discovered that it was so outrageously high that we decided to repeat the test. The second reading was as high as the first one. The professor advised the patient that he should take the test seriously and listen carefully to what the reverend would be saying. He suggested this is not only a fundraising exercise.

I counseled the "patient" and suggested that he might wish to drop by the medical clinic on board immediately. It would close in a few minutes, and I suggested he might wish to show the doctor on duty the little paper with our figures. I asked him to do us a favor and to come back to report to us if our test was reasonable.

Some fifteen minutes later our "patient" reappeared. He excitedly told us that according to the doctor down below, his blood pressure was so excessively high that he had received immediate medication. He also got several instructions, the last one of which was to go back to us and thank those "dilettante physicians" upstairs for alerting him, just in time, to see the MD at the clinic since he was "walking on a cliff's edge." He exclaimed, "Thank you so much. I think, maybe you have saved my life! I am the *happiest man* on board!"

At night, I once again was requested to preach the message to the Christian Fellowship. A small group of about eighteen Philippine and Indonesian people attended to study the Bible. They had developed a very strong biblical conviction and they felt that their lives had to be in complete harmony with the Word of God: No images, no icons, no making the sign of the cross, no beads; only the Word of Christ coupled with a devoted and morally acceptable Christian lifestyle.

I preached the sermon, and they were encouraged by the biblical orientation. At the close of the ceremony, which took place at midnight and ended at about one thirty in the morning, one announcement was made that seemed to create a small but hardly noticeable stir. Brother Alfonso had been in charge of the Christian Fellowship Bible Study Program every Sunday night. He had done very well, and his ministry had been much appreciated. We were headed for Mumbai in India and we were told that Brother Alfonso was scheduled to go on leave.

The brethren, who functioned as the leaders of the Christian Fellowship, had approached Sister Angela. (Interestingly, the participants referred to each other as brothers and sisters.) She was a very active Christian girl who was in charge of the musical part of the meetings by writing out the hymns and projecting them on an overhead, so she was a real blessing to the Fellowship. Now, she had been asked to be in charge of the Christian Fellowship meetings as soon as Brother Alfonso left. She had accepted and the change was announced.

Two "brothers" approached me after the worship service and asked if they could talk to me privately. Since we had met in a room adjacent to the theater, I suggested we meet in the theater. At two o'clock in the morning the theater was a quiet place. They came directly to the point: They appreciated Sister Angela but felt they could no longer worship with the Christian Fellowship, because they believed that a woman should not be in a position of leadership in the church.

Their question was: "Should they inform the fellowship that they did not wish to continue with them or should they just quietly drop out?" I thought, "Here I am on board of a cruise ship, in the middle of the Indian Ocean, in the dead of night, and the issue of 'Women in Office' pops up and seems to have placed two brothers in an awkward position." I prayed for Solomon's wisdom. The Spirit of God, as always, richly provided.

I told them that it seemed to me they needed the fellowship for the support and strengthening of their faith. They responded by saying that they were considering to form their own Christian Fellowship more biblically based. I appreciated their well-intended thoughts, but it pained my heart. I said, "How many people does the Christian Fellowship have?" "Well, tonight I think there were thirteen," said one of them. So I said, "Is it correct to say that there are about one thousand three hundred seafarers on this ship?" They agreed.

I continued, "Thirteen out of one thousand three hundred is one percent." They agreed. I said, "If you leave, a number of people on board will hear that the Christian Fellowship has split. They do not know why, and they don't care, but the testimony that goes out to them will be, 'A dozen people of the Christian Fellowship cannot even stay together. Is that Christian unity? Should we join a group that splits?' A Christian Fellowship ought to continue to give a 'united testimony' to the seafarers. This testimony should be: 'In Christ we are one!'"

I added, "Sister Angela will be in charge for only a limited time. She too will go on leave, five or six months down the road, so would it not be an inspiration to the rest of the group who knows your position that you want to support them and preserve integrity and unity before the rest of the crew on board? Don't you think that God understands your predicament? Could he not bless you in your display of unity to the honor of his name and cause by staying with the Fellowship Group?"

They got the point and responded immediately: "You are right; we should stay with them and we will. Thank you for speaking to us! We agree with you."

For them it was a happy conclusion of the night.

EXORCISM ON BOARD

She was married to a European officer. She herself was from Singapore. Anyone who gets married may wish to remember that one of the chief factors in maintaining a good relationship is understanding each other and each other's needs. If you marry someone from a different part of the world, or from a different nation, sensitivity in this area is altogether a most significant and beneficial factor.

All of us have to learn that. For some of us, that does not start to blossom until the Spirit of God overwhelms us, and in a real sense calls us to order in this aspect of married life.

There is another biblical matter we are to take note of *before* we get married. It is not easy to digest, but there are pills in the Sacred Scriptures which are hard to swallow and even harder to digest. This is one of the hardest ones, because love may interfere. "Do not be yoked together with *un*believers ..." II Cor.6:14–18.

Irrespective of what the Bible says, there are countless people who do marry without having the spiritual dimension harmonized, and many discover that, as the Bible warned, it can bring them into perplexing situations. For both of them, this was not the case in point. They were deeply in love with each other. They had been married for a few years, and they were fortunate to be sailing on the same ship. He worked in the technical department, and she worked in one of the stores. Both of them were well equipped for their jobs and enjoyed what they were doing.

Her husband had acquired, in Africa, a large wooden sculpture of a head which had been carved like a demonic face with some bones sticking out from behind the ears, giving it the expression not merely of an angry man, but of a powerful demon. In fact when he bought it, he especially liked that aspect and said that he was going to hang it up in his cabin. In his job, he had to deal, at times, with difficult people as well as with difficult situations, and he felt that this demonic powerful figurehead would inspire him daily to face up to the frustrations he had to cope with.

He said he did not believe. That referred to a belief in God, because obviously he did believe in the Devil.

It has always intrigued me that many people who say they do not believe and confess to have no faith in Christ still display a real belief in particular aspects of the teachings of the Bible. He felt the "representation" of the devil would be a source of power and so in a sense, he acknowledged the Devil.

Many people who do not believe in God use the name of God repeatedly. Though they do not read the Bible, they refer to the biblical references of Hell, and at times, suggest to certain people that they should go there. So, that suggests that there may well be some kind of awareness of the biblical teachings. They may not believe in Christ but for what they believe they leave the door open.

The whole thing came to my attention, because she talked to me about it. I had met him already and had discovered that he re-emphasized his position that he did not believe in God. He did confirm that there was power in the demonic however.

I sensed that she was uncomfortable. Her mood, her attitude, her face reflected her distress. When I inquired what the problem was she explained that this wooden "mask," which her husband liked so much, was hanging in their cabin and it bothered her enormously.

She could not feel at ease with this piece of wood on the wall, because to her, it had become more than a mere piece of wood. She really felt that either the devil was in it, or it emanated the power of the devil precisely as her husband had said. So, she had become distressed. Every time she walked into their cabin that mask on the wall became a frightening presence to her. It caused her to be unable to sleep.

Her husband did not want to have the mask removed. She could not live with where it was hanging. So, the relationship between two people who loved each other and were married, was in a state of stress because of "a piece of wood" bought in some market in an African port.

Now various prophets in the Bible speak about this. Actually God speaks through them. Take Habakkuk 2:19 for example, "Woe to him who says to wood 'Come to life!' or to lifeless stone 'Wake up!' Can it give guidance?" But in Isaiah 44, God gives the most revealing exposition. I could summarize it, but it is far more expressive in the direct version:

> "Half of the wood he burns in the fire; over it he prepares his meal, he roasts his meat and eats his fill. He also warms himself and says, 'Ah! I am warm; I see the fire.' From the rest he makes a god, his idol; he bows to it and worships. He prays to it and says, 'Save me; you are my god.'
>
> They know nothing, they understand nothing; their eyes are plastered over so they cannot see, and their minds are closed so they cannot understand. No one stops to think, no one has the knowledge or understanding to say, 'Half of it I used for fuel; I even baked bread over its coals, I roasted meat and I ate. Shall I make a detestable thing from what is left? Shall I bow down to a block of wood?'

He feeds on ashes, a deluded heart misleads him; he cannot save himself or say, 'Is not this thing in my right hand a lie?' (Isaiah 44:16, 17, and 20)."

However, the officer was not ready for this. He had hung that mask in his cabin. Now it was interesting that he "saw" something in that piece of wood, but he did not "hear" the cry of his own wife with whom he lived in the same cabin. It frightened her, and she wanted it removed. She was thinking, *"Put it under the bed or in a suitcase, in the corner even, but do not hang it on the wall, staring at me."*

So I tried to console her by saying, "It is just a wooden block hanging on the wall. It has no value. I am sure your husband chopped off half the price before getting it, so it is a *cheap* piece of wood." She did not see it that way, because she "saw" something in that cheap piece of wood: a demonic display.

It made me reflect for a few moments on the whole world of imagery and the value one has attached to all sorts of items. Why would the guitar of Elvis Presley be so extremely valuable? It is just an ordinary guitar.

Let me stay in my own ecclesiastical circle: Why do people hang a little cross from the mirror in their car? In many cases it is also made of a plain piece of wood. Can it save you from a car accident? A piece of wood?

Why do people open up their wallet and show me a picture of the Virgin Mary with child, or a small photo of an icon representing a saint, and revere it? Their mother gave it to them before they left to set sail. It is just a reminder of Christ and His care. Yet, in the context of their religious orientation they treasure such symbols.

Why do I see people kiss an icon in the church? Is it not a painter's artistry on a piece of canvas? We have a deep-seated urge to cling to something physical and visible which reflects the magic and power of God and his Son Jesus Christ. Yet Isaiah 44 points out clearly that we are to worship only God.

Frequently one notices that in a discussion, when the word *hope* is used, someone knocks on wood, to express that what he hopes for will really come about. Most people do not actually know where this originated. The fact is however, that in the historic naval world, the huge sailing ships had their largest mast placed toward the rear of the ship on the "poop deck," which is what this wide open area was called. Frequently a cross or a crucifix was attached to this mast. It was acknowledged by crossing oneself or by touching the mast, when one passed by. Most people were well aware that neither the cross nor the crucifix, or the acknowledgement of them, could bring about the thing hoped for. It was a reminder that Christ, who had hung on the cross, could well influence the situation positively. So the piece of wood was a reminder of Christ.

In the Greek Orthodox tradition December 6th is St. Nicolas Day. He is called the Patron Saint of Seafarers. When I board a Greek ship, frequently I see an icon of St. Nicolas hanging on the bridge. It is indicative of the fact that deep down in the hearts and souls of some seafarers, there is the search for support and protection particularly when you face wind force twelve and twenty feet waves.

Is our hope and protection in one who is "gathered with the fathers" as all the saints are? Biblically we get an even greater vision: our hope is in the One, in whom even our fathers and saints have a new, an everlasting life.

My friend ought to be inspired by this and get her comfort from it. But she didn't and said, "It is just as if that piece of wood is alive. I know that someone carved the eyes in it, but they are now really looking at me. That demon might do something to me, so I am afraid."

I understood that perfectly, so I asked her, "Does it always bother you and do you always feel it is staring at you?" She gave a redemptive answer: "No, not always, but often. As a Christian, I know I should not get worried." Did I hear that correctly? Did she suddenly refer to her Christian orientation?

I said, "In that case I'll give you an absolutely guaranteed solution. Whenever you are bothered by that mask, walk up to it and do what Martin Luther did when he was plagued by the devil: Confront him! Go to the mask, stand in front of it, look directly at it, and say out loud: 'I believe in the LORD Jesus Christ, who will reign over all his enemies. That includes you, Devil!' Then spit at the mask on the wall, as forcefully as you can. That is the best form of displaying your rejection. You'll discover that the mask loses its effect and power over you immediately, completely, and permanently. Guaranteed!"

When I walked into the store two days later, she smiled and thanked me saying, "It worked, Reverend. It really worked. Thank you very much!" The devil was "exorcised" from a piece of wood hanging on the wall…

Most oil tankers dock at isolated, far away docks. They are huge and need very deep water. With millions of gallons of fuel on board, they are to be carefully protected. I have often concentrated my ministry on such tankers because of the isolation of the crew. They have come to an outlying port and cannot go into town or to a Seafarers Center, unless we transport them, so I visited the "Golden Sunbeam."

The Golden Sunbeam had no gold, unless you would call the fuel gold, so there was nothing to retrieve. I went to visit this tanker, in an absolutely forsaken area, to minister to the officers and crew. The ship had just arrived and was low in the water, unlike some of those car-carriers with six thousand automobiles on them, where you may have a gangway with sixty-four steps up.

As I came to the top of the gangway of this tanker, I was greeted by a very nice guard, a young fellow from the Gilbert Islands, which used to be under English control. I was always delighted when they would come to our chapel service, for they had the gift of singing a cappella in voices from high soprano to deep base. They sang in a manner that was emotionally very touching. They were terrible shy and would stand in a circle not daring to look at the audience in the chapel. They needed time to gear up, but once they sang, one was deeply moved.

The guard warmly welcomed me and suggested immediately that I ought to speak to the others on board who were just sitting down for their mid-morning break. He closed the gate at the gangway and proceeded to lead the way to the rear of the ship. Instead of walking straight to the back of the ship, he made a peculiar roundabout at mid-ships. It turned out that there was no obstacle and with the motion of his hand, he indicated that I should make the same peculiar round-about.

I asked myself why we did this, for he then proceeded in a straight line to the back of the ship. So I stopped and called out to the guard, who politely came back to me, again making that peculiar round-about at the very spot where I had stopped. I asked him, "Why do we have to make a round-about here even though there is absolutely nothing on the deck?" He said, "There is a demon there. The assistant boatswain fell there three days ago and broke his leg, so I do not want to walk there. Nobody walks there."

The assistant boatswain's broken leg had become the "flag" for all on board not to walk in that specific spot anymore because there was a "demon" sitting there who would break the leg of anyone who dared to walk across. Nineteen men on that ship had their path redirected by what some people adjudged to be a "demon" on a flat piece of steel on this tanker. It seemed to me, that the Word of the LORD could bring deliverance here and that the LORD challenged us to embrace his word.

I reviewed my theological training. I had learned how to understand the Sacred Scriptures and to apply the teachings of the Bible to the practicality of life. That's what a theological training is all about. But it is true that I had not been briefed on the biblical teaching of exorcism. That's peculiar particularly since at the very start of the ministry of our LORD himself we see the confrontation with the devil addressed in a powerful way (Matt.4:1–11).

Nineteen men should not be deluding themselves. They were aware of the presence of the devil in that particular spot on the deck of their tanker. He may have been in other areas as well and have had some of his cronies take charge of the thoughts, the eyes, the minds, or the mouths of some of these nineteen people, but the focus here was on a flat piece of the steel deck. That is a challenge for us as Christians. And that is what Ministry to Seafarers is about: To straighten out not only their path if they go in the wrong direction, but in this case to straighten out their walk on deck.

So, I addressed the guard: "In the Bible we are told that Jesus Christ is King. That includes the deck of the Golden Sunbeam. Nineteen of you, created in the image of the King, cannot spend the rest of your lives on this tanker in anxiety about a devil who could break your legs. In the Name of that King the devil is to go, and we claim this spot of the tanker to be under the sole control of our Lord Jesus Christ."

I then proceeded to walk with my size fourteen shoes straight through the spot that was under demonic control. The guard stood there and saw me walk forward first and then to give him complete reassurance, back to where he stood. When we came to the crew's mess room, the guard told everyone present there all about it. I could not understand a word of what he said because I do not speak their dialect. But we all did praise the Lord!

They were embarking passengers. That's always a hectic time on a cruise ship. Everyone is at their station catering to every whim of those who are boarding. The wine steward is at his elaborately decorated wine table. The staff of the spa is inviting you to enjoy a time of relaxation with massages. The sports department staff is suggesting good and healthy exercises. The casino dealers are reminding you that the moment we have left port, the doors will be open and you will have a chance to become very rich.

I was heading downstairs on one of the busiest stairways on board of this cruise ship. I meet people when they are relaxing at their break time. I then preach my "mini-sermons," extend a word of counsel, invite people to stay in touch with the LORD Jesus Christ, and hand out a devotional or even a Bible, depending on the time, the circumstances, or the setting in which the staff is at work.

The one thing I have learned in my years on board is not to postpone my action. When I am talking in the staff dining room at one table, I have learned that others, at other tables, listen and suddenly get involved. That's what happened on Saturday. I turned around to get a copy of the Scriptures out of my bag, which I had parked near the entrance of the dining room, and as I turned around, one man at the table behind me looked me straight in the face and said, "God must have sent you here today, because my mother died yesterday."

That meant that at that very moment I was called to "rise to the occasion" with consolation and inspiration in the life of someone who could not go home to bury his own Mother. He had work to do and a schedule to follow. He had to turn to and do whatever was required of him. We could not arrange a get together later somewhere else. Now I had to speak. Now I had to console and inspire. Now I had to lead in prayer.

I continued down the busy stairway with passengers running up and down. Up came the hotel manager, a girl with four stripes on her shoulder. As she saw me, she called loudly on the name of God. Ordinarily I say in a case like that, "You mean: Oh my Reverend," and they catch on that they should keep the identities distinguished.

Her surprise was that she met me on the stairway. In fact, I sort of just walked into her. Characteristic of the seafarer, this hotel manager immediately placed before me the matter that bothered her. "My Uncle has pronounced a curse on both of my parents and they are in big trouble. They are deathly afraid. They have asked me to come home. I cannot go home. They don't know what to do. They are at a loss. So Reverend, please pray that the curse be removed. I will phone them and tell them."

There was no point in trying to find out on the stairway why this uncle did this, what the relation with this Uncle was, what kind of religious background her parents had. Here was a call, "Nullify, exorcise this curse, so that my parents will be out of their imprisonment and can breathe again."

I grabbed her hand on the stairway and with the passengers racing up and down, I prayed for the deliverance, at that very moment, of her parents from this demonic power, in the name of Christ the Savior: Exorcism at twenty thousand miles away from where the curse was demonizing these people.

As I was about to continue with the activities of the day, I heard confirmation of what I had already figured out in my own mind: *"What are twenty thousand miles on earth to the Creator and* LORD *of the universe?"* My friend, the hotel manager, said. "I am going to the phone immediately to tell my parents that they have been set free of the curse." That is a positive reaction: "They have been set free of the curse."

That'll be a real surprise for the uncle!

FORGIVE US OUR DEBTS
AS WE FORGIVE ...

On a piece of wrapping paper near the body of a dead child in the Ravensbruck concentration camp, where ninety-two thousand women and children died, this prayer was found: "Oh Lord, remember not only the men and women of goodwill, but also those of ill will. But do not remember all the sufferings they have inflicted on us. *Remember the fruits we bore, thanks to this suffering*: our comradeship, our loyalty, our humility, the courage, the generosity, the greatness of heart, which has grown out of this, and when they come to judgment, *let all the fruits we have borne, be their forgiveness.*"

I read this absolutely stunning prayer as an introduction to a session called "A Chat with the Clergy" during the World Cruise on a beautiful cruise ship. It was a popular one hour discussion held on sea-days for all interested passengers. I had introduced it on board of this particular cruise ship which had never had this type of program before. On the World Cruise of another cruise ship, it had become so popular that we had run out of time and space.

I was asked to lead the first discussion. So, as an introduction, I read that amazing prayer which had obviously been written by a Jewish person. Had she possibly tasted something of the very essence, the very heart of the Christian gospel, shortly before her own death in this concentration camp? Had she tasted something of the forgiveness by the greatest Jew, who at his own crucifixion shortly before his death, said, "Father, forgive them, for they do not know what they are doing" (Luke 23:34).

When I had finished reading the prayer, there was a brief moment of total silence in that spacious lounge filled with people. Then one passenger jumped up and shouted, "I totally disagree with that prayer! Those, who committed these atrocities, should never be forgiven. They should burn in hell!"

A lively discussion about forgiveness, which is the very heart of the Christian gospel, followed. Christ the Messiah taught us "The Lord's Prayer." It can be prayed by Christians as well as by Jews.

There is one phrase in that prayer which received his special attention: "Forgive us our debts, as we also have forgiven our debtors." Of all the lessons in that prayer, Jesus elaborates only on that one when he says, " … If you forgive men when they sin against you, your heavenly Father will also forgive you," but then there is the other side to that: "If you do not forgive men their sins, your heavenly Father will not forgive your sins" (Matthew 6:15). We can put that in our pocket! *God is going by our records.* We do well to pay attention!

The violent reaction of the passenger reminded me of Ishak, an Indonesian Chief Dining Room Supervisor, and a man in charge of some hundred and fifty stewards. I met him in the officers' bar of a cruise ship, which was docked for disembarkation and embarkation. Ishak was on his coffee break.

He actually shocked me with his mere appearance. Physically he looked a wreck; pale, worn out, unusually skinny, and with a look of frustration on his face. I greeted him and asked him how he was doing. In the true tradition of the personnel on board he answered, "I am fine." I sat down across from him and said: "Are you telling me the truth?"

Without an apology he immediately started with, "I am livid with anger. Six weeks ago I got a letter from my wife. We had a good marriage and two children. A friend of ours, who lived close by, looked after them during the long periods that I am away at sea, usually for eight months at a time. I felt confident that my family was safe and protected. But now it turns out that this friend has become the lover of my wife. Can you imagine that? Your life gets destroyed while you are some twenty thousand miles away from home."

He continued, "I am going home, and I will kill this man. I am Indonesian. I have to do this. How can I stay on board? How can I do my work? I can't eat anymore. I cannot sleep. I have already asked the crew purser to get me a ticket to fly home, but he cannot get a replacement for me on such short notice, so I have to wait as yet. But I have no choice; I must kill that man."

Every word that I would say, if he did hear it, would be weighed over against the fact that he was in a profound crisis. I could sympathize, empathize, and do everything possible to have him change his mind. But he was the one who had to deal with it. I said, "Your name tells me that you are a Christian. Am I right?" He answered, "Yes, but what does that have to do with it? People, who commit the kind of crime that this man has committed, need to be punished. Wouldn't you agree? He has to die. Right?"

I have come across this type of crisis more than once: One's commitment to the Lord, one's Christian faith is suddenly pitted over against one's crisis. Ishak knew deep down in his heart that his Christian commitment would not allow him to kill that man, but he figured there was justification for it. He looked me straight in the eyes and said with all the conviction he could muster, "I am going to kill him."

He kept looking at me. Did he expect some sort of benediction? I said, "Ishak, in that case I suggest you take some medication." "What are you talking about?" he asked; "Do you want me to go to a doctor?" I pulled out my Bible and read: "Do not take revenge, but leave room for God's wrath, for it is written: 'It is mine to avenge, I will repay,' says the Lord" (Romans 12:19).

He looked at me and said: "Why should God get the satisfaction out of getting even with that bastard? This is my business. I want to get the satisfaction. I must kill him and I will." With that conviction firmly rooted in his mind, he stood up and said: "I must get to my job. I'll be back by 2:30."

I saw a ray of hope. He did not say that he was no longer interested in pursuing the discussion. He would be back. For what? For part two of my sermon? At three fifteen he showed up. He was still convinced of the correctness of his intentions to disembark, to go home, and to kill the man.

There are times that I think it is easier to preach from a pulpit, in a well established church, to the people in the pews. Here I was, sitting across from just one man, but he has already stated his case. I could preach as much as I wanted, but the mere look on his face was saying: "You are not going to convince me with any pious talk." Only the Spirit of God could bring about a change.

Earlier I had served Romans chapter twelve to him. It had had no effect. So, now I prefaced Luke 6:35 and 36 with an introductory sentence. "Ishak, I have one more pill for you. You are not going to like it, so open your mouth and swallow it immediately or you'll choke on it. It is a pill especially for Indonesians who are on their way to kill someone. So here it comes:

'Love your enemies, do good to them. Then your reward will be great and you will be sons of the Most High, because he is kind to the ungrateful and wicked. Be merciful, just as your Father is merciful.' Now swallow this and digest it. When you arrive home, remember your Heavenly Father who is merciful. When you embrace your children, remember your Heavenly Father. When you see that evil man, before you kill him, remember your Heavenly Father who is merciful."

I got up and went to the faucet in the adjacent galley, picked up a glass, and filled it with water. Then I put it in front of him and said: "Drink it or you'll choke on that pill."

Immediately I filled another glass with water and put that on the table too. "What is that for?" he asked. I answered, "It's for me."

"Why?" he questioned. I said: "I feel so miserable and I so sympathize with you that I am about to choke on it myself."

Ishak went home. Indonesian Airlines was the carrier with Indonesian personnel on board and Indonesian food on the menu. Indonesian determination to deal with the crisis was alive and well… Of course it had absolutely nothing to do with Indonesia or being an Indonesian. It had to do with one man's justified anger.

One year later, to the day, I had the opportunity to visit a sister ship of the same company. As I walked into the officers' dining room there sat Ishak. I could not believe my eyes. He smiled. He had gained some thirty pounds. He looked healthy. Soon, my curiosity was satisfied with just the one sentence he offered as a greeting: "My wife and I are together again."

He was apparently back on the job, judging by his uniform, and not in a maximum security prison because of the murder of a man who had brought destruction into his home and into his life to the point, that he had lost not only thirty-five pounds, but got locked in the grip of the spirit of revenge. How did he get out of that? What had happened? Did Ishak get caught by Romans 12:19? "Do *not* take revenge … I'll do that."

Ishak did not elaborate. He left me with that one sentence. But I suspect that the Spirit of God went along with him to Indonesia and persuaded him to deal with his crisis in the way Christ spoke about this in Matt.6: 14. "If you forgive men when they sin against you, your heavenly Father will also forgive you." The word men, obviously included that "bastard" Ishak wanted to kill, but didn't.

FIVE CHRISTIAN FELLOWSHIPS ON ONE CRUISE SHIP

Among a number of Christian Seafarers on board of ships, there is a desire to fellowship and "commune in Christ the LORD" with other Christians. They form "The Christian Fellowship." On many ships, it is in the lower ranks that the "Christian Fellowship" blossoms.

Only on Korean cargo ships did those in a higher position join those in a lower position in the Christian Fellowship without any qualms or trepidation. It is also notable that in most instances, the attendants of the Christian Fellowships have been converted to an evangelical church. They are frequently well versed in the Scriptures and deeply concerned about the maintenance of a distinct biblical orientation in their Christian Fellowship.

One aspect was brought to my attention: On this huge cruise ship they had not only one, or two, but five Christian Fellowships. I can understand that, because what keeps these groups separated in most instances is their language.

Whenever I have been invited to lead their worship service I speak in plain, non-colloquial, well-articulated English. I know that English is their second language. It is also my second language. For many of them it is still difficult to understand English.

The Fellowships on this ship were excited about Trudy and me joining them. All five fellowships approached me to lead their worship service and to conduct Holy Communion. It was an exhilarating experience. They met on different days and all of them started at midnight since all attendants were then available.

The first group we attended came from Indonesia. Somehow linked up in their ecclesiastical tradition with the Netherlands, they followed a pattern that was familiar to us. They mustered a lectern from one of the musicians for me to use as the pulpit. All chairs were set in straight rows. The leader made it a point to whisper to me that I should not forget to announce the offering, which was for an orphanage in Indonesia. Imagine, here are these seafarers setting aside money from their limited wages for the ministry to an orphanage in Indonesia. I thought that was inspiring. "One more thing, Pendetta, (that is Indonesian for pastor)" whispered the leader, "Do not forget the Benediction."

A church service, in which we all stand before God, needs to be capped by his benediction! Of course! In my more than fifty-year career as a pastor, I had never been confronted with that kind of request in any church, but at least half a dozen times in the Indonesian Christian Fellowship Services on board of ships. "Do not forget the benediction."

The second group was made up of people from the Philippines. For the first thirty-five minutes we stood and sang. We praised the Lord, and we sought to emotionally get ourselves to a higher level. We stood with hands raised and desired the inspiration of Christ whom we all worship.

Then we prayed after which the Scriptures were read. Everyone read a few verses in Tagalog, their language, while I read in English and preached, after which I invited them to Holy Communion. We all stood in reverend silence remembering Christ's broken body and shed blood while eating the broken crackers and drinking the Coca-cola which took the place of bread and wine. Somehow, it was a moving ceremony and we all felt truly strengthened by God.

The third group was from Jamaica and St. Vincent. We just plunked down where ever there were chairs and we praised the LORD for being together, informal, relaxed, rejoicing, and having a time of real fellowship in Christ. The message, which I was to deliver, was prefaced by a time of singing vigorously, loudly, and so dynamic that the sound reverberated. This was followed by a time of testimony.

I had at one time studied at Gordon College in Boston, Massachusetts, before switching to Calvin College and Calvin Seminary in Grand Rapids, Michigan. At Gordon College, I had become familiar with the service of testimony. Here I could see it again in its full glory. One seafarer after the other stood up and testified to God's working in his or her life.

The applications for us, the audience, were direct, and I felt that this time was as valuable as the proclamation of the Word of God. They all referred to the Scriptures and preached a mini sermon. The audience participated with loud "Amens," and with frequent references to the praise of the LORD. It inspired the speakers to conclude with a prayer for us all, as they sank to their knees, inviting us to do the same. It was an inspiration of magnificent proportions!

The fourth Christian Fellowship represented the people from Goa, India. We met again in the same room, where all the others had met. It was set aside for this purpose.

As I entered the room—and I thought I had come early—some twenty-five gentlemen were already in attendance in a setting which I hardly recognized. The table was covered with an immaculate white tablecloth. It was set with lit candles on either end, with flowers, a chalice of sorts, next to a bottle of wine, and a plate with communion wafers. A crucifix, as well as an old but pompously looking Pulpit Bible, had been placed in the center. Here I was in the true Anglican/

Catholic tradition where the formality of the service and its décor had significance. All twenty-five attendants stood up as I entered.

In a devout manner, we all participated in a beautiful Anglican Order of Worship in the responses, the prayers, the Apostle's Creed, and the LORD's Prayer. In the other services, one was not expected to join in on the recitation of the LORD's Prayer.

The Jamaicans had all knelt in prayer using the seats of their chairs to lean on. No particular denomination has a "patent" on some liturgical expression in the church. Some kneel, others raise their hands, some stand while singing, some cross themselves, and others recite the LORD's Prayer in unison. Christ said, "…the true worshipers will worship the Father in spirit and in truth, for they are the kind of worshipers the Father seeks…" (John 4:23).

The last group we met with was from a variety of South American countries. Their Pentecostal background, combined with a highly spirited South American musical orientation, made this one of the most extraordinary experiences. Not only their singing, all in Spanish, enlivened by vivacious dancing, but even their praying in "concert" was musically and physically illustrated.

They did not talk to God; they "shouted" at him, both in their thanks and in their requests. It lasted not only three minutes but carried on for almost fifteen minutes and was followed, mysteriously, by an exceptional calmness and quietude, until finally the "Leader" concluded not with the traditional "Amen," but with "Praise the LORD."

I have heard that phrase many times in all sorts of places flippantly used, but at the conclusion of the period of silence at the end of that extremely "heated" prayer in which everyone had talked at the same time, in what seemed to me total confusion, this final "Praise the LORD" took on a different form. I was exhausted, as were they, but the peace of God overwhelmed us. Here were all these South Americans in worship with us, and we felt one with them in the LORD, as we had felt one with all those other fellowships.

The next day, one of the senior Philippine persons asked me, "Reverend, did you attend all the Christian Fellowships?" I replied, "Yes, I have been to all of them." Then, he came back with another question, which I have never forgotten: "Have you also been to a 'white' Christian Fellowship?" I replied, "No I did not find one." He continued, "Isn't it peculiar that you as white people who have come to us as well as to South America, India, Jamaica, the Philippines, Korea, China, and Africa to bring the gospel of our LORD Jesus Christ do not have a 'white' Christian Fellowship on board? Half the crew here is European, North American, and Australian, all white."

In our twenty years at sea, I have only run into half a dozen "white" people who attended an existing Christian Fellowship. One was an English drummer. One was a South African beautician. The American ship's doctor was the third one. An American beauty parlor manager and an Australian purser as well as a Canadian comedian made up the rest.

We have been in touch with many Christian crew members working in different areas—in offices, in engine rooms, on the bridge, in the theater—but in an attempt to recruit them for a Christian Fellowship, where they could function as a witness and a testimony to others, we have not had much success except on one large cruise ship.

This ship was sailing on a Saturday. I thought this might give me the opportunity to lead the worship service for the passengers on Sunday morning. I e-mailed the cruise director and offered my services. He replied that they had a positive Christian group on board which looked after the worship service. I did not need to make any arrangements except to preach the sermon.

When we came on board we learned that a group of seafarers, headed by the chief dancer of the cast, was in charge of the worship service for the passengers. As we entered the auditorium, we were presented with a proper order of service. We discovered that not only the chief dancer, but the drummer of the orchestra, two TV technicians, and the sound technician, as well as two guitarists, led the worship services. The hymns were projected on a large screen. After the scripture lessons, my name appeared in large letters on the screen as today's preacher.

We were delighted, and after the church service we learned that all participants were recently converted Christians. The cruise director had discovered them. They asked us if we could provide them with a couple of sermons and inspire them for the following weeks which we did. We praised God for these Christians; all of them hailing from Canada and the USA. In fact, all of them were white Christians.

The fleet of cruise ships is huge. So I live in the hope that there may be other cruise ships where crewmembers of every color may let the testimony of God's salvation in Christ ring out for the passengers as well as for the crew.

FINAL FAREWELLS

The chief officer had passed away and I was called to conduct a funeral service. The crew was from Africa, but the master was English. We alerted everyone that the funeral service would be conducted in a distinguished funeral home in the city.

It turned into a deeply emotional experience. Everyone was dressed in full regalia because of the importance of the occasion. But since the funeral service was to take place in the funeral home, everyone felt the need to fortify himself with the fruit of the grape to relieve the tension.

At the funeral home I conducted the worship service. I highlighted the biblical direction that, irrespective of our age, the LORD determines our agenda, and he is always near us:

"What is your only comfort in life and death? That I am not my own but belong with body and soul, in life and death, to my faithful Savior Jesus Christ..." Heidelberg Catechism, LORD's Day 1.

When I had prayed for the LORD's guidance and for the family of the chief officer, I invited the members of the crew to quietly come forward and pay their last respects to the chief officer. Together with my wife and her Aunt and Uncle from Holland, I retreated to the Clergy's dressing room to disrobe.

We had just entered it when the funeral director, pale as a sheet, suddenly barged into the dressing room and in desperation alerted me that he was afraid the crew might take the body of the chief officer out of the casket. He said, "I have talked to the master of the ship, but he calmly tells me that since they are not on the ship he has no authority over the crew whatsoever. That's why I come to you."

I immediately rushed back with him to the parlor where the chief officer's body was displayed. There, to our amazement, the entire crew was crowding around the body. A few of them had hoisted the body up. Some of them were wailing and crying while others were speaking loudly to their former chief officer expressing their regret and offering their profound apologies for negligent behavior in the past.

The funeral director, now supported by two of his assistants, stayed in the back of the room close to the door. They were all horrified by the spectacle they were witnessing.

As I approached the center of the group, with the captain about three feet away from the action, I put my arms around two crew members and slowly pushed my way forward to where the body of the chief officer had been raised to a sitting position. At that very moment I received insight from the Spirit of God:

"Here are African people saying their farewell to the one man every single individual on board has had contact with in one way or another. With some of them it was a good contact, but with most of them that contact was burdened by misunderstanding, unwillingness to follow through on the chief officer's advice and commands, or by having responded in a most improper manner.

Now he had passed away. The body will be shipped to Africa, but before that happens, every single person has to make a statement of some kind expressing his apology for whatever has gone amiss in the relationship. It has to be voiced loudly and clearly, accompanied by some distinct physical contact. That is not your tradition and culture. It is theirs and it has meaning for them. So allow them to give full vent to their emotions. They will calm down."

With that wisdom, I approached the staff of the funeral home assuring them that in another ten minutes they would quiet down. Fifteen minutes later, totally exhausted from the experience, everyone returned to their seats in the chapel, and awaited my instructions to board the bus and to return to their ship.

Their captain, completely under control, simply remarked, "You must have witnessed this before, because you kept your cool." I replied, "It was the Spirit of God who gave insight and wisdom which enabled me to keep my cool."

It is of course natural that we wish to pay our respects to those who have gone before us. St. James goes even beyond that when he instructs us, "Religion that God our Father accepts as pure and faultless is this: To look after orphans and widows in their distress..." (James 1:27). Since I had alerted them to this message of the LORD, they now got the hint that they are called to put James 1:27 into practice when they return back home, where the chief officer also lived.

The distress mentioned here is not merely a physical distress, although if we look at our society and note the incredible suffering and misery in so many countries, the need to respond to physical distress is beyond measure.

But there is also the distress of the heart and soul of people. I understand that there are special courses given to those who professionally deal with people who have sustained a loss in their home, enabling them to meaningfully console and comfort them.

The message I found in my mailbox on board the ship was rather straightforward, "Passenger wants to have a ceremony to dump her husband's ashes. Uittenbosch, can you help?"

There are of course people who have had a profound relationship with the sea as for example, professional fishermen, who during their lives have expressed the wish to be buried at sea.

I consented to deal with it and after having made the proper legal arrangements with the Ship's master, who was most cooperative, we decided that the ceremony should be performed in private on the aft-deck below the passenger deck.

One of our table mates was a young man in possession of the appropriate machinery to determine exactly where the ship would be situated at the time of the disposal. Our other table mates had little awareness of the Christian characteristics associated with burials.

It became a moving ceremony as I preached about the comfort of God, not only at this time, but in the years ahead for the passenger who had lost her husband. I also focused on that exceptional message of Christ about the life hereafter. The Scriptures are rather limited about life after death, but there are some amazing instructions of Christ we should never forget:

"Do not let your heart be troubled. Trust in God, trust also in me. In my father's house are many rooms. If it were not so I would have told you. I am going there to prepare a place for you …" (John 14:1–2).

That is a message to the disciples of Christ and by extension to believers everywhere. So we see that isolation is most definitely eradicated when we die "in Christ."

The passenger was much encouraged and interestingly our table mates who heard my message during dinner from our "technical expert" were inspired as well, because the "Word of the LORD is living and active …" (Hebrews 4:12).

There is despair in the lives of many people with which they are unable to deal.

While I was awaiting a ship, passing through the St. Lambert Locks, a lady had entered the restricted area of the road above the locks. From where I stood, at the point where the two lock-doors came together to allow the ship we were awaiting to enter, I noticed that the lady on the road above us had come out of her car, stepped over the railing, and had attempted to jump into the river. But she missed her target, and instead of ending up in the water, she landed on the opposite quay from where I stood.

At the very moment that she jumped, the two lock-doors had joined, enabling me to run across to reach the other side where this horribly wounded lady was lying at the very edge of the river. It was a shocking sight. When I approached her, she urged me to push her off the quay edge into the river. Moments later, the ambulance arrived and took her to the hospital where she passed away.

I was devastated. Here I was for just a few moments with her and she had but one wish: *to end her life.* May God have mercy on her soul!

On the ships, there are also people who in their despair have taken their own life. Whenever I am called out to such a tragedy, I experience an enormous pain.

If I would have been there just a day, an hour earlier, I could possibly have been of help and prevented the tragedy.

CAST YOUR BREAD
UPON THE WATERS ...

In the laundry room of a huge cruise ship, the only language spoken was Mandarin. Seven mainland Chinese people worked there. With intense speed, they washed and dried thousands of towels, sheets, pillowcases, tablecloths, and napkins. It was boiling hot in there despite an air conditioning unit blowing with the wind force of a hurricane.

My Chinese vocabulary is extremely limited, but I have learned the greetings, the courtesy expressions, and the benediction. The greetings and courtesy remarks got little reaction other than their appropriate response. But the benediction knocked them off their feet. They looked surprised and they immediately identified it with the Christian religion, as some of them imitated it magnificently with folded hands, and bowed heads, and then looking up to the ceiling.

The language barrier has never bothered me. The Spirit of God is able to reach people of every language, either directly or through his messengers. A detailed record of that can be found in Acts 2.

One other incident encouraged me.

The late Rev. J. Wristers, a seafarer's chaplain for most of his life, was elated when I had accepted the call to become a minister to seafarers. He and his wife came all the way from New Orleans, LA, up to Kingston, ON, Canada, in his old car and talked to us for almost twenty-four hours uninterruptedly. He convinced us of the enormous need of spiritual care for the seafarers.

One of his extraordinary stories made a deep impression on us. He was called to the hospital to visit a Chinese seaman who had had an accident on board a ship and was rather seriously wounded. He visited the gentleman, but he could not speak a single word of Mandarin. He brought him flowers and copies of the National Geographic magazine. If you cannot read the language, the pictures speak loud and clear.

At times, he also brought some Chinese delicacies picked up in a Chinese restaurant. The most significant gift he presented was a copy of the Bible in Mandarin. It created a contradictory reaction: excitement because it was in Mandarin and fear because he was not permitted to have a Bible in his possession. But he did accept it. Maybe he intended to hide it later.

The reverend would sit down at the patient's bed for at least twenty minutes and in pantomime "talk" to him. Every visit he concluded by rising to his feet, bending slightly over the patient, and placing his hand upon the patient's forehead. Then he prayed in English. He did this just about every other day for six weeks until the patient was released to go home. Not a single intelligible word was exchanged that made sense to both of them. It was at all times a monologue on the part of this pastor. The Chinese patient just smiled. To smile was a unique display for a Communist Chinese person.

Almost two years later, Reverend Wristers received a letter. It was written in Mandarin. But someone who spoke Mandarin as well as English had been kind enough to add the translation of the letter.

It was a thank you note from that Chinese seafarer who had been in the hospital in New Orleans. It is of course never too late to say "thank you" but that was not the only purpose of the letter. The real purpose was to inform the reverend of what could not have been said when they were together because of the language barrier. He lived in a fairly small village outside the hustle and bustle of the enormous Chinese cities with millions of people in them.

He had not returned to sea but was now working at a simple job in the country. He liked it and was thankful that he could stay with his family. His broken bones had healed and he was doing very well. But something else had happened. He not only wanted to thank the Reverend Wristers for his visits, which he had appreciated, but he wanted to thank him especially for the prayers that had been said. And what made him altogether thankful and delighted was the copy of that Bible in Mandarin. He had read it very extensively and he had come to Jesus Christ. That changed his outlook totally. Then that Bible had come into the hands of his family and friends. In fact, it circulated in his village.

The details were not mentioned, but he wanted the reverend to know that as a result not one, not two, but *all* the people had become followers of Jesus Christ; *the entire village.*

So, here on board, despite the language barrier, we somehow seemed to hit it off. Every time when I came down, these Chinese wanted to shake my hand. They complimented me on the pronunciation of the five words I spoke in Mandarin. They laughed at my size fourteen shoes. They stared at my clerical shirt while one of them repeatedly—somewhat mockingly so it seemed to me at times—greeted me by attempting to make the sign of the cross, proud of his knowledge that he had pegged me as a man of God. But every week when I returned they furtively looked if I had brought again some Chinese Christian reading material. I had managed to get a daily devotional in Chinese, published by the multimedia ministry of the *Back to God Ministries International.*

When I concluded my visit, one of them always took on an increasingly devout pose as I pronounced the blessing in Mandarin. I thought I should perhaps take a course in Mandarin to disciple him, catching myself that I was still too limited in my capabilities to bring him to Christ. I had my eyes on only one person, the "devout" one. The LORD, however, counted seven.

During the fall season, their ship came every week from New York to Montreal. It stopped in Quebec City where Trudy and I boarded her, at the request of the ship's officers and the company, to minister to both passengers and staff during weekends as she sailed back and forth from Quebec City to Montreal.

Following two seasons of pastoral care among them, still continuously hampered by the severe limitation of our knowledge of Chinese, I nevertheless ventured to preach a sermon one evening when they were all gathered for a time of relaxation. With their help, it was not too difficult, because the Chinese language displays in pictures the meaning of many words.

Moreover, the gospel of salvation in Christ is embedded in the Chinese language in at least one hundred thirty-nine expressions. I concentrated on only one that evening. The key to our salvation is that we must be made righteous. That's an awesome thing. How can we ever become acceptable to a Holy God? How do we get cleaned up? Only God can right the wrong in us. He does it through His Son Jesus Christ. We are told to believe that, to take him at his Word. That's the heart of the Bible.

I pointed to the copies I had brought along for them and tried to clarify to them Romans chapter 3. That's an effort in a Mandarin Bible. The righteousness of God comes through faith in Jesus Christ, to all who believe. Jesus Christ is called "The Lamb of God, who takes away the sins of the world" (John 1:29).

The Chinese people display that in a more lively form than we do, because their language is pictorial. The picture for the word "me" gets another picture on top of it, which means "lamb" and there you have the word "righteous" in Mandarin. Think of it: When the LORD God almighty looks down he sees the lamb before he sees me.... I am hidden by the Lamb. He is my salvation....

It seemed to me that there was more theology here than my seven friends could handle in one sitting when they begin to discover who that lamb really is. The LORD God decided that it should take two sittings.

On one of those weekly voyages, a Chinese Christian couple sailed on the ship with their elderly parents. One of the stewardesses noticed that they were reading Chinese newspapers. She asked them if they did throw those papers away after having read them. When the answer was in the affirmative, she asked if she could give them to the people working in the laundry. Imagine, here is a Polish stewardess asking for some used Chinese papers to give away to people in the laundry. Little did that girl realize that God had put her in this strategic position for a special purpose.

The couple was surprised to hear that there were Chinese people on board. The public never sees the crew working in the bowels of a cruise ship. So they asked their stewardess if it would be possible to meet the Chinese people at night sometime. She informed them that she would ask the hotel manager. She did, and he granted them permission.

He knew how valuable it would be for his Chinese crew members to be in contact with some Chinese passengers. Unaware, the hotel manager had also become a tool in the hands of God to do his work. The message got through to the Chinese crew members, and arrangements were made by one of them who took the lead in getting together with the Chinese passengers.

The young couple went down one night and were welcomed by the seven Chinese crew members. They all sat in the cramped quarters of a small cabin for two people.

Throughout the evening, Trudy and I were visiting various seafarers in their cabins witnessing to Christ the LORD. Late at night I suggested that we should drop by the section where the Chinese crew members had their cabins. As we came closer we noticed that the door of their cabin was open and that quite a discussion was going on. We stopped and looked inside. We were immediately welcomed with loud exclamations by all of them. They made space for us to sit down. They introduced us to the Chinese passengers by talking rapidly and by displaying some Chinese devotionals as well as the Bibles we had given them and by pointing to both my clerical shirt and my size fourteen shoes.

Then we really got into the presentation of the gospel. Trudy talked extensively with one group. She was supported by the Chinese passenger who translated every sentence for her. His wife translated for me. So, this time with her help, I preached my little sermon about "the lamb of God above me" once again.

We had a unique time of testimony with our seven friends and we all sensed the presence of the Spirit of God. We spoke and prayed— with every sentence articulated and translated—until deep into the night, and when we left the passengers stayed behind in the cabin. We were convinced that the LORD would use them mightily to his glory, with their Chinese language, culture, and manners, to touch the hearts of our friends.

He did so most exceptionally. He had set "a whole crew" in motion to bring about Salvation, and to fulfill his purpose. It makes you realize how every person has a place and function in the vast plan of the LORD.

Just look at this letter, which was slipped under the door of our cabin in the middle of the night:

> Dear Rev. and Mrs. Uittenbosch,
>
> It is with great joy that we'd like to report to you that four of the seven Chinese crewmen have accepted Jesus Christ as their personal Savior tonight.
>
> We believe it was a fruit of your hard labor of love and much prayer in the past two years. The remaining three think that they need some more time.
>
> May he receive all glory—Amen.
>
> As we look back to the happenings tonight, we find it amazing and beautiful to see how the Holy Spirit had worked things together to bring salvation to these crewmen.

1   My stepmother's Polish stewardess asked us for the Chinese newspaper for the crewmen on Tuesday.

2   My stepmother wanted to talk to them to ease some home-sick feelings of them. Fu-Ying called and made the appointment for 5:00 p.m. today.

3   I felt prompted to ask Fu-Ying after his meeting with my parents if he and his six friends would like to meet my husband and me to learn about Jesus tonight.

4   We didn't know you have been ministering to them for the past two years.

5   What's more amazing was, you chose the same night to visit them when we were visiting tonight to confirm the message of love.

6   What's most amazing is that we were just trying to explain what "righteousness" (from Romans 10:9–10) means when you knocked on the door. Without knowing our private conversation, you told them the meaning of a "lamb over me" as the Christian interpretation of the Chinese character for "righteousness."

We just want to bow our head and worship the wonderful work of the Holy Spirit.

What a joy to see how God used us as a team without any foreknowledge of each other's work!

We'd like to follow up with the four of them for growth.

We need to pray for the remaining three for their salvation.

We taught them some Chinese hymns and encouraged them to meet weekly to sing hymns, to pray and to read the Bible you've given them.

They need the Chinese translation of the NIV Study Bible.

Please pray with us and seek God's help in building these young brothers up in the LORD. They need church life.

God bless you,
J and W.

Early the following morning Trudy and I went back to congratulate our Chinese friends and to welcome them into the Christian community. We were greeted in the laundry room, where they were all on duty, with a song.

They were using the song sheets, which they had received the previous night. And they were making a serious attempt to sing: "Jesus calls us o'er the tumult of our life's wild restless sea. Day by day His sweet voice soundeth, saying: 'Christian Follow Me.'" We couldn't understand a word of it. It all sounded "Chinese" to us, but we knew what it was all about, so we sang along in English.

The most moving moment, however, came when the one person who always seemed to so mockingly make the sign of the cross, by drawing a big circle around his face and chest, suddenly stepped away from the machine he was attending. It was right in the middle of our hymn sing when we had arrived at stanza four: "Jesus calls us by Thy mercies; Savior may we hear thy call. Give our hearts to Thine obedience. Serve, and love Thee best of all."

He raced up to us and stood at attention in front of both of us for a priceless display. He again made the "sign of the cross" two times—once for Trudy and once for me—with considerable excitement, pointing at us, like he always did, and said: "You, you!" Then he concluded his demonstration with the three choicest words of his extremely limited English vocabulary, as he made the "circle" for the third time around his *own* face and chest, and said: "Now *me* too!"—For which we praised the LORD.

ZERO IN ON
WHAT YOU SEE AND HEAR

I could hardly believe my eyes, but when I walked up to the young Argentinean man serving in one of the bars of a magnificent cruise ship, I noticed the name on his name tag. His name and function were neatly engraved on it: "Jesus, Bartender."

I frantically searched through the niches of my preacher's mind to see if I could justify the closeness to each other of these two words. I concluded I could. So I launched into a mini-sermon with three points, which I preached to Jesus.

1   Is not our LORD Jesus the supplier, not of the spirits, but of the Holy Spirit, who unlike any bottle on earth, truly refreshes us and in fact renews both body and soul?

2   Is it not true that he who drinks of the *living water* will never thirst again? Which bar can make that claim?

3   If your name is Jesus, however common that name may be in South America, does that not place you in the awesome responsibility to live up to that name? "Be perfect as your heavenly Father is perfect" (Matthew 5:48).

Jesus and I became friends. What is more, I gave him a copy of the New Testament, which has recorded everything about his namesake. It ought to keep him in touch.

A CHINESE MISSIONARY?

"You do good thing, you save people," said Xiang, a mainland Chinese seafarer. He was courteous, gracious, but theologically incorrect. Xiang had seen us at work in the huge staff and crew dining hall on this cruise ship. He was eating his late night dinner. So I responded, "Xiang, not we, but God saves people." I am not certain that he got the theological meaning of my answer. He had been watching us. He had heard us talk. He saw us giving the Word of God to people with whom we had had a conversation. That is the beauty of this work in the setting of a mess room: Other people see you. They may not be involved at all, but they spy you out. They are curious, because you are professionally outside their circle, yet you move about in their circle and you seem to be at ease in it.

Xiang did not react to my answer, but he did pick up just one word: God. That prompted him to state his position, even though he respected and complimented our ministry. He wanted to show where he stood. "I do not believe in God and I know little about God, but my niece believes in God."

That was a curious answer; he confirmed that he was not committed. He softened that statement by saying that he hardly knew anything about God. Why did he say that? Was he asking indirectly for some information? Was he asking, "Maybe you can steer me into the right direction?" He referred to his niece, thousands of miles away, in an environment where it is a threatening situation to express your belief in God. So, was he asking, "You are on the level of my niece, because you are doing a good thing—telling people that they need to be saved?" He had not yet discovered that the real issue is an acknowledgement and a following of God.

With his two sentences, he opened wide the door for an introduction to Jesus Christ. What was a blessing to his niece—despite the fact that she might be an isolated individual in the communist community in which she lives—could conceivably become a blessing to him. So we sat down together and discussed extensively who God is and what he expects us to be. He wants Xiang to become acquainted with him. We gave him a copy of the Scriptures in Chinese, together with our instructions where to start reading. He seemed to appreciate our talk.

A late night announcement was made that the ship was due to sail very shortly. "Will those who are not sailing please leave via the gangway on deck four?" We had a large amount of reading material, both Bibles and devotionals in Chinese, scheduled to be delivered to the Chinese crewmembers working in different departments on board.

Our engagements in the mess room took so much time that we did not have the opportunity to go down to every department, yet now the ship was ready to sail. So I said, "Xiang, your Chinese is better than ours. Maybe you can go down to the other Chinese crew members, and be kind enough to deliver this material to them?"

He responded enthusiastically, then I added, "Imagine, you are now a missionary distributing the Word of God." He smiled at that remark. With his hands and arms full of Bibles, Xiang walked out of the mess room unaware that if he would read the Bible it could well change his life, enabling him to see eye to eye with his niece.

The chief purser on a cruise ship came down the escalator in the terminal. She was armed with two boxes of tickets and with whatever other paraphernalia is required to usher in the thousands of passengers who stood ready to board the ship.

I was about to go up the escalator. As I assisted her in carrying the boxes to the proper place, I noticed that she had two chains around her neck each with a cross. I asked her: "Why do you have two necklaces with a cross? Don't you feel linked up to Christ with one of them? Forgive my curiosity." She said, "Funny that you should ask that. The one is from my mother and the other from my boyfriend. But neither one is doing the job. I am out of touch with Christ and I had hoped that the crosses would get me back to him."

While she unpacked her boxes and put the stuff in the right slots, we talked. I said that I liked the crosses, but I agreed with her that they did not do the job. I challenged her with the thought that I should get her a third cross. Perhaps that might solve her problem. She laughed at that, aware that I was kidding.

Then I said, "Cross number one is from your mother, who gave it to you in the hope that you would stay in touch with Christ, the one who has died on the cross for you, right? Cross number two, the one from your boyfriend, is saying the same thing. I am happy you have a boyfriend who believes that one's priority is to stay in touch with Christ Jesus. Obviously he must be a Christian. So, both of them left you with a reminder to stay in touch with Jesus."

I continued, "There is a story in the Bible that touches on the same principle. It's a long story. So I'll spare you the details, but what I like about it is that the person in the story decided he would return to his Father. Never mind what he was wearing, or what he had done: *He went back.* The story can be found in Luke 15; check it out."

She had no Bible. I pulled one out of my bag and handed it to her. The line of passengers began to move, so she now stood at attention and I mounted the escalator to board the ship.

When people are dressed in casual clothes, they at times display their appreciation or allegiance to the current stars in sports or in music. "Follow the rock stars," "Attend the winter Olympics," could be T-shirt titles.

A young Jamaican came into the staff dining room with an interesting T-shirt, "Hang out for Jesus, for he hung out for you." I liked it and so I immediately approached him. I asked him, "Do you belong to a positive Christian Fellowship on board?" He looked surprised and asked me, "Why do you ask me that?" When I pointed to his T-shirt he responded, "I could not find another one. I don't even know what this one says." When I read it out loud to him he said, "I bought it from some Jesus freaks in the Barbados. It was cheap." Bless the freaks! Good price and an even better message.

When I asked him, "Does it mean anything to you?" it turned out that he had no allegiance to Jesus and wasn't "hanging in with him" or "hanging out" for him at all. In fact, he even had a hard time "hanging in" on board of the ship. The job was so stressful that he felt "hung up." The pressures of the cruise ship were wearing him down. So, we talked about relief from pressure. He seemed willing to listen. His burden was amplified, however, by his need to drink a lot. I suggested that might cause a "hang-over," whereas he was to follow the instruction of the T-shirt, and "hang out for Jesus." He thanked me for the message but did not make any promises. Instead he said, "I would like to hear more, but I have to return to my job. I can't hang around here any longer." I wonder if today he is still "hanging in" on board or "hanging out" with the best "company" on earth.

"Ask me about Bellari." That's what it said on a beautiful ribbon the store clerks had attached to their name tags. It was a PR gimmick. I believed Mrs. Bellari herself was expected to come on board to advertise her exquisite jewelry. I jokingly asked the manager of the ship's stores why I had been excluded from receiving such a nice ribbon. To my surprise, he said, "We shall be delighted to get you one. Please come back tomorrow at this time."

I asked myself, "Why do I have to come back tomorrow? Don't they have a pile of them in a drawer? Couldn't they give me one of those?"

On board of cruise ships we do not question orders or rules, so I kept quiet, but I did return the next day. Four jewelry shop clerks came together when they saw me arrive. They showed me a little box, which they presented to me with pomp and circumstances. When I opened it, there was a very nice ribbon in it, but it did not say, "Ask me about Bellari." Of course not! My job on the ships was not in the jewelry stores. The staff knew that very well. That's why I got a special ribbon, which stated, *"Ask me about God."* I found it intriguing that they had assessed my being on board so appropriately.

He had fallen down in the hold and had injured himself, not seriously, but he needed to be dragged out of the hold. I just walked by when it happened. He was a German seaman.

I speak German fluently, so when I had gone down into the hold I spoke to him. I then looked up and noticed that a huge crane, used to bring in the containers, was overhead.

It fortunately was not in operation, but I was moved to alert my German patient to just look up to the top of the crane where the Company's name appeared in clear letters.

It read: "Lieb Herr." That is a well known make for cranes, but I pointed out to my friend, the patient, in his suffering and discomfort that there was a message for him in that crane's name which, translated into English, means "Dear LORD."

So we called on our Dear LORD.

There are people who do have a Bible on board. There is a variety of reasons explaining how they got it. It is not important, although we salute the people who gave it to them.

A faithful organization, aside from devoted family members, is the Swiss Seamen's Mission located in Marseille, France. Their exclusive ministry is the distribution of Bibles to Seafarers. There are many seafarers who have received a copy of the Bible from them. Imagine, the landlocked country of Switzerland has a well known Ministry to Seafarers in Marseille, by the sea.

The point is, of course, to get the people to read the Bible. I have learned that we need to create curiosity about the Bible by giving an intriguing example which might challenge people to read it. When I ask: "Do you have a Bible?" I might get the answer, "I do." When

I then ask: "Do you read it?" I might get the response, "No, I don't." I try to heighten the suspense by saying, "In that case I have something special for you." I then get up and walk to the washbasin. In every staff dining room on board there is one since it is a requirement to wash your hands before you start to eat.

I pick up a paper towel and return to the table where I write on the white paper towel: "Please use this to wipe the dust off the Bible before you read it. Then read Romans 10:8 and 9." I might add a few other suggestions, but as an opening shot I begin with this. Now many people have no idea what it says in Romans 10, but the fact that everyone in the circle is curious about the nicely folded napkin, which I have given to this one person, creates so much curiosity that they all want to read it. It invariably brings about loud laughter from everyone present.

Interestingly some people reported to me that after having received such a little note, they did start to read the Bible, even rather regularly.

On board of cruise ships when one is in touch with the staff, an appropriate name tag is always required. These name tags change in their design from time to time.

On one ship, I used to have a very nice name tag with my function marked underneath my name. The company then decided to change the design of the tag and to include a photograph of the person wearing it. I suspect that had something to do with the increased security.

I was known simply as the priest to the people in the office where these tags were designed. Trudy needed to have a revised nametag as well. So we asked the office if they could prepare one. The gentlemen in charge didn't toy around with a title for her indicating her function. One of them said to his colleague: "She is the wife of the Priest, so we'll simply write on her name tag 'Priestess.'" That's what they did.

However you look at it, the fact remains that her function on board could well be classified as priestess. I think it makes more sense than the remark of my kind Indian steward who tagged her as the "Priest's girlfriend."

> Dear Rev. Hans,
>
> My name is Margarita. I come from Brazil. Do you remember that I met you on board of the largest cruise ship of the Company? It is large alright. I am still at a loss about how to find my way around. It was my first week on this ship when you came into the crew mess, where my friend and I were sitting. I was considering quitting because I missed too much my family and I thought I hated the ship life.
>
> That night you talked to me about God and the Bible. But the thing I most remember is a passage of the Bible you mentioned: I Peter 5 line 7. I looked it up and it said "Cast all your burdens on him for he cares for you" And I threw all my problems to him, and that gave me the strength to finish my contract.
>
> You gave me your card and your e-mail and you told me: "In six months you will write me and tell me that you will have finished your contract...?" So sure you were of the effect of that Bible passage. I am doing it now. Here is my e-mail. I just wanted to let you know that your words that night helped me every time I was thinking of quitting.
>
> Thank you, Margarita (from Brazil)

When an e-mail like this comes to my attention, I again receive confirmation that the Spirit of God, through the Word of the LORD, has influence in a person's life which gives light, hope, and perspective. Whenever I make the suggestion to read 1 Peter 5:7, I remind the person I am talking to that it is very easy to remember this verse:

Just think of the odd numbers: 1, 3, 5, 7. Replace the 3 by Peter and you have it.

Then you follow the invitation and start "throwing" your concerns, your worries, your anxieties, and all your burdens to the One who stands ready to catch them.

"You are *sinning* in front of your people, padre."

As a member of the law, catching me going over the speed limit on a Sunday night, when I had no volunteers assisting me and had stuffed our twelve passenger mini bus with twenty seafarers to get in time to my church service, he used proper ecclesiastical language.

He was a member of the private police force on the waterfront. In fact I knew him well. He was also gracious. After my explanation he said. "You know that the speed limit here is thirty-five miles per hour. You were going almost twice as fast. Might I suggest that you stick to fifty miles per hour?" I called that "grace" in the law.

My relationship with the private police force had always been very positive.

One of the inspectors invited me for lunch one day. When I received the assurance that the police would pay for it, I accepted the invitation. Admittedly I was a bit suspicious.

After all, if the police force invites you for lunch what could possibly be behind it? I figured I would get a lesson about speeding on the waterfront.

The luncheon was delicious. The remarks after the luncheon were encouraging:

The Chief of Police said, "Padre, we appreciate your being on the waterfront. Your clerical shirt functions as a restraint for misbehavior such as stealing."

When he said *that,* I recalled an incident I had witnessed years ago when the cargo was being brought in on open skids. There was one skid loaded with canned hams, but every now and then, when the skid was not hoisted out of the ship carefully, some cans would fall out on the dock.

I noticed how two cans were picked up by a longshoreman, but instead of replacing them on the skid, he opened the motor-cap of a little fork-lift, which was just passing by, threw the cans into the open space next to the engine and immediately closed the cap again. I thought, "This is the first time that I am a personal witness to what appears to be theft." In my naiveté, however, I thought, "When the driver gets into the shed, he most likely will take the tins out of the fork-lift and put them properly on the skid. So this is perhaps just a 'transportation matter.'" But my surprise caused me to stop and take a good look. That caused another longshoreman to ask, "Why are you staring at that fork-lift? Is there anything wrong?"

Not certain of the situation and giving them the benefit of the doubt I replied: "No, but I just never knew that these fork-lifts were running on canned hams."

The Chief continued, "We have decided to give you a special name."

I asked, "What is it? Something like 'sinbuster'?" After all that would be a fitting title. Fundamentally, my job is to *bust* sin, to break down that awful barrier which prevents us from getting peace with God. I am theologically well aware that *a lot* more has to happen to bust sin. It needs to be forgiven through the sacrificial death of our LORD Jesus Christ.

The Chief reacted by saying, "No, that is not the name we thought of. We have taken into consideration your Dutch national heritage. So we have decided to call you *'Our Dutch Cleanser.'*"

For a moment, I was taken aback. I am being compared to cleansing powder? Should I feel insulted? I decided to graciously acknowledge their choice of my new name.

When I checked what Dutch Cleanser really was, I discovered that it was a cleansing powder with the claim that no spot was so dirty that it could not be removed. I became greatly encouraged:

That is exactly what my job as a preacher is all about. No sin is so great that it cannot be forgiven.

The Islamic people must cleanse their hands, faces, and feet before going into the mosque for prayers. The cleansing fountains are just outside the mosque.

The *Hagia Sophia* (The Saint Sophia), a huge Christian church located next to the Blue Mosque in Istanbul, Turkey, also placed a circular fountain close to its entrance.

Fittingly a sign was placed on it in Greek. *"NIPSON ANOMHMATA MH MONA NOSPIN."* When translated it means, "You must not only cleanse the outside, but also the inside."

It was his birthday, so we celebrated. While talking together, all nine of us in one small cabin, with the owner absent for a while because of his responsibilities, we did not deal with anything serious. We were just kidding around.

The scene changed when the owner returned, plunked himself down on a very small seat and blurted out, "It is as hot as hell here." Since none of us had been *there* we could not support his statement with certainty, although we were tempted to agree, because it was indeed boiling hot in that small cabin.

No one answered, so I decided to raise the question, "Where do you get the idea that hell is so hot?" Suddenly noticing me, hidden in a corner, he said, "Oh, Padre, I am sorry, I did not know that you were here already. I should not have said that in your presence." I replied, "Don't worry. I am just curious to find out if what you say is true. Is hell hot?" He repeated, "I apologize."

That started the discussion. Everyone got involved in it because I, as the preacher did not *seem* to readily agree that hell was hot. Admittedly, the negativistic character of hell was, to some of them, sufficient support that it had to be an uncomfortably hot place. Interestingly in the New Testament the word hell is used a dozen times, eleven times by Jesus himself. Luke 3:17 refers to hell as the "unquenchable fire" where the chaff is going to be put and burned up. That gives a clear portrayal of the heat of hell.

It became a "heated" discussion on this birthday as we focused on the biblical other side called *heaven,* a dimension seldom in focus for many of them. Heaven in their minds seemed to be a "cool" place. But hell was somehow more familiar to a number of them, presumably because the word was used far more extensively. When we returned to what the Bible has to say about it, we discovered that the word took on an ominous character as it refers to "eternal and unquenchable fire."

In Luke 12, reference is made that in the last analysis we should not be afraid of those who kill the body and after that can do no more. But then an almost shocking statement is made: ..."Fear him who after the killing of the body has power to throw you into hell..." (Luke12:5). That is a summons to live in acknowledgement, devotion, and obedience to God. After Job has been stripped of everything he had and was visited with physical torment, he makes a most astonishing observation when he quoted, "The fear of the LORD, that is wisdom, and to shun evil is understanding" (Job 28:28).

So we concluded that hell is, in reality, considerably hotter than the heat in that cabin.

GOD HAS FORGOTTEN ME

"God Has Forgotten Me." That was the reaction of a very nice young girl who functioned as a dining room stewardess on a cruise ship. She had just selected her lunch and walked with her tray to one of the few empty tables. I was coming from the opposite side and we met at that table.

She addressed her remark obviously to me while she was still walking towards the table, so I sat down with her. I suspect my clerical shirt prompted her to say what she did say. As we sat down she added, "You must know what that means. You try to get in touch, but you cannot get through. There is no answer, no sign, and no reaction. There is nothing, so God must have forgotten me."

I listened to her story. There was misunderstanding. There was pain. There was an inability to shake her worries. She had a contract on the ship and realized that she was there basically for the money, but she found herself isolated from her home, her friends, her culture, and her traditions. Her home was in Lithuania. That's another world. Even with twelve hundred staff and crew members on board you can feel isolated.

I decided to tread carefully. I agreed with her, that God and forgetfulness are indeed linked up. I figured that would give her encouragement. But I added, "It is a special kind of forgetfulness. This is what I read in the Bible, 'I, even I, am he who blots out your transgressions, for my own sake *and remembers your sins* no more' (Is.

43:25). How about that? God cleans up our record completely and on top of that he says: 'I have forgotten the past. I don't remember it anymore.' That's, of course, almost unbelievable. We might have made some dreadful mistakes in our lives, and we talk to God about them, asking him, 'What about those mistakes?' He will answer, 'I have forgotten all about those and I don't want to remember them either.' That's what he will be saying."

I continued: "But God forgetting *you*? I suggest *you* forget that! In the very last line of the gospel of Matthew it says: 'Surely I am with you always.' Do you know Greek? No? Well, the New Testament was written in Greek and I looked at what it said in Greek. It says it even more specifically, 'I am with you each and every day.' That includes good days and bad days, happy days and sad days, healthy days and sick days, birthdays and even death days. That's what 'always' means. And guess what: God himself says in Isaiah 49 something that is especially for people who think He has forgotten them."

> But Zion said, "The LORD has forsaken me, the LORD has forgotten me." Can a mother forget the baby at her breast and have no compassion on the child she has borne? Though she may forget, I will not forget you! See, I have engraved you on the palms of my hands.
>
> Isaiah 49:14–16

We talked about it a bit more extensively. The limited time of crew members permits us to talk with them only briefly. It is therefore significant to get to the heart of the matter as soon as possible, while at the same time being sensitive to where the people are at, both culturally and spiritually.

I gave her one of my biblical "prescriptions," neatly written on the back of my calling card on how to deal with her worries. I said, "Look at what the Bible tells us: 'Do not be anxious about anything, but in everything, by prayer and petition with thanksgiving, present your requests to God and the peace of God, which transcends all understanding will guard your hearts and your minds in Christ Jesus' (Phil.4:6–7).

That's the formal version. Put in simplified English it says: 'Don't worry about a thing. If you need something ask God and he will give you peace.' Do you have a Bible?"

The answer was negative. I swung around to grab my briefcase, which I had parked on a seat behind me. I pulled out a New Testament and presented it to her with the blank back cover facing her. She turned it over and to her stunning amazement it was in Lithuanian. She checked the inside to make sure it really was. She then turned to me and asked, "How is this possible?"

I suggested, "It might have something to do with God *not* forgetting you. Here you come into the mess room for lunch. I come from the opposite direction and meet you right here, next to this table, where you made that statement. There are more than one hundred and twenty-five tables in this room. You sat down at this one, and I joined you because you said something to me about God.

My briefcase had only a few New Testaments left in it. One 'happened' to be Latvian. You have no Bible and you are Lithuanian. Now you have God talking to you through His Word. If he *had* forgotten you, he would not have bothered to send his Word to you and he would have steered me to another table."

She had to go back to work. She shook my hand. All she managed to say was, "It's amazing!"

IDOLS OVERBOARD

Every now and then, we are privileged to witness how the reality of the gospel penetrates the hearts of people on board. Some pause to listen, some stop to examine the claims more carefully, some come back to get further guidance, some are still sitting on the fence, but some perceive "the light" and then … through the inspiration of the Holy Spirit, commit themselves to Christ!

For years, I had met Korean seafarers, but always only on board of cargo ships. They distinguished themselves in a number of ways:

- They maintained immaculate living quarters and never entered their cabin with shoes on.

- There was often a group of committed Christians on board. They met for Christian fellowship and worship regularly. Interestingly, there never was any hesitancy among them to openly interact, despite the fact that there were seafarers from different ranks in attendance. Ordinarily, a junior officer, a sailor, an engine room assistant, or a steward would not dare to voice his opinion about the teachings of the Bible in the presence of senior officers. That would be out of step with the ship's protocol. But this was not the case among Koreans. The Christian gospel had influenced them to realize, that even though they had different functions on board, in Christ they were all one.

- They would sing together the traditional Christian hymns.

Commitment to the LORD meant that they had to be "clean," before they could align themselves with him. One engineer pointed this out to me, "I must wait till I have stopped drinking and smoking before I can be baptized." Six weeks later he came to me and asked, "Will you please baptize me now? I am clean." He was baptized in a festive church service and welcomed into the community of Christ.

Mr. Sung was the only Korean on the cruise ship I was visiting. When I met him, I discovered that communication was difficult because of his lack of English and my lack of Korean.

He could hardly communicate outside the area of his immediate responsibilities. Socially, he did not have any contacts. Since he was undoubtedly very lonely, I went to great length to get through to him. I doubted he had any books at all. So what better book to give him than the Bible? With pantomime and my limited Korean vocabulary, I made an elaborate presentation of a Korean Bible.

His Korean sense of courtesy demanded that he refuse my gift at first. Mr. Sung had never seen a Bible. His religion was characterized by the presence of many "charms" with which to ward off evil, as well as danger. Although he did not dare to share this with me at the time, he construed the Bible as a threat to his "charms." He therefore put it aside in his cabin and did not read it. He even toyed around with the idea of throwing the Bible overboard, but since the ship was due to return to Montreal, where he might see me again, he did not think it wise to do that just yet. Moreover, there are laws against that. All those thoughts prevented him from taking such a drastic action. Then an amazing thing happened ... the Bible started to challenge him. As he reported to me much later, every time he entered his cabin the Bible seemed to say, "Read me!"

Fearful that his "charms" and "spirits" might harm him, he dared not pick it up, but finally one day he *did* pick it up and started to read a few pages. He returned to it the next day and got caught up in its message. He then proceeded to read it seriously for hours on end. One night, he read for eight hours straight, he told me. Imagine that!

In the process, he met the LORD and Savior, Jesus Christ, who reshaped his heart so radically, that he threw "overboard" all the idols that he had worshiped for so many years.

As he continued his examination of the Scriptures, he was challenged by its call to be baptized. When his ship returned to Montreal, he sought me out and testified to the miraculous workings of the LORD in his life. In halting English, he explained the change that had come about, because he had come into personal contact with Christ. He had come to "the Light." He longed for baptism and asked if he could be baptized when the ship returned. When his ship did return, I immediately visited it, eagerly looking forward to seeing him again, but on a cruise ship it is easy to miss one another. I met all kinds of seafarers, but not Mr. Sung!

In the meantime, back at the Seafarers Centre, my wife Trudy met a Greek officer who introduced himself as Theodore. "Oh," she exclaimed, "that means 'Gift of God!'"

Theodore responded, "I don't believe in God!"

Trudy, undisturbed, asked, "Would you like to get to know him?" and offered him a Greek New Testament.

He answered, "I have read it, but I do not believe it." So, for him we can only pray that he may come to "the Light."

Just then, Mr. Sung entered and asked, "Is the Padre in?"

"No," she replied, "the Padre has gone to the ship to look for a Korean seafarer. *You* are Korean! He is undoubtedly looking for you. Do sit down. He said, 'I'll be back in half an hour,' so he should be here in an hour."

Mr. Sung said, "I like to talk about baptism."

She asked, "Your own or someone else's?"

He replied, "My own!"

So, as soon as I returned, Trudy told me, "Mr. Sung likes to talk to you about baptism!"

That very same afternoon, Mr. Sung was baptized in our magnificent chapel upstairs in the presence of seafarers from Hungary, Russia, India, China, England, Greece, Indonesia, and the Philippines. Some young people had come to our Seafarers Centre to help spread the "Good News." They witnessed the sacrament of baptism as well. And what a witness it was to all those present, Muslims, Buddhists, Hindus, Catholics, and Protestants, to hear this former Buddhist acknowledge Jesus Christ as his LORD and Savior! Mr. Sung then knelt down and was baptized in the name of the Father, the Son, and the Holy Spirit. Afterwards, the assembled "congregation" congratulated Mr. Sung and we celebrated with him right there in our Seafarers Centre. It was August 14, 1988.

Pressured by his duties on board, he soon returned to his ship. The ship sailed. She did not return to Montreal, but traveled around the world with Mr. Sung on board. Years later he immigrated to the USA. Unfamiliar with the presence of a variety of Korean Christian churches of North America, he initially met with other immigrants of Chinese and Philippine background. He even led them in Sunday worship for a while.

Then coincidentally, or as Trudy had taught me to say "God-incidentally," since God is in control of all events, Mr. Sung came into contact with a Korean church. After he had attended a number of Sundays, he asked the pastor of the Korean church, the Rev. Koo, if he could become a member of the congregation. They prayed and talked together tracing the history of his entrance into the Christian community.

His concern was: Would his baptism be valid? It was performed by a man, dressed in a navy-blue robe, twelve years ago. The Rev. Koo, hearing the reference to the kind of garb of the person who had baptized him, suspected for a moment that he had been caught in the web of some cult, so he asked if Mr. Sung had received a Certificate of Baptism. He had received one, and he promptly produced it.

When Pastor Koo looked at it he exclaimed: "Now this is almost unbelievable. The pastor who baptized you is not only of the same denomination, but he is also a personal friend of mine. He happens to be close by at this very moment and lives only three minutes from here. We shall contact him."

They did and we immediately invited Mr. Sung, together with Pastor Koo and his wife, for dinner. Almost completely hidden behind an enormous bouquet of flowers, Mr. Sung came up the stairs of our apartment. Here was one of my seafarers resurfacing after twelve years. For some reason I had to think about a verse from the Book of Ecclesiastes: "Cast your bread upon the waters, for after many days you will find it again" (Eccl. 11:1).

On a Sunday morning a few weeks later, Mr. Sung testified to the miracle of God's salvation, of his struggles as demons tried to wean him away from the Christian life, and of the way in which God triumphed. He stood on the stage of that same church. The congregation in attendance at this time was English-speaking. Mr. Sung spoke in Korean, but Pastor Koo translated for him.

It was a moving testimony in which he gave account of his own strong opposition when he received the Bible. What had made an almost miraculous impression on him was the fact that, though he had not dared to dispose of the Bible, its very presence in his cabin disquieted him so much that he finally opened it and started to read it. Though he did not understand many aspects of the Bible at first, it created a real peace in him as he continued to read.

In fact, that was the point of his message to the young people present: "I should have examined that book immediately. It has answers to all the questions that plagued me so continuously. Of course there were times that I drifted back to my old lifestyle, but that book, that fascinating book, called me back to order.

I challenge you: Read that book. Read it again and again. Digest it, and you'll experience its dynamic power. My life has changed, because I gained the knowledge of Jesus through the reading of the Bible. He gave me Light in my darkness."

THE MARRIAGE PRESCRIPTION

Marriage is "in" again. I rejoice in that. For many years the theme was: "We just live together." I remember an officer on board whom I asked if he was married. He replied: "Reverend, where have you been? We don't get married anymore today. We just live together." It is advertised on TV: The world of "stars" is frequently characterized by it. In the ordinary sitcoms and soaps on TV it is considered part of "the normal thing to do."

The staff and crewmembers on cruise ships are suffering. The shipping world is an unnatural environment for a healthy marriage and family relationships. Among the officers, the policy ordinarily is to work for three or four months and then to have two months off. Most of the staff and crewmembers, even though many of them are married, have contracts for six to nine or ten months.

There are a number of professions in which absences from the home and family for a longer or shorter period of time are demanded. But nine or even six months? That is not healthy. You are married and you live like a bachelor most of the year. You expect fidelity from your wife for eight months and God says to you: "Stay faithful to her."

Family relationships are under stress on board. Marriages are in danger. People begin to struggle with what is right and what is wrong. As one man said to me, "In our heart and soul we know of course what is right and what is wrong, but we are being tempted. That's why I have joined the Christian Fellowship. I need the support of others, who are committed Christians, to withstand the temptations." Excellent solution!

She sat there almost in tears. What was the problem? She was a single mother working on a ship. Did she divorce her husband? No. She never had a husband. But now she has a son at home. Who looks after her son? Her own mother. God bless the mothers who sacrifice for their children's mistakes.

Now her life had become more complicated. She was pregnant again. Did she get married this time? No. Who was the "father?" Someone from another country. He had just left because his contract had come to a close. Had he made any arrangements for her? No. She asked him to pay for the birth of the child. He did not commit himself in any form. Is that love? Is that devotion? Is that loyalty to someone with whom you have become that close?

She had to get back to the job. She was an assistant dining room stewardess. Pregnant and having to carry those enormous trays with ten to twelve plates? Would she do damage to the unborn child? That was her concern. Would she be able to stick it out for another six weeks until her contract was finished, or would she have to quit earlier and finance her own flight back to her country? She did not even talk about the possibility of something else: That other kind of "damage."

If he forsakes and forgets her, the mother, her child may never get to know his or her own father. How will the child react to that when the child comes to maturity? "Dad, where is your love and care for my mother? Where is your heart for me, your child...?"

The Bible says: "What God has joined together let man not separate."

As a result of this is there now a re-vitalization of commitment? We march into church, seeking the blessing of God, following a declaration of commitment to each other, which uses million-dollar words like, "in sickness and in health, in poverty and in wealth, when near each other and when far away from each other on a cruise ship…"

Marriage is "in" again. On board of many ships, people are looking for something that has value and permanence.

In the course of time, I have developed a very simple but relevant prescription for a healthy marriage. I preface my suggestions with the statement that I have been married for many years. My clerical collar might cause some people to suspect that I am a Roman Catholic Priest. Trudy is not always with me in the area where I minister on board. She might be in another part of the ship in discussion with people I have perhaps not even met.

The clerical collar has value while I present myself as a Man of God in the midst of seafarers and passengers. It makes very little difference what kind of denomination I represent. Most people are not interested in that. They want to know what *God* has to say. It may possibly cause some confusion to people, who are familiar with the Protestant or Evangelical church, when they see a Protestant pastor with a clerical collar.

I still recall our visit to one particular cruise ship. Trudy was accompanying me. The ship was in the process of embarking the passengers. I had visited the staff of this ship by myself a number of times. Now we were visiting the ship together. We were walking through the passenger area, adjacent to the main entrance. We were scheduled to meet with someone, so we were in a hurry.

Ahead of us was a steward from Goa, India. He was immaculately dressed in a white jacket, dark blue slacks, and white gloves. He carried the hand-luggage of a couple to whom he had been assigned as an escort to their cabin. It was a lovely sight to see this young man, with his black hair and bright smile, in the priceless setting of this splendid ship with a beautiful flower arrangement on a glass pedestal, two mirrors reflecting it, and the well dressed passengers nicely following their escort.

I happened to know the steward personally. As we rushed past him, both of us briefly turned and I greeted him by name. He recognized me. In his excitement he responded with: "Oh, hello, Father." We kept walking. But I will never forget what he said to the passengers he was escorting: "That is *our* Priest - with his girlfriend." At that time I had been married to my "girlfriend" for forty years.

When people approach me and mention marriage in the near or distant future, I make it a point to provide them with a prescription for a successful marriage. I congratulate them with their intentions. I inquire about the person he or she is going to marry. We discuss it in detail.

I tell them: "My visit with you is similar to a visit to the doctor. He talks to you, examines you, and then he pulls out his pad and writes a prescription. The difficulty with his prescription is you cannot read it. You cannot even keep it. You give it to the pharmacist. My prescription you can read and you can keep."

Then I take my calling card out of my pocket and write specific passages from the Bible on it, usually complete chapters, which I feel might be meaningful for the person I am talking with. I avoid making references to specific verses only in the Bible, for two reasons: In most instances the people I come into contact with do not know what a "verse" is. The second reason is that I do not wish to have people concentrate only on a few sentences in the Bible.

The second engineer from a Soviet ship once whispered in my ear, "Why are there all those numbers in this Book?" I replied, "For easier identification and to help in locating certain sections."

The Bible is a book in which God speaks to us in the context of the lives of people, not in the context of isolated dogmatic statements. The personal interaction is of primary importance in the Bible. God speaks to me in my setting. My sorrow, my sin, and my longing for salvation are addressed in it.

That's why I never quote the well-known verse John 3:16, which is found on the first three or four pages of certain Bibles in a hundred different languages. It is a key verse. It is the heart of the gospel. It is a sparkling diamond. It is the summary of the Christian message, but I am speaking to my seafarers, who do not know the gospel, who are not familiar with the heart of the message, who do not know why this verse is a key verse.

If I stay with John 3:16 only in my proclamation, I am suggesting this is a statement in and by itself, without the context, in which it is said. I would like to have the person, who does not know Christ, come to an understanding that here is a discussion between Christ and a person called, Nicodemus. He was supposed to know what Christ was talking about, since he was an "insider." Yet he did not understand the heart of the matter and needed clarity.

So I say instead, "Here is the gospel of St. John. Take a look at chapter three. Begin with it." I might add, "The doctor will suggest that you take your medication three times per day, so allow me to mark certain passages you might like to read three times as well. Why three times? After the first time you may ask yourself, 'This sounds like a fairly rough story. Why did the pastor suggest that I should read this?' After the second time you might say, 'That's interesting; Nicodemus had a problem and in verse ten he is told to smarten up.' But you discover that it is all a bit more complex than you thought."

I then continue: "During the third reading, the Spirit of God miraculously reveals to you that the whole thing is aimed at *you*. That takes a while to sink in. But there comes a time that the light goes on. You are challenged to believe in Christ which ties you up to something you have never even thought of: Eternal Life! That's something nobody has ever talked about and you may have never dreamt of. That's a prescription your medical doctor does not even have in his file."

When I give the "marriage prescription," I again take out my calling card, flip it over, and write on the back the following letters in capitals: A, B, G, L, ILY, IAS. Underneath this I usually write: 1 Corinthians 13 and Colossians 3. Next I explain the letters:

The "A" displays a triangle. At the top there is God. One of you is at the bottom right, the other at the bottom left. Marriage is a "triangle" relationship, with God at the top. So we begin with him, who is number one. You can tell your friends, "I am going to get married, but it will be a triangle relationship." You'll discover that everyone will want to know what you mean by that.

If you should slip away from God, who is at the top, you are also slipping away from each other. Stay close to God and you are staying close to each other. You will begin with God, most likely in a church, with a priest or a preacher. He pronounces upon you the blessing of God for you have made oaths in his presence. You have sworn loyalty to His Word and to each other. So keep the triangle tight.

The "B": If you want to keep that triangle in shape, you need guide lines. They are all found in the "book," the Bible. There are so many valuable and practical lessons in the Bible, even beyond the relationship between the two of you. Read together at least a chapter a day and you'll discover this "book" has something to say about everything. Consider it the specifications to the blueprint of life in all its ramifications.

It talks about our personal lives and about our relationships with others in the society and in the community. It has something to say about the political world as well. It talks about disasters. The matters of life and death are clearly described in this "book." So use it. As my Pakistani Muslim boatswain said when I had given him a copy of the Urduh New Testament, "This book is gold!"

The "G" refers to a very sensitive word, gentle. In our actions and words gentleness should dominate. It is a very tender, but expensive word, because it has a tendency to fly right into the face of our own ego, particularly when we are expressing our convictions. To be gentle in what we say and in how we say, it is an art that has to be acquired. Few people are born with it. There is an incredible statement in 1 Peter 3:15, where we read, "… Do it with gentleness and respect."

The letter "L" invariably causes people to guess that this letter refers to love or lust. But I assume that if you wish to get married, you do love each other, so I would not want to belabor that subject. It does not refer to lust either. It stands for something extremely difficult, particularly for us men. It refers to the word "listen."

Whenever the fiancée is present in the little session, when I raise this, her face lights up. Signs of total agreement are made, for she had already discovered, that this was particularly *his* problem. But there are two sides to this:

God has created us with two ears to listen to him and to each other. That is not easy. In many instances men do have an extremely hard time with listening. Could that be because women, upon occasion, do not mean what they say? In some instances they do not say what they mean either. So let's get to the heart of the matter. How do we as men learn to listen? We must learn to listen with a hundred and fifty percent attention, not with thirty percent. So put the paper away, turn off the TV, forget the blackberry. Look at her. Give her the full one hundred and fifty percent. That's why the letter "L" is included here.

When Trudy is with me, when I present this prescription to a couple, I look to her for some confirmation. She is always very helpful by informing the couple that *we* have been married for half a century. Then I will say to the couple, "Ask her how *I* am doing."

If they do, she will respond, "He is making progress."

The three letters "ILY" stand for something so simple and yet so often ignored. We need to encourage each other more frequently with the three words, "I love you!" We as men ought to take the lead here. When you are not yet married, that expression is used repeatedly, but when you are married, you forget to use it. Do not assume that special services you might render, like mopping the floor or cooking the dinner or fixing the broken screens are sufficient as a substitute for your verbal expressions of love.

Finally we have "I A S." There are occasions when you have a conflict. It can explode without you having intended that. Somehow a sharp disagreement causes you to have words with each other. These change the way in which you look at each other. They are on the level that, even years later, it still pains you that you have said what you said.

In an argument with each other, you might try to console yourself with the fact that you were right and that your spouse was wrong. But with your insistence on being right, you are breaking down the marriage relationship. So wake up! You are right. And guess what: She is right. But remember these words—again from the Bible, "Do not let the sun go down while you are still angry, and do not give the devil a foothold" (Eph. 4:26–27).

So, apply the key formula: I A S *"I am sorry!"*

Today is perhaps a rather late date, but it is never too late to say: *"I am sorry."*

I'll spell it out and you'll see that God hits this nail on the head with Col. 3:12–14.

> Clothe yourselves with compassion, kindness, humility, gentleness, and patience. Bear with each other and forgive whatever grievances you may have against one another. Forgive as the Lord forgave you, and over all these virtues put on love which binds them all together in perfect unity.
>
> Col. 3: 12–14

I have always been impressed by the appreciation displayed by so many people after I had submitted this prescription to them. The manner in which they reacted, sometimes in almost reverent silence, the care wherewith they stuffed away my card, the words they expressed all indicated that they saw at least some value in it, and they were impressed by having received these guidelines.

In 2004, I had the privilege to function as chaplain for passengers and staff on the Maiden Voyages of the Queen Mary two. It was one of the most breathtaking experiences we had ever had in our more than eighteen years of sailing.

Between the European (England to Ft. Lauderdale) and the North American (Ft. Lauderdale to the Caribbean) Maiden Voyages, the ship stayed for about a week in Ft. Lauderdale to host dignitaries and travel agents. It was a very busy week with almost every night a festive dinner. I was on board as the chaplain and though we did not attend every dinner we had occasion to be part of most of them.

One night stands out: Having dined with various dignitaries, all associated with the shipping world, we greeted a number of them, when the festivities had come to a close. There had been almost a thousand of them in attendance. As they exited the Commodore and the Chiefs of Staff were at the exit to say farewell. We happened to be at the exit as well.

A couple in their thirties approached the exit. The gentleman, recognizing me, exclaimed loudly, "It is you, Reverend!" Then he graciously explained who he was. "I am now the chief officer on that cruise ship, which sailed through the Suez Canal, when you were with us on board and we had to divert our voyage because of some trouble in the Middle East."

He refreshed my memory with his name and then said, "At that time I was the Second Officer." Then he continued, "Do you remember, I was about to get married at that time, and you and I had a long discussion about marriage and you gave me your prescription?" He continued, as he introduced us to his wife, "This is the person to whom I got married."

At this point she took over. "Oh, so you are the pastor who gave that special 'marriage prescription' to my husband. He gave it to me, shortly after he had received it from you. Well, I want you to know, we have adopted the instructions you put on your card and we check that card daily. It is now hanging on the fridge. We have been happily married for the past three years. Thank you so much! You are an inspiration to both of us."

I was much encouraged. May the LORD bless them with his presence "until death do them part."

ESTHER DISCOVERS ESTHER

She was Welsh and worked in the spa, a charming girl, with her name tag in place. The spa was quiet. Most of the passengers were engaged in other activities, so there she stood alone, almost with a sense of boredom. The clock ticks slowly when you are not occupied. The hours seem longer than when the place is packed with people. There was no special program either to draw in the crowds. So she left to take a break, and that was when I met her.

I displayed surprise and excitement when I greeted her, with a slightly louder voice than normal, using her name. "You have a fascinating name. It is known around the world. Did you know that there is a certain amount of fame associated with that name?" She said, "Where do you get that?" "From the Bible," I said. "In fact, there is a book in the Bible called 'Esther.'"

She bent slightly forward and lowered her voice, as if to be sure that no one could hear her and said, "I apologize, but I have never read the Bible, so I did not know that my name is in it." I did not react to what she said, but instead continued with: "It is an absolutely beautiful story. In fact, it is a love story. It is very short, but I am certain you will want to read it."

"I do not have a Bible," she answered, "and I would not know where to get one here on board." That made sense to me. In the cabins of the officers, staff, and crew members of cruise ships you will ordinarily not find a copy of the Bible. The occupants come from many different nations. Upon occasion you may find a personal Bible left behind by the previous attendant of your cabin.

Esther had no Bible, and when I said that I would get her one she said: "Do not get me a big one, because when I am heading home I could not possibly take any more baggage." It struck me as ironic. The Word of God, which tells us about the way to unburden ourselves of any excess "baggage," was construed as extra baggage. "All right, Esther, I'll get you a very small one." But, I thought, *When she is going home soon, will this not be a unique occasion to give her at least a New Testament, possibly with the Psalms and the Proverbs?* I would inscribe it with my prescriptions in the hope that it would lead her to Christ while suggesting that she purchase a complete Bible eventually, in order to read the story of "Esther." Here I ran into a nasty problem. I had no more New Testaments although I had brought along quite a number of them. I checked the dwindled supply in my own cabin. All the English copies were gone.

The ship on which we sailed had a huge "main street," Fifth Avenue style with stores and restaurants of every description on each side. At both ends there were four sets of glass elevators. It was a pleasure to go up and down in anyone of them. You could see where you were going and observe the different decks you passed; it was a fascinating design.

In the vicinity of the reception office, near one of the elevators, a group of eight well dressed passengers stood talking to each other. As I was the chaplain on board, I felt it would be nice to just stop and greet them. I do that often. I approach a group of people and exchange a few remarks, which in one way or another, might inspire them to come to the church service I will be conducting, or I could answer some questions they might have.

They were extremely friendly people, four couples traveling together. Noticing my clerical shirt, they asked if I was the chaplain on board. When I confirmed it, they asked me what that responsibility entailed. I told them that I would conduct the worship services for the passengers. I gave them the time and place and added that I would conduct daily meditations as well and invited them to attend those. I further explained that I would visit the sick and be available for anyone in need. But since I am professionally a chaplain to seafarers, I mentioned especially that I spend the rest of my time contacting the more than one thousand seafarers.

They asked, "Do you conduct church services for them, or do you have Bible studies? How can you handle so many people in the limited time that you are on board, or are you staying for a number of cruises? Do you have time to relax, sit, and read like some of us do and enjoy the cruise?"

I launched into a brief description of my ministry on board. "Yes, at times I conduct services for the crew. I also regularly conduct worship services and Bible studies for small groups of about twenty members, all committed Christians, once or twice per week, late at night from midnight until about two o'clock in the morning. That's the only time they can attend. I also double check the hospital every day and visit seafarers who are hospitalized."

I continued, "At times I get a hint from one of the doctors to contact someone who has a personal struggle, is depressed, or is grieving because of the loss of a close family member. The rest of the time I visit the people in the mess rooms, the officers' dining room, and the staff dining room. I visit with crew members of the spa, of the stores, and of the casino when the staff is without any responsibilities and on a break."

I added the following, "I visit the entertainers and their technical staff during their time off. In short, I try to acquaint myself with all the crew members. Pastoral ministry is of course vital. Many people like to talk about their personal lives, their homes, their children, and their dreams for the future. I could put it in one sentence: When they see me, although they would never put it in this typical biblical language, they are asking, 'Is there perhaps a Word of the LORD for me?' After all, you are the spiritual guide here.

Most people are looking for some direction, some perspective, some encouragement, and some wisdom. I garnish my remarks and advice and wisdom with the directives of the Scriptures. I want them to experience the peace that is in Christ Jesus and I steer them in that direction. I am deeply aware, that this has to be done in a very sensitive, courteous, and gracious manner. At all times I have to remember that I may be speaking to someone, who did not grow up in the Christian context, yet whose heart is open to its message."

I do not wish to force anyone to a decision. Our LORD ordinarily talked to people by referring to an incident or a story, and let them draw their own conclusions. Never did I see him force anyone to a decision. So everyone is always respected, but he would become aware of "the way of the LORD." Especially in our contact with Asiatic people, who at all times would like to accommodate the speaker, it behooves us to give them space and time. Never should anyone feel forced into an acceptance of Christ. Our LORD looks for the heart and for the genuine commitment of one's spirit.

I always accompany my remarks with references to the Scriptures and I ask them if they are familiar with the Bible and have a copy of it. After all, the whole drama of our misery is given perspective with the liberating acts and peaceful direction of our Savior, clearly exposed in the Word of God. So I hand out Bibles in the languages of the people with whom I am in contact, particularly when they are curious about it.

I told these eight passengers that today I had a measure of frustration, because there was one very special person I wanted to give a New Testament to, but I had run out of them. One of the gentlemen put his hand into his pocket and out it came with a New Testament. He handed it to me and said, "Your need has been met." He added, "I am a Gideon, so I always carry a New Testament in my pocket for situations like this." His friend confessed that he was a Gideon too, but he did not have anything in his pocket.

We praised the LORD for this meeting. I joyfully continued my trip to the spa. Before I had reached my cabin, I ran into Trudy who said that she had just talked to one of the cooks who had asked for a New Testament. Trudy, unaware of the shortage we were facing, had assured him that I would provide him with one. She left me with the message, but I thought: *In this huge ship with fourteen hundred members of staff, I could perhaps steer clear of that cook for a few days, after which I would hopefully have a new supply of Bibles and New Testaments.*"

On my way to the spa to just deliver the New Testament, another girl stopped me and asked if I could briefly talk to her in the staff dining room which was empty and deserted at this time. While we talked a gentleman came in. Judging by his uniform, he was a cook, a cook in a hurry, because without wasting any time he cut into our conversation and said, "Your wife promised me a New Testament. I am here to pick it up."

The New Testament was in my pocket, scheduled to go to Esther. I could not say, "I do not have one." Trudy had promised him one, so I said: "Right, here it is," and out of my pocket it came into his hand, whereupon he immediately turned around and raced out to attend to his duties.

I carried on with my talk with this girl. We analyzed her problems, very complex stuff, but we prayed for light and direction and I set out some beacons for her stormy sailing. I could not even give her a Bible or a New Testament, since now I had indeed not a single one in my possession, so I left her with some biblical prescriptions, written on the back of my calling card.

I made my way to the spa to inform Esther, that I had not been able to find a copy of the small Bible I had promised her and to apologize to her. To get there I had to go via "Fifth Avenue" again. I passed by the reception desk and saw the glass elevators swoosh up and down. But now a miracle took place: The glass elevator, closest to the reception desk, came down and stopped at the fifth floor at the exact moment that I was passing by.

It was packed with people. Mysteriously no one came out and no one went in. Just before the doors closed a lady's hand, with a New Testament in it, was extended in my direction. I instinctively took the New Testament from her. I did not see her face. The elevator was too crowded. The doors closed and the elevator disappeared.

To this day I do not know who that lady was and what prompted her to act as she did. I suspected that she was connected with the "Gideon" group. She surely did not know that the first one had been given away already. But it may well be that the LORD had suggested to her, "Take one along, because the pastor needs it. And I will steer him onto your path." The distance from this elevator to where Esther was working was somehow much shorter, presumably because I walked on air.

However you look at it, you cannot deny that God continuously involves himself in our outreach. He operates in miraculous ways and not infrequently involves a whole army of people to be part of his scheme to accomplish his goal. We will be enriched when we have an eye for that.

Esther left with a minimum of "extra" baggage, but with the message of Matthew 11:30: "My 'baggage' (yoke) is easy and my burden is light."

DELIVERANCE ON A BENCH

In this account, a number of extremely distressing factors surface. The reason it is included is fundamentally three-fold:

1 It is not an isolated matter. Many people continue to become involved in similar situations.

2 The exceptional spiritual pain and emotional distress is extremely devastating.

3 It is precisely in the redemptive message of the Gospel that relief and restoration are richly provided.

Near the entrance to the cruise ship stood several crew members with their suitcases. They had arrived from different parts of the world, some of them about to board for the very first time. I made it a point to briefly talk to each one of them in order to welcome them; especially those who are there for the first time.

A short distance away, under a tree, stood a bench on which two girls were seated. I have always been convinced that the LORD mysteriously leads me to the very people he wants me to contact as was the case on this particular morning. I walked up to that bench and greeted the two girls. One of them stood up and excused herself, explaining that duty called her back to the ship.

That left one girl who said, "When I saw you walk toward the gate, I thought, *Maybe the other girl will leave when they see a priest or pastor, or whatever you are, coming toward us.* That would give me a chance to talk to you, although I don't know you at all. Do you have time? Or are you in a hurry?"

I assured her that I had time for her. So she continued, "I would really like to ask you for help, because I have a terrible problem. I have been thinking about it and trying to find some relief, but I don't get anywhere. I can't sleep anymore. I cannot talk to anyone about it. My problem is breaking my heart."

She continued, "You see, I work in the administrative department and all the other people there have their own concerns. They are all very nice people and I enjoy working with them, but I could not possibly talk to any one of them about this. When you are on a cruise ship like this, with over a thousand people, you can still feel totally alone. Does that make sense to you?"

She added, "I struck up an acquaintance with someone from another country. He is an officer on board. Our countries are more or less neighbors, but aside from that, you know how it goes. We kept meeting every now and then in the officers' bar. We liked each other as soon as we met. At one time, we both had an afternoon off in one of the ports. We took a tour on our own with a taxi. We had a great time. We were away from the ship and I discovered I still liked him."

She went on with her story; "When you are on board all the time, you become half blind. The world around you is continuously a world of work and more work without much of a let up. The whole atmosphere on board, as you well know, is a bit unreal. Moreover, I have no other friends even though there are about a dozen girls from my country on board. They are working in the stores and in the casino, but I have hardly any contact with them." She noted, "We eat together at times in the staff dining room or have a drink once in a while, but I did not develop a close friendship with any of them. I was attracted to this officer. We started to like each other more and more. Oh well, I'll be honest. I fell in love with him. By the way, are you a Catholic Priest?"

I said, "I am a Protestant pastor and I have been married for a long time. I have two sons and a daughter. They are all more or less your age." That seemed to put her at ease. So she continued, "We liked each other. I felt I was getting dependent on him. It is strange, you know, on a ship. But when a love-relationship develops, you become anxious, because you are afraid that it may break off and then you are back in that terrible pit of being alone again. Imagine, alone on a ship with so many crew members. It sounds crazy, but that's the way it is. I believed he was in love with me as well. We became very close!"

She added, "I might as well be honest; we fell in love and we started to make love. In the course of time, we became careless when we made love. You know what I mean? But then one day I discovered that things were not as they usually are with me, and that made me decide to take a test. The test showed that I was pregnant. I could not believe it, but I could not deny it either. I was pregnant. I was shocked! My world suddenly collapsed."

She continued, "Here I am in North America having this job on the ship. I came here to make money and to change my life. In a few years I planned to go back home and possibly settle in a nice apartment, which I could then afford to buy, and to get back into the circle of my family and friends. When you get pregnant you cannot stay on the ship. You are dismissed and you must pay your own flight home. Where would I get the money to fly to my country?

So I talked to my boyfriend. Then I got a second shock, because I used a word that was not in his vocabulary. That was the word 'marriage,' I had suggested: 'Let's get off the ship together and live ashore.'" Her story continued with the following: "But we had not even thought about where we would live. Living in his country away from my family would be dreadful. I am too close to my family and could not live without them. Moreover, if I would come home and we would have to arrange immediately a wedding, because I was pregnant, what kind of reaction would my parents, my whole family have? They would be devastated. They would ask: 'Where are you going to live? Will this boy support you? How will he do that? He earns his money on a ship on the other side of the world.'"

Then she said, "When we discussed all these questions a third shock hit me. My boyfriend was not willing to go ashore with me—pregnant or not. In fact, he did not want to think nor talk about being married and living in either one of our countries. When all of this started to hit me, it dawned on me that I got myself into an enormous problem with no way out. I was terribly frustrated and furious with him and with myself. I became desperate. The feelings of my boyfriend for me suddenly seemed to cool off."

Her story didn't stop there, "It was shock after shock and it became almost impossible for me to do my work. I had a terrible time concentrating and not making any mistakes. I did not know where to turn. Then I came into contact, right here ashore, with a girl from another ship. She had gone through a similar experience and she suggested that I get an abortion." An abortion? I could not believe my ears. "She said, 'I had one. It is a hellish experience and you feel totally rotten but only for a couple of days. Then you realize you are still on the ship. You still have your job. After a couple of weeks you are your old self. You don't have to tell your parents or anybody, and life goes on.' So I got an abortion, right here in town, because I really did not see any other way out."

She shared, "It was awful, frightening, ghastly, terrible! But it was true what that girl said to me. I got back to the ship in time. In fact it was on a Saturday. I felt sick and disgusted for the next couple of days. But I still had my job. I didn't have to tell my parents anything. I wondered how my boyfriend would now feel. That girl had said life would get better after a couple of weeks. Today we are eleven weeks further. Physically I have recovered I think, but did life get better? It did not. Life became worse! That's why I need to talk to you."

She added, "For some reason my boyfriend had lost interest in me. Here I had gone through something that concerned both of us. Now he doesn't even look at me anymore. Can you imagine that? But what is worse is that I cannot sleep anymore. I read about abortion and that it is actually a real life that has been cut off. Dreadful, that is murder. I committed murder? As I read more and more about it, I have become aware that millions of abortions take place almost every year. There are even organizations that are proposing an abortion to anyone who needs one. But I also read about Christian people, who keep talking about the value of a human life. So this murder thing keeps going through my mind."

She said, "I realized I had become one of those who had the human life in them destroyed. I feel I really have committed murder. That thought almost chokes me. I am Orthodox. I don't go to church and I don't practice my religion, but I suddenly have this terrible fear that God might send me to hell for this. So I toss and turn every night, and I see demons, maybe the devil himself, reminding me of the terrible thing I have done. And I cannot do anything about it. What is destroyed is destroyed. My own peace and happiness and joy in life are also destroyed. I feel I am dead myself. God must hate me and be furious with me."

She concluded, "I think during the rest of my life he will see to it that I will never forget this, never! I killed a child, but I am at the level now that I think I should have killed myself as well. So tell me, what can I do?"

Since we sat next to each other and I really had not seen what she looked like, I turned slightly and looked at her. She was a lovely girl, but I could see the strain and pain grooved into her face.

Then I said, "At the end of your story, you suddenly mentioned that you are Orthodox, but that you do not go to church. You also mentioned God. So to you, as an Orthodox girl, though you don't practice your religion and don't go to church, God has suddenly appeared. But he seems to have come in a frightening form, angry and bent on revenge, pursuing you with demons. You experience it daily. That's what you said. Am I correct?" "You are absolutely right. That is how it is," she said.

"Now, listen carefully," I continued, "It is God, who sent me to you at this time, eleven weeks after you had an abortion. So, let's get to the heart of the matter. There are three things you have to consider. Number one: You came to know somebody from the opposite sex, and your friendship developed into love, although it was a shaky love, because genuine love is linked up with loyalty, trust, and support of each other permanently. When you get married, expressions are used such as: "in sickness and in health, in riches and in poverty, we stay together until death do us part." That's expensive language. It highlights faithfulness to each other forever.

Now number two: If we go by the directions of God and by the Bible, which is his word, we are reminded that we are to give our bodies to each other only *within* that bond of marriage. Only then are we able to build on a sound foundation."

I added, "We live in a society, in which something else has taken its place and it is called "sex." Now, if you separate sex from the bond of marriage, from faithfulness, and permanent devotion to each other, you end up with a few moments of physical satisfaction, which may well destroy your life. You are not to look at a man as a sex object, fit only for physical satisfaction. You ought to look at him with permanent commitment, faithfulness, and trust. Then you are talking love! That is what God intends for us. That goes for men and women alike."

I added the following, "There is the whole realm of emotions and interacting with the other person on a constant, permanent human basis where one has respect and allegiance for each other as well as a willingness to sacrifice. But when you get into the trap, which you got yourself into, there is only one way out and that is genuine confession to God."

I said, "Now we get to number three: You got pregnant. That illustrates that this whole business of sexual involvement with each other can develop into the creation of a life. That is miraculous and designed by God for within the bond of marriage. Words like children, training, education with the support of a father and a mother for the children, make up the family as God intended. Both of you walked away from that. When you discovered that you were pregnant, you could not make a joyful announcement to your friend. You were shocked. You did not explode with joy that you are going to be a mother and that the two of you are going to form a family. Instead, because of your lack of support, you were driven to a 'solution' to your pregnancy. That solution was an abortion. Now God enters into the picture.

God comes back to you through this awful act of destroying the life of what could have been a beautiful child. With this, God is saying to you what it says on a large billboard: 'We need to talk—God.' That explains why I am here to say to you, 'The heart of the matter is God wants to talk to you.' So listen closely: There are many instances in the Bible where people have blown it. But God sent me down here to let you know that there is a way out, because God is a forgiving God. That in itself is miraculous. No matter what you do, you can never make undone what happened, but God directed me to sit down on this bench to hear your story. You are aware that you sinned against God. You are crushed because you went through this abortion. You are wondering if God will ever forgive you. And I am here to tell you that God is prepared to forgive you!" She started to cry.

After a few minutes I said, "Shall we now speak to God about all of this, tell him that you have sinned against him, ask him to forgive you for having had an abortion, and beg him to ban the demons since you promise to return to a life of obedience to him?" We prayed. The Spirit of God touched her heart. It brought about a smile and an almost visible peace to her eyes bathed in tears. It reflected her heart.

She returned to the ship with a new allegiance to God, forgiven and with joy and hope. I thanked God for the bench. It became the surgical seat of spiritual deliverance and of a renewed life.

HIDDEN TREASURES

Whenever I board a ship, whether a cargo ship or a cruise ship, I carry a bag with Bibles in as many different languages as I assume will be spoken on that particular ship. In my forty-five years of ministry, this has been a unique benefit because so many people were blessed precisely by the immediate presentation of a copy of the Bible out of my bag in their own language.

After most of my cruises or my visits on cargo ships, I walked off the ships without Bibles, since they all had been given to those who desired to have one of their own. In fact, in many instances I had run out of them well before we reached our home port, particularly when I was on cruise ships.

Once in a while, there were exceptions when it turned out that the composition of the crew was different from what I had anticipated. But since I assumed that those Bibles, which had not as yet been given away, would be picked up at a later date by someone who spoke its language, I left a few copies on board in highly accessible places such as in the library for the officers or for the crew. I would place those Bibles there, partly hidden by a popular magazine or a book, praying that sooner or later they would be found by the right person.

Dimitri was a Ukrainian electronics engineer on a large cruise ship. He had become acquainted with a most charming front office attendant, a girl from South Africa. When I met them, I noticed that this was something more than a mere shipboard romance. There seemed to be a genuine relationship of loyalty, love, and allegiance that was most inspiring.

Monika was a committed Christian, educated in the Orthodox Reformed tradition and seeking to practice her faith in all her contacts with passengers and staff. On a cruise ship, that is a most commendable display of one's commitment to the LORD. In her contact with Dimitri, she mentioned quite early in their relationship that she felt the need to have a genuine bond with each other in the LORD.

In many instances when people have fallen in love and like to see their relationship formalized with a marriage ceremony, they come to me with misty eyes assuring me of their profound love for each other. Very seldom do I run into people who give the spiritual relationship priority. Most couples assume that this dimension will fall into place automatically, because they are so deeply in love.

It is on this level that I might be able to give some guidelines. The spiritual relationship will function as the foundation of the marriage when they both have put their trust in the LORD and are prepared to be guided by him in their marriage relationship.

Monika prioritized the spiritual relationship and informed Dimitri that she was in the habit of reading her Bible regularly. This inspired her and drew her closer to God. Dimitri was orthodox by tradition, but had not as yet applied his religious heritage to any aspect of his practical life. So Monika suggested that he obtain a Bible and proposed that they should read it together. She thought that if they followed this procedure, she might be able to give him guidance and direction into a closer relationship with the LORD.

Dimitri reacted favorably, but felt left up in the air since he had no idea where to get a Bible in his native language, because however you look at it, reading the Bible in your *own* language gives you a deeper understanding of its contents and so exposes you more thoroughly to its truth.

Dimitri was called into the office where he was instructed to transfer for a period of six weeks to another ship to deal with a complex electronics problem. Changes and transfers do happen frequently on board, so it did not surprise him. He packed a bag and was all set to get off the ship at the next port. When he arrived at the next ship, it turned out that the problem was somewhat more substantial than he had been led to believe. So the six weeks turned into two months.

When he returned, I met him again and asked him how his time on that other ship had been spent. He then told me, that it had been a miraculous transfer. Not only had he dealt with the electronics problems, but one evening he had been looking around in the officers' library with a friend. When the friend had left, he had rummaged through magazines and books and made an amazing discovery.

There, to his stunning surprise, almost totally hidden by some magazines, he found a brand new Ukrainian Bible. It had no nametag. In fact, it looked as if it had never been opened, which was not surprising, because on that ship there had been no other Ukrainians during its last voyages. They had been replaced by Hungarians, so Dimitri felt that he could take that Ukrainian Bible and consider it his own.

He figured Monika would be surprised and very happy, but his own surprise was to have found a Ukrainian Bible on that ship, tucked away among some magazines in the officers' library. He wondered how it got there.

I explained that I had put it there. That to him was even more surprising. I had not been sailing on that ship. So how could I have put it there? I explained that a long time ago I *had been* sailing on that ship and because there were no Ukrainians on board at that time, I had put it in the library, praying that one day a Ukrainian might come on board and be blessed by it. Well, God had answered my prayer, one *had* come on board. His name was Dimitri.

I found this once again a clear indication of how God works in amazing ways to reach a *specific* person. Monika and Dimitri are now reading the Bible together and I look forward to their ecclesiastical wedding ceremony where they will solicit the blessings of the Lord … in Ukrainian and in Afrikaans.

As I was walking out of the officer's dining room the pianist was just coming in. "Am I ever happy to see you," he said. I wondered what he wanted to see me about, so I turned around and decided to sit at the table he had chosen for eating his dinner.

As happens almost always on board, he came directly to the point without a lengthy introduction by asking, "Do you know what Psalm 139 is all about?"

I answered, "I do. It is one of the most fascinating Psalms, illustrating that God is ever present in our lives. I'll give you the very heart of its message. Let me quote it to you:

> "Where can I go from your Spirit? Where can I flee from your presence? If I go up to the heavens, you are there; if I make my bed in the depths, you are there. If I rise on the wings of the dawn, if I settle on the far side of the sea, even there your hand will guide me; your right hand will hold me fast. If I say, "Surely the darkness will hide me and the light become night around me," even the darkness will not be dark to you; the night will shine like the day, for darkness is as light to you.
>
> Psalm 139:7–12

"My good man, this is one of the most dynamic testimonies in the Bible. We had to memorize it in the Seminary and I have never forgotten it. But why on earth are you asking me about this?"

He responded, "As you know I am the piano-bar man. You have been there, right? That's where I play the piano and compose songs for the passengers. It is always packed in my area. Now there was a passenger who came up to me just as I left for dinner and asked if I could compose a song about Psalm 139. I have never looked in the Bible and I think I would not even know where to find this Psalm. So I am happy that you introduced me to it. Is there more to it, or is what you quoted the whole shot?"

I replied, "No, there is more to it. Actually you will want to read it from the beginning to the end."

"How can I?" he asked. "I don't have a Bible and if I had one I would not know where to look, but this passenger wants it tonight."

So I said, "I'll get you a Bible right away and I'll mark it for you, but now I have a commitment, so where can I find you?"

He said, "I'll tell you what to do. Put it in the piano and put the cover down again. I always close the piano when I am not playing. You are familiar with the ship, right? You know where the piano bar is? I shall look for the Bible in the piano and compose a song for that passenger."

I suggested, "Make it a hymn, then you can sing it during my Sunday Worship Service." He smiled and I took off.

Armed with a duly marked Bible, open at Psalm 139, I went to the piano bar.

The place was empty, or so I thought, but to my surprise at the very moment that I was maneuvering with the lid of the piano, the voice of the cruise director interrupted me, "Are you the replacement for our piano bar player?" he asked. "In fact what are you trying to do there? Are you trying to tune the piano?" I responded, "No. I am just putting a Bible in the piano."

"A Bible in the piano?" he exclaimed, "I have never heard of anything like it. I know they put Bibles in Churches, but to put one in the piano is for sure a first. May I see it for a moment?"

I showed him the Bible and as he paged through it I noticed he was becoming increasingly more excited. "Do you have another one?" he asked. I said, "Not with me, but I'll go back to my cabin and get one for you."

I never got to his office for as I walked in the hallway I ran into him and I had the chance to present it to him then and there. His reaction was expressed by calling on the name of the LORD.

The enthusiasm that is expressed when some people get into touch with the Bible is frequently characterized by their calling on the name of the LORD. When that does happen I ordinarily make a comment about the biblical instruction not to use the name of the LORD in vain, but deep down in my heart I sometimes think that the awareness of the presence of our LORD begins to become a reality in the life of such a person.

As yet the cruise director was still a stranger in the Christian orbit, but he had come a step closer because of the book he now held in his hand. "I'll be frank with you," he said. "I do not belong to any church or group. I have never bothered to become interested in religion. But when I see someone put a Bible in the piano of all places, I think there must be something to it that might be worth my while to find out about and that I should take note of. Thank you very much."

GOD IN THE CASINO

It is at all times a bit awkward when I, as a clergyman, walk through the casino. The tendency on the part of some passengers is to challenge me, "Father, bless me so I will win!" That blessing has nothing to do with a relationship between God and the person. In many instances the people, who so approach me, may perhaps not even have much of a relationship with God.

Deep down, they are aware though that there is more between heaven and earth than we can see. The spiritual and invisible world has, in one way or another, bearing on us. Who knows but that it can be utilized. In the book of Acts, in chapter 8:18–24, there is an interesting incident recorded which deals with an individual who wanted to buy what he saw displayed in the "actions" of Peter and John. Fundamentally, his request for a blessing was an attempt to get more money.

As a representative of the "spiritual" world, I am therefore approached to be of help with what is customarily perceived to be an aspect of the methodology of the church: to issue a blessing.

On some ships I was requested not to appear at all in the casino. It was felt by the senior staff that the presence of the clergy, particularly when dressed in clerical garb, might be an embarrassment. On board of ships it is significant to maintain the rules of "the house" and to agree with the suggestions made by those who are in authority. So when I am requested to stay out of the casino, I comply.

"Would you be kind enough to contact the Hotel Manager?" asked our dining room steward when he presented the menu to us.

I asked, "Immediately?"

The steward answered, "No sir, he suggested that you first enjoy your dinner, but he is expecting you right after dinner." I thanked him.

I figured if the Hotel Manager wanted to see me most likely there was a problem with one of the passengers. When I arrived at his office, he asked me to sit down. That in itself put me on guard. Ordinarily one just walks in, and in about six sentences the issue is settled.

He reminded me that he had requested me not to appear in the casino during the voyage. I wondered why he raised this matter again. He then said, "I do not think I can find another person though to whom I could talk about this, but to you. Have you met the manager of the casino? It is a girl." I informed him that I had met her in the officers' lounge where we had talked briefly. He then proceeded by saying, "Well, I think you may wish to talk to her again, because we just received a telegram from the ship where her husband works. It informs us that he has suddenly died. We are wondering if you would be willing to inform her."

Imagine, you are on board and you get notice that your husband on another ship is no longer alive. Your life totally changes. Your ideas, ideals, and future are falling apart and the world around you will never be the same.

For days, both Trudy and I talked with her and tried to console her, reminding her that God will not forsake her, but that he will extend his comfort to her. She testified that she was experiencing some of this already.

Even though the casino was officially out of bounds for us, death had brought us in. It was an extremely tragic experience. It reminded us anew that there is more to the casino than slot machines, playing tables, and a crowd of passengers. The very people who are at work there on a daily basis are people, who like anyone else, behoove the care of the LORD in their lives. I have since made it a point to contact the people who work in the casino while they are off duty. Many people have needs. We can function pastorally by being a sounding board and by giving meaningful advice.

As I walked through this one casino, someone asked me if I would be kind enough to contact a person who was working there but happened to be on break. I contacted her and made arrangements to meet her in one of the restaurants. Like almost everyone else, she came directly to the point. "A passenger came up to me at my table about six or seven days ago. My table was still empty, but she did not want to play. She just leaned over the table and pointed her finger directly at me. It seemed to me that she was angry, because in a rather firm voice she told me, 'You should not be working here. In fact you should get out of here, because God does not want you to stay in this job.' Then she walked away. Now I have been in touch with all kinds of people and sometimes they make unusual remarks, but this remark was very strange."

She continued, "What is worse is that it has begun to bother me. In fact there are times when I wake up at night and get upset all over again. So I think perhaps that lady is right, I should get out of this job. I have been trained for it and it has enabled me to make a reasonable amount of money, particularly when you come from a former communist country like I do. But I never became excited about working in a casino. To me it was simply a job, and it enabled me to be on a cruise ship and to see something of the world. But now I have become restless because of this strange remark. So I am happy you contacted me, because I would like to ask you, What is this? Should I quit my job? Why was that lady angry? Why did she mention God? What is your opinion about all of this?"

First I thought, *There are all kinds of passengers who immediately express their feelings when they do not get what they want or need on board.* For example, when they cannot find the place where the towels are kept for the swimming pool, they approach the first person who wears a uniform, and they ask him or her demanding almost immediate satisfaction for their needs. They can upon occasion be a bit rude and display an attitude of "I paid for this cruise. I demand an immediate answer."

But then I realized that this was not the case here. This woman had mentioned God. The second thing I realized was that the girl felt she had to refocus her life. She was asking for a clear interpretation.

I answered her by saying, "The attitude and the tone of certain people might not endear us to them, but the fact that this matter keeps bothering you would lead me to conclude that God is perhaps indeed involved in this and is using this lady, with her stern approach, to alert you that you might consider this a call from God to refocus and to redirect your life. You sort of hinted at that yourself, right? You might well find peace in that. Why else would this message continue to bother you?" You do not wish to continue to be plagued by the matter that lady raised when you go to sleep at night.

Without even so much as a moment of reflection she answered, "You are right. This could well be from God. I have never felt at ease in my job even though I liked the money. But God may want me to come back to him and redirect my life. Yes, I think you are right. I think I'll finish my contract and then I will sign off. Thank you for clarifying it for me."

Somewhere it says in the Bible that we must discern the spirits. The lady who spoke did not speak to anyone else in the casino. The reason she spoke to this particular girl remains a mystery. She had never met the girl before. She did not check if the girl reacted in a manner acceptable to her. She came, spoke, and left. But the reaction of the girl was the result of what the lady had said. In the midst of it all the guidance of the LORD came across.

What his purpose is for this girl remains a mystery as well, but here again is confirmation that God is involved in our lives and there are times that we are alerted to it, sometimes even rather bluntly. For this lovely girl this was such a time!

In our Seafarers Centre, there was a magnificent chapel on the second floor adjacent to a large social lounge. All around this entire second floor some remarkable paintings and symbols were displayed to intrigue seafarers. When a seafarer had made a telephone call, I made it a point to invite him briefly upstairs to find out if the contact with home had been good or bad, particularly when I suspected that he had made a stressful call.

Upstairs, in the middle of the day, he would sense that he was in a distinctly different place with a chaplain escorting him. That frequently provided the opportunity to share some of his personal concerns in a relaxed setting. Or I would point out some of the artifacts, displayed in the lounge and chapel, which not infrequently led to some interesting discussions, stimulating to the mind.

He had looked rather serious when he came out of the telephone booth, so I suggested that he come upstairs to see the chapel and the social lounge. I did not know his position on board. He had not introduced himself.

In the course of my work with seafaring people, I have discovered that unless they introduce themselves, they prefer anonymity. Therefore, I rarely ask a person what his name is. If I know his position, I might address him by his title or function.

We walked around and noticed a set of three very old, but extremely heavy boards welded together with iron bands, and I asked him if he could identify what that set was. Like almost everyone to whom I had shown this, he was unable to identify it as part of the deck covering of a very ancient sailing vessel.

We stopped next at the large, beautifully designed logo of the Seafarers Centre which I had designed years ago. I have it on my business card as well. It displays a combination of a cross and an anchor. An open book, representing the Bible, is in its very center. The anchor and the cross are often understood to refer to the shipping world. That is indeed the case, but the combination has a somewhat different background.

The cross is to remind us, of course, of our LORD whose death on the cross gives life to anyone who believes in him as the risen Son of God. That is the miraculous design of becoming a Christian.

The anchor I used as a word play on the Greek word "Kyrie," which refers to God. In certain oratorios or cantatas, when sung in Latin, the glory of God is expressed in the sentence "Kyrie Eleison," which means, "God be praised."

If a 150,000-ton ship will remain steady when it has been anchored, any person "anchored in God" will not be swayed. He will remain steady in God.

After I was finished with my explanation, and realizing that people on board of cruise ships are always pressed for time, I said, "Since we are standing here close to the chapel, may I offer a prayer to God for you?" Without awaiting his answer, I walked slowly to the front of the chapel where we had a small kneeling bench on the stage next to the altar. The stage itself was only one step higher than the main floor. I noticed he had followed me to the front. Before I knelt down on the kneeling bench, I felt I should have his approval of my intentions. Standing at the edge of the stage, he confirmed my intention by asking, "Shall I kneel here?" I replied, "Please feel free." I then knelt down and offered prayer on his behalf. After the prayer, he rose to his feet with wet eyes and made a challenging statement:

"I am the manager of the casino on board. I do not belong to any church. I just came in to telephone my wife. Then you invited me to come upstairs and now you prayed for me. That floors me. You don't know anything about my life, you don't even know my name, but you are the first person in my life who gives a damn about my soul. That is incredible. I thank you from the bottom of my heart. No one has ever done anything like this for me."

He looked at his watch and said, "I must go." I ushered him to the door downstairs and remained behind with his exceptional expression about the "care for his soul." I have never forgotten it. I reflected that fundamentally this is the cry of so many people on board, and I am sure ashore as well.

It may not be expressed in "ecclesiastical" language, but I discerned it to be a cry from the heart.

Is there a word of the LORD, *for me?*